*The Origins and Onset of the
Romanian Holocaust*

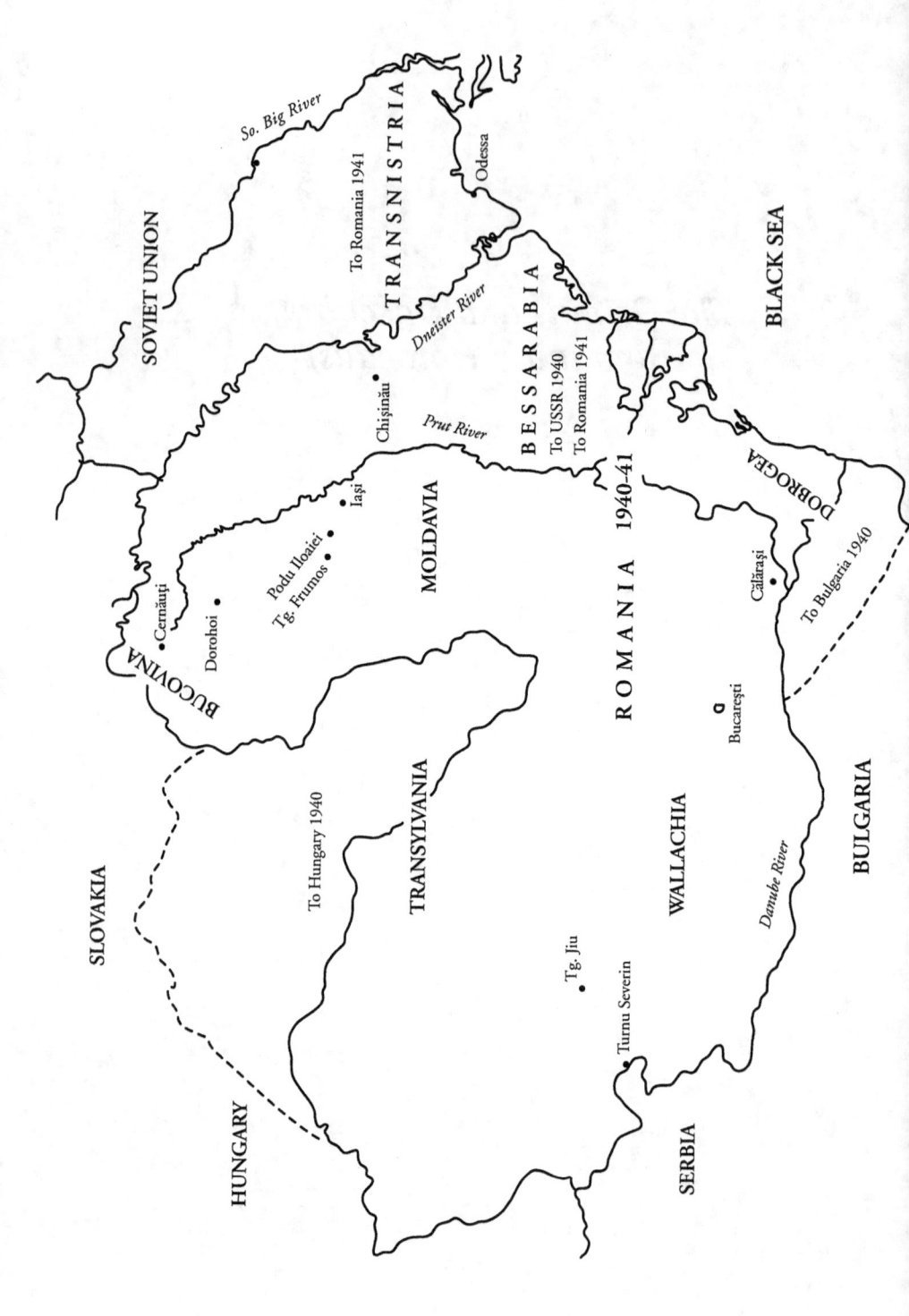

The Origins and Onset of the Romanian Holocaust

Henry Eaton

WAYNE STATE UNIVERSITY PRESS DETROIT

© 2013 by Wayne State University Press, Detroit, Michigan 48201. All rights reserved. No part of this book may be reproduced without formal permission.

17 16 15 14 13   5 4 3 2 1

Library of Congress Cataloging-in-Publication Data

Eaton, Henry L.

The origins and onset of the Romanian Holocaust / Henry Eaton.
   pages cm
Includes bibliographical references and index.
ISBN 978-0-8143-3872-8 (pbk. : alk. paper)—ISBN 978-0-8143-3856-8 (e-book)
1. Jews—Persecutions—Romania. 2. Jews—Romania—Iasi—History—20th century. 3. Holocaust, Jewish (1939–1945)—Romania. 4. Antisemitism—Romania—History—20th century. 5. Romania—Ethnic relations. I. Title.

DS135.R7E23 2013
940.53'1809498—dc23

2012040558

All photographs are from the United States Holocaust Memorial Museum. The views or opinions expressed in this book, and the context in which the images are used, do not necessarily reflect the views or policy of, or imply approval or endorsement by, the United States Holocaust Memorial Museum.

Typeset by Newgen North America
Composed in Adobe Garamond Pro and Walbaum

publication was made possible by
Jewish Federation of Greater Hartford

Contents

Preface ix

Introduction 1

1. Iași 9

2. Unification and the Jewish Question 17

3. Romanian Jews 29

4. Fascism and Antisemitism in the 1930s 43

5. The Rumble of Violence 55

6. War and the Mass Execution at Stânca Rosnovanu 71

7. *Duminica ceea* (That Sunday) 81

8. *Trenurile mortuare* (The Death Trains) 95

9. Victims 111

10. Perpetrators 121

11. The German Connection 139

    Conclusion 149

    Notes 157
    Bibliography 175
    Index 179

Preface

The Romanian Holocaust began in late June 1941. On the twenty-seventh of that month officers and soldiers of the Romanian 6th Cavalry Regiment executed 311 Jews (men, women, and children) at a place called Stânca Rosnovanu in northeastern Romania. Next evening, June 28, in the nearby city of Iași, the government's intelligence service, simulating an attack on German and Romanian troops in the city, ignited a pogrom. In the chaos that followed, policemen and German and Romanian soldiers joined civilians in the murder of several hundred Jews. Of those who survived some 2,700 perished while being evacuated from the city in the freight cars of two trains. The focus of this short study is on these mass murders and their origins. This means looking at immediate circumstances (e.g., Romania's ties with Nazi Germany) and looking back, especially at the growing presence and volatility of antisemitism in Romania from the mid-1800s and the transformation that occurred between the two world wars when anti-Jewish actions turned increasingly violent and finally genocidal.

For about fifty years following the publications of Marius Mircu's *Pogromul de la Iași* (București: Glob, 1945) and Matatias Carp's *Black Book* (1946–48) there was nothing published in Romania that dealt with the Iași pogrom and related events objectively and in some full measure. One slender book, published in 1978, concerned itself directly with the subject: A. Karețki and M. Covaci, *Zile Însîngerate la Iași (28–30 iunie 1941)* (Bloody days in Iași [28–30 June 1941]) (București: Politică, 1978). It differed from other texts by apologists and deniers in its attention to certain important details. But its message was the same: Germans were in charge of the massacre; they and some local scum were the killers. Real Romanians were blameless, and the number of Jewish victims was relatively small. Still, it was remarkable that a book on the pogrom, one of many subjects Romanians did not talk freely about during the Ceaușescu dictatorship, was published at all. Sometime in 1982–83, when I lived in Iași, a friend placed the book in my hands without comment.

PREFACE

Historians in Romania have often characterized their country as protecting its Jews during World War II and have described wartime dictator Ion Antonescu as a savior, pointing out that he rejected a German plan to deport Romanian Jews to the Belzec death camp. According to the *Historical Dictionary of Romania*, "while Antonescu deported 150–170,000 Jews from Bessarabia and Bucovina to Transnistria, he resisted German pressure to send Romanian Jews to Nazi death camps, as a result saving the lives of over 300,000 Jews."[1] What the authors of this dictionary and other apologists fail to point out is that when in October 1942 Antonescu canceled an earlier agreement with Germany to have Romanian Jews deported he was conducting his own genocidal operation, set in motion by his own dictatorial regime. That operation included mass killings by Romanian soldiers during the invasion of the Soviet Union, brutal deportations of survivors by Romanian gendarmerie, and death camps in Transnistria (between the Dniester and Bug rivers) administrated by a Romanian governor and his police officials. It was to these camps that nearly all the above-mentioned "deported 150–170,000 Jews from Bessarabia and Bucovina" were sent. Apologists sometimes make a further claim that the Antonescu regime, unlike the Hungarian government, not only saved its own Jews from German death camps but also gave asylum to Jews escaping from Hungary and other nearby countries. These apologists depict an innocent nation and heroic leader squeezed between opposing powers, Nazi Germany and the Soviet Union. Some even scoff at the idea that antisemitism was deeply rooted in Romania and so, having dismissed the fact of a Romanian Holocaust, also dismiss its primary cause.[2] Such views are likely to be with us for some time, but what has been a rather solid wall of denial has taken some hits. Most significant in this turnabout has been a wave of good scholarship and publication on the subject. Even the Romanian government has backed away from denial. On October 12, 2004, President Ion Iliescu, speaking publicly, admitted Romania's participation in the mass extermination of Jews. Supporting the president's report was a lengthy summary of (and excellent introduction to) the Romanian Holocaust, created for him by an international commission of top scholars in the field, headed by Elie Wiesel and supported by the Holocaust Martyrs' and Heroes' Remembrance Authority in Jerusalem (Yad Vashem) and the United States Holocaust Memorial Museum in Washington, DC.[3]

Indispensable for understanding long-term causes of the Romanian Holocaust are Carol Iancu's works, especially his history of Jews and antisemitism in Romania: *Les Juifs en Roumanie (1866–1919): De l'exclusion à l'émancipation* (Aix-en-Provence: Université de Provence, 1978) and *Les Juifs en Roumaine, 1919–1938: De l'émancipation à la marginalisation*

PREFACE

(Paris: Peeters, 1996). Iancu's second volume is complemented by two excellent monographs: Leon Volovici's *Nationalist Ideology and Antisemitism: The Case of Romanian Intellectuals in the 1930s,* translated from Romanian by C. Kormos (Oxford: Pergamon Press, 1991) and Irina Livezeanu's *Cultural Politics in Greater Romania: Regionalism, Nation Building, and Ethnic Struggle, 1918–1930* (Ithaca, NY: Cornell University Press, 1995). The first full-length study is Radu Ioanid's *The Holocaust in Romania: The Destruction of Jews and Gypsies under the Antonescu Regime, 1940–1944* (Chicago: Ivan R. Dee, 2000); Ioanid devotes some thirty pages to the Iași pogrom. Accounts of pogrom survivors may be found in the archives of Yad Vashem. Of published survivor accounts, one of the most interesting is Adrian Radu-Cernea, *Pogromul de la Iași: Depoziție de martor* (București: Hasefer, 2002). Official reports by civil and military officials around the time of the killings may be found at Yad Vashem and in the United States Holocaust Memorial Museum (especially RG 25.004M), and in volume 2 of Matatias Carp's The Black Book.

Carp's three-volume *Cartea Neagră: Suferințele evreilor din România în timpul dictaturii fasciste, 1940–1944* (București: 1946–48), or The Black Book: The suffering of Romanian Jews during the fascist dictatorship, 1940–1944, is the cornerstone for scholarship on the Romanian Holocaust. As secretary of the Federal Union of Jewish Communities in Romania during the war, Carp (1904–1952) was well situated to draw on and assemble basic information. Volume 1 of The Black Book documents the depredations of the National-Legionnaire State (September 1940–January 1941) that ended in a mass murder of Jews in Bucharest. Volume 2 primarily concerns the Iași pogrom and death trains. Volume 3 bears on wartime mass killings in Bucovina and Bessarabia and in the labor-death camps of Transnistria. These volumes first appeared between 1946 and 1948 then generally vanished from public view, part of an effort, it seems, to keep the national honor unsullied. It took nearly half a century and collapse of the Ceaușescu dictatorship for Carp's work to be reissued in Romania in 1996.[4]

Several volumes of documents on the history of Romanian Jews, including the 1930s and '40s, have been published by the Center for the Study of the History of Romanian Jews (Centrul pentru studiul istoriei Evreilor din România), a branch of the Federation of Jewish Communities of Romania (Federația Comunităților Evereiști din România) in Bucharest.[5]

Jean Ancel (d. 2008) has been the most prolific author of scholarly articles, books, and published document collections on the Romanian Holocaust. His *Preludiu la asasinat: Pogromul de la Iași, 29 iunie 1941* (Iași: Polirom, 2005) and volume 2 of Carp's *Cartea Neagră* are the two most important works on the Iași pogrom. Some other very important contributions by Ancel to the study of the Romanian Holocaust are: *Documents Concerning the Fate of Romanian Jewry during the Holocaust* (New York: Beate Klarsfeld Foundation, 1986), 12 vols.; *Transnistria* (București: Atlas, 1998), 3 vols.; and *Contribuții la istoria României: Problema evreiască* (București: Hasefer/Yad Vashem, 2001–3), 2 vols. Primary sources and the critical evaluation of official documents are constants in Ancel's work.

I appreciate the support given me by the University of North Texas to work in the library and archives of Yad Vashem, by the Fulbright Program to spend the 1990–91 academic year in Iași, and by the Russian and East European Center of the University of Illinois (Urbana) to work in the university library's excellent East European collection. The staffs at Yad Vashem and Illinois were kind and helpful. Despite its relative newness the expanding collection of the library and archives of the United States Holocaust Memorial Museum was useful to me. I very much appreciate the help of Professor Ralph Fisher of the University of Illinois, who always encouraged me in my work and who read my manuscript and suggested improvements. Thanks to Andrei Cretu for correcting my faulty diacritical marking of Romanian words. No one has given more support to this book project than my wife Kate and my sons Stephen and Jonathan. I owe many thanks to members of the Jewish community of Iași, especially those who recounted for me their recollections of the pogrom, and to Professor Odette Caufman-Blumenfeld and her father Dr. Simion Caufman, late president of the community.

Introduction

This is a brief study of the origins of the Romanian Holocaust and the first mass killings of Jews by Romanian authorities. It addresses two questions. First, why did the Antonescu government set out to exterminate Jews, those who lived in Romania and those in areas annexed by Romania during the Axis invasion of the Soviet Union in World War II? The war, the invasion, and Romania's alliance with Nazi Germany certainly accommodated a genocidal campaign, "ethnic purification" in the jargon of government leaders, but the war and Axis alignment were not compelling circumstances. Of the Third Reich's allies, only Romania took that course; in Hungary and Italy the systematic destruction of Jews required the intervention of Himmler's SS. So why did Romania set out to destroy the Jews in its territories? To answer this question one must look at Romania's antisemitic history, the subject I take up in the first half of this study. The second question concerns the initial mass killings of Jews by Romanian government agencies—where did the killings take place and when? who were the victims and perpetrators? and who gave the orders? The later chapters of this work are concerned with answering these questions.

The first massacres occurred in late June and early July 1941. On Sunday afternoon, June 29, 1941, in the city of Iași, several hundred Jews were shot to death in the courtyard of the municipal police station (*chestură*). Policemen, soldiers, and civilians began rounding them up the night before: invading and ransacking homes, stealing valuables, extorting money, beating and murdering residents. Many survivors of this assault were marched to the police station, some women and children but men for the most part, arms raised, jeered at, spit on, beaten, and shot if they fell behind or dropped their arms. Those who got to the chestură were driven into its courtyard between rows of soldiers beating them with wooden clubs and iron bars, wounding many, killing some. Women and most children were freed around the noon hour. Then, about 2:00 p.m., at the sound of air-raid sirens, the gates were closed and the shooting commenced, lasting off and on for some four hours. That evening and early Monday morning, survivors of the massacre and others, held in the chestură building or elsewhere in the city or caught up in the continuing raids, were herded to the central train station. Here the prisoners, crazed by thirst, some savagely beaten or wounded by gunshots or bayonets, were jammed into the boxcars of two trains. In the intense summer heat each car became a suffocating prison, doors locked shut and air vents closed or boarded over. More than fifteen hundred died in the foul and oven-like wagons of the first train, which meandered south on a halting, weeklong journey to the town of Călărași, ordinarily a trip of no more than a day. Nearly twelve hundred dead were removed from the more crowded cars of the second train, which took some eight hours to reach the town of Podu Iloaiei, only 15 miles (25 kilometers) west of Iași. Approximately 2,713 perished in the trains, but the total number of those murdered is not known. Romania's Intelligence Service reported one of the highest estimates, a figure of 13,266, including 40 women and 180 children.[1] Romanian Jews call the day of mass murder *Duminica ceea* (That Sunday) and the trains *Trenurile mortuare* (The Death Trains).

Another massacre of Jews occurred a few miles north of Iași two days before "That Sunday." Soldiers of the Romanian 6th Cavalry Regiment, during a skirmish across the Prut River, had entered the Soviet border town of Sculeni. Before retreating they rounded up some of its residents and brought them back into Romanian territory. Jews were then separated from the rest, and on June 27 at a place called Stânca Rosnovanu two regimental officers and a few soldiers robbed them, forced the young Jewish men to dig burial trenches, and executed them—311 men, women, and children. When Colonel Matieș, the regiment's commander, was later questioned about the killings he dismissed the victims as deserving no consideration and claimed he had commanded the execution "in conformity with superior orders."[2]

On the one hand these mass murders at Stânca Rosnovanu and Iași and in the death trains are part of Romania's long and often violent antisemitic past. What they signaled, however, was an extraordinary escalation of violence. They were the first of many such actions Romanian military and police units carried out during the invasion of the Soviet Union (1941–44). Whether acting alone or with German SS mobile killing commandos, the

INTRODUCTION

mission of these units was the "ethnic cleansing" of those conquered territories that were to come under Romanian rule: Northern Bucovina, Bessarabia, and Transnistria. Had the Axis powers defeated the Soviet Union and come to dominate the whole of the European continent, the Jews of Romania proper, the *Regat* or Old Kingdom, almost certainly would also have been exterminated.

Iași (pronounced *yahsh*), capital of the former principality of Moldavia, is in northeastern Romania, spread along the Bahlui River Valley and among the hills that flank its course. It lies some 10 miles (16 kilometers) west of the Prut River, Romania's border with the Soviet Union in June 1941 and after the breakup of the USSR its border with the Republic of Moldova. In the late nineteenth and early twentieth centuries Iași and neighboring towns and cities such as Fălticeni, Dorohoi, Suceava, and Botoșani had large Jewish populations whose shops, homes, schools, and synagogues represented lively, if not wealthy, communities. That side of Romanian life is all but gone now due to the cataclysmic events leading up to and including World War II, the persistence of antisemitism that followed the war, and opportunities for Romanian Jews to go elsewhere. In the territory that comprised Romania after World War II (i.e., excluding Soviet annexed Northern Bucovina and Bessarabia), Romanian Jews were reduced in number from about 450,000 in 1930 to about 26,000 in 1977.[3] In the late nineteenth century and up to World War II, Iași was a major center of Romanian Jewish culture with a community of 30,000 to 40,000 persons and more than a hundred synagogues. In the course of the war and its aftermath those numbers were reduced to a few hundred persons and one main temple.

Deniers and apologists have explained "That Sunday" and "The Death Trains" as the work of Germans. True Romanians, they say, did not take part in such a monstrous crime; instead, they risked their lives to help the victims.[4] But the eyewitness accounts of victims and others show that, in the first place, while they did not act alone in the killings, Romanians, from the highest officials to the dregs, initiated, participated in, and advanced, each stage of the action. Secondly, there is a long history of ill will and violence by Romanian Christians against Jews, including mass murders. The Iași pogrom is part of this record, the fruit of centuries-old hatreds that, during the troubled years between the two world wars, nurtured the most extreme solutions to Romania's so-called Jewish question.

Such solutions, supported by some of the country's most influential political, intellectual, and religious leaders, gained wide acceptance in the 1920s and '30s and were finally put into general practice, beginning with draconian anti-Jewish legislation in January 1938. Mass violence against Jews soon followed. In late June 1940, Romanian soldiers, forced by the Soviet Union to retreat from Bessarabia and Northern Bucovina, vented their anger and frustration as they withdrew by plundering and killing Jews. Hardest hit of several communities was the city of Dorohoi where more than fifty Jews were murdered. In November Iron Guardsmen murdered eleven Jews in the city of Ploieşti. A few months later more than a hundred Jews were massacred in Bucharest during the Iron Guard rebellion of January 21–23, 1941. Thus the first mass killings of the Romanian Holocaust in late June 1941, at Stânca Rosnovanu and Iaşi and in the death trains, was not so much a beginning as an escalation of deadly violence against Jews.

Victims of the Iaşi pogrom were still dying on the Călăraşi death train as Romanian and German forces, making up Army Group South, began their attack (Operation München, July 2, 1941) into Soviet territory. On the German side, killing Jews was the special task of Einsatzgruppe D, the mobile unit Himmler assigned to the southern military zone. On the Romanian side, extermination was primarily the work of soldiers, policemen, and agents of two government intelligence services: SSI (Serviciul Special de Informaţii) and Section II (military intelligence) of the Supreme General Staff. German exterminators occasionally reported on the actions of their Romanian partners, especially their sloppiness (leaving dead bodies strewn about), cruelty, and greed. Regarding an action of July 1941 in Bessarabia, Einsatzgruppe D reported that "during the past days and nights, considerable excesses were carried out repeatedly against Jews by Rumanian soldiers."[5] Jews were murdered or imprisoned, tortured, raped, and robbed; thousands were killed in Cernăuţi (Czernowitz) and Chişinău (Kishinev), the major cities of Bucovina and Bessarabia. Romanian commanders, at Ion Antonescu's urging, carried out one of the largest single mass murders of Jews during the war in and around Odessa on October 22–24, 1941. Many survivors of this and other massacres died while being marched to labor-death camps in Romania-controlled Transnistria (between the Dniester and Southern Bug rivers), and most of those who reached the camps died there, victims of execution squads, typhus or other diseases, starvation, exposure, or multiple afflictions. The fact that the same state agencies responsible for the killings of Jews at Stânca Rosnovanu and Iaşi continued the wholesale killing of Jews during the invasion of the Soviet Union shows these events to be part of the same "cleansing" operation.[6]

Who ordered the Iaşi pogrom and subsequent mass murders? There is one credible answer—those who had the power to make those decisions, dictator Ion Antonescu and his top civil and military officials. Most likely the order was given some days or weeks before the invasion of the Soviet

INTRODUCTION

Union. Around that time Ion and his distantly related second-in-command Mihai Antonescu described the upcoming struggle in their speeches as a war of machine guns and ethnic purification. The likely first action taken by the government to put its genocidal plan in motion was to send to Iași, on June 18, 1941, a special unit of SSI, the state's intelligence service, the task of which was to spark a pogrom in the city by simulating an attack on German and Romanian troops stationed there. The staged attack could hardly fail, preceded as it was by two Soviet bombings of the city and allegations that Jews (already demonized as enemy aliens) had signaled the bombers to their targets. Perpetrators of the pogrom came from all social classes and included SSI agents who not only set it off but also, exceeding their orders, joined in the killings. Officers and men of Romanian and German military units in the city, local and district policemen, and civilians also participated. Greed was one of the chief motivators; at one end of the plundering frenzy Christians grabbed their Jewish partners' share of land and business property, at the other end scavengers stripped cadavers of their clothing and shoes.

What lies behind the descent of Ion Antonescu's government into genocide? Nazi Germany showed the way by its remarkable rise to power and relentless campaign against Jews. Romanian leaders generally admired the Führer's regime. An obvious connection between the antisemitic policies of the two countries occurred in August 1940 when the government of King Carol II enacted legislation patterned after the anti-Jewish Nuremberg laws of 1935. As for the German plan to invade the USSR, that offered Romania the opportunity to crush its Soviet enemy, recover territory that it claimed rightfully belonged to it, and at the same time mask the crime of genocide.

The path Antonescu's government took had its origins in the age-old hatred of Jews, sharpened in the 1860s and 1870s when the country became unified and independent. Three things rather clearly mark this circumstance: first, an already deep-seated Christian antisemitism; second, the growing number and commercial prominence of Jews in Moldavia in the mid-1800s; and third, the question of Romanian citizenship for Jews. Leading the antisemitic movement, from the 1860s to the 1940s, were the country's elite: statesmen, poets, historians, philosophers, theologians, journalists, lawyers, university students and their professors, scientists, government ministers, and hierarchs of the Orthodox Church.

The aftermath of World War I was an important moment in this history, featuring protests by Christian university students against Jews and their political emancipation. The climax came in a nationwide student demonstration in December 1922 that helped generate a number of fascist-

INTRODUCTION

nationalist-Christian-antisemitic parties or groups. Doubtless the racism of these students was rooted in the country's enduring Jew-hatred and encouraged, from the turn of the century, by writings and speeches of the country's most prominent men, but some were also frustrated by the competition they faced from Jewish students. They demanded a reduction in the number of Jews admitted to, or even their elimination from, the universities. *Numerus clausus* (restricted admission) and *numerus nullus* (no admission) became major slogans in the interwar period inside and outside the universities. Not only were Jews excluded from public schools (only five were admitted to the University of Iași for the 1939–40 academic year), they also became targets of laws that took away their political rights, property, and employment. They were also more likely to be targets of violent crimes when, as during the interwar years, violence (including murder) became part of the Romanian political landscape. Officials of Carol II's government murdered leaders of the Iron Guard. Guardists responded by killing government officials. Iron Guard founder Corneliu Codreanu, having murdered a police official, was treated by the jury that acquitted him and by much of the public as a hero. Codreanu was himself murdered on King Carol's orders in November 1938; two years later legionnaires took their revenge, executing sixty-three persons they alleged were involved in his killing. Violence as a way of solving political problems became the way for antisemites to vent their own particular hatred. Besides mass killings there were many actions against individuals or small groups of Jews: robbery, extortion, torture, murder. Such actions acquired a momentum, bolstered by deeply entrenched hatred, nurtured in the climate of growing political violence, and meeting little moral resistance from a generally acquiescent Christian public and government. In this way a bridge was built leading from occasional, random, and private (perhaps even spontaneous) murderous actions against Jews toward a state-administered genocide.

The next-to-last chapter of this destructive process, the effort to make Romanian Jews aliens and drive them out of the country, began in earnest with the Citizenship Revision Law of 1938, legislated by the government of poet Octavian Goga and Professor Alexandru C. Cuza (not to be confused with the unifying prince of Romania, Alexandru I. Cuza, who died in 1873). The law canceled citizenship for nearly a quarter-million Jews, some of whom were then stripped of their jobs and threatened with expulsion from the country. Anti-Jewish terror accompanied Draconian legislation. The government, which had long tolerated acts of injustice against Jews, turned a permissive eye on the mass murders committed by soldiers who ravaged the towns and villages of Bucovina in the summer of 1940. Some seven months later Ion Antonescu held back his military forces while legionnaires tortured

INTRODUCTION

and killed Bucharest Jews during the rebellion of January 1941. Finally, as the time for invading Soviet Russia approached, mass murder became state policy. The first such killing operations involving military, intelligence, and police agencies, were the mass murders of Sculeni Jews at Stânca Rosnovanu and the Iași pogrom and death trains.

CHAPTER 1

Iași

Elie Wiesel spoke at the National Theater in Iași in late June 1991, marking the fiftieth anniversary of the pogrom and death trains. As he began, a woman sitting in the front row shouted out that he lied. Wiesel paused for a moment while she was escorted out of the building and then calmly went on speaking. It was the woman who lied, but what she said was not surprising given the time and place. In 1991 swastikas were still occasionally spray-painted on building walls in Iași, and most Romanian historians, as well as their country's president, Ion Iliescu, had not yet admitted to any such thing as a Romanian Holocaust. As for the theater itself, it has not been immune to anti-Jewish slander. It is true that among the sculptures of prominent theater people that ring the building is a small pedestal-mounted bust of Avram Goldfaden (1840–1908), "father" of Yiddish theater, which he first staged in Iași at the Green Tree cabaret in 1876. Goldfaden's bust, a rarity in Romania, representing a Jew, reminds us of the city's and country's once vital Jewish community. But the dominating sculpture, one that stands at the building's entrance, is a larger-than-life statue of Vasile Alecsandri (1821–1890) after whom the theater is named. He is a much admired national figure, one of his country's founding fathers but known best for advancing Romanian literature as publisher, poet, and "father of Romanian drama." He despised Jews, depicting them as "village bloodsuckers," greedy merchants, and cowards, reinforcing images that became, alongside established Christian myths of deicide and blood libel, fixtures of Romanian antisemitism.[1]

Between 1848 and 1878 revolutionaries, including Alecsandri, united the principalities of Moldavia and Wallachia into the independent state of

CHAPTER 1

Romania. These national heroes tended to be highborn and well educated, to be historians, journalists, playwrights, and poets as well as political activists. They not only brought Romania into existence but, as lawmakers and ministers, fixed its direction. They appeared at first to favor a broadly inclusive political system, proposing in 1848 that Romanian Jews be granted citizenship in the new state. This was, however, a proposal made to attract support for their rebellion, not to emancipate Jews. Once in power they not only denied Jews citizenship but assaulted them with numerous hostile laws and policies.

When the government, pressured by European allies, did most reluctantly grant citizenship to Romanian Jews after World War I, the opposition was again led by the intellectual and political elite and by Christian university students. Among the most prominent and influential opponents were University of Iași professors: Romania's most respected historian Nicolae Iorga (1871–1940) and political economist Alexandru C. Cuza (1857–1944). It was Cuza's student, Corneliu Codreanu (1899–1938), who in 1927 created the Legion of the Archangel Michael (known also as the Iron Guard). It took some fifteen years, from the 1923 constitutional revision (granting Jews citizenship) to the Goga-Cuza government of 1937–38, for the unrelenting antisemitic clamor to move state leaders toward dismantling the political rights and economic means of Romania's Jews and to put them on a path of destruction.

A few blocks north of the National Theater is Union Plaza (Piață Unirii) where stands a bronze statue of Moldavian prince Alexandru Ioan Cuza (1820–1873). Plaza and statue commemorate the uniting of Wallachia and Moldavia in 1859 when assemblies in each principality elected Cuza as their prince.[2] Over the next several years, constitutional and administrative unification were worked out and Romania was born. Cuza's reign was brief and extraordinary. Assisted by his prime minister, Mihail Kogălniceanu (1817–1891), the two worked to achieve independent statehood, reduce the power of the church, establish foundations for free and compulsory public education, and bring about reform that, along with peasant emancipation, would reduce the immense gulf between rich landowners and poor debt-ridden farmers.[3] The prince even sought to lift legal restrictions from Jews and create a constitutional path for their gradual naturalization. Unfortunately, his opponents, helped by scandals in his government and private life, were able to drive him out of office and from the country in 1866.

A few blocks farther north on a street called Copou is Alexandru I. Cuza University, Romania's first university (established in 1860). It and the advancement of public education in general were major achievements of Prince Cuza and Kogălniceanu. A statue of the prince's minister, representing him reading aloud from an open book, stands on a high pedestal in front of one of the university's main buildings. The intellectual life of Iași as well as the unification and independence of Romania are, in some important measure, the work of this man. In 1848, in opposition to the Russian-sponsored regime of Moldavian Prince Mihail Sturdza, Kogălniceanu proposed, with the backing of other revolutionaries, a list of demands that would have created a unified and independent democratic republic; freed Jews from various civil, political, and economic restrictions; and made them citizens.[4] As Romania approached independent statehood, however, he and his cohorts opposed granting them citizenship and, as interior minister, issued directives in 1869 proposing to local authorities that they drive Jews from the villages. Kogălniceanu even boasted that his anti-Jewish actions, which encouraged Christian villagers to attack Jews, were more effective than those of his revolutionary cohort and ministerial predecessor Ion Brătianu who had issued similar directives.[5] In front of another entrance to the university's main building is a statue of A. D. Xenopol (1847–1920), "Romania's first great modern historian." Like Kogălniceanu he stands on a high platform as if about to address the students and professors who pass below. His answer to "the Jewish question" in Romania was one-way assimilation, the path taken by his father, a Jew who converted to Christianity.[6]

North of the university is an area of nice houses and Copou Park. This part of the city reminded Nicolae Iorga of a splendid past, aristocratic and harmonious. "I passed spellbound through the magnificent gardens surrounded by iron balustrades," he wrote, "with wide avenues adorned by the monument, erected at the time of Mihail Sturdza, the Russian Protector."[7] The monument, a thirteen-ton stone obelisk, was put up by Prince Sturdza in 1834 to commemorate the Règlement organique. Following Russia's defeat of the Ottoman Empire in 1828–29 it became the dominant foreign power in the two Romanian principalities. One result was that new fundamental laws for their governance, a Règlement for Moldavia (January 1832) and a nearly identical one for Wallachia (July 1831), were worked out by the Romanian nobility under Russian guidance.[8] Xenopol claimed that antisemitism in Romanian party politics appeared only when Jews began to pursue citizenship in the 1860s.[9] Still, located in the Moldavian Règlement is a paragraph (chapter 3, article 94) representing Jews not much differently than we find in racist propaganda a century later: "Without question the Jews, who are everywhere in Moldavia and whose numbers increase daily, live mainly at the expense of the natives and exploit nearly all resources to the detriment of both industrial progress and public well-being. In order to avoid this problem, if at all possible . . . the census report will record the circumstance of every Jew so that those who have no status, lack authorization, and are not usefully employed, may be got rid of and those like them no longer be allowed to enter Moldavia."[10] Carol Iancu points to this passage as a key to understanding the tragic situation of Romanian Jews—identified in law at the country's inception as invading parasites who exploit the country and its people to no good end and are "to be got rid of." This is not just a law that points toward anti-Jewish sentiments far down the road. This particular article of the Moldavian Règlement was revived in the 1860s by ministers of the united principalities, including Kogălniceanu, to provide legal authority for driving Jews from villages and out of the country. Clearly the aim of Romania's founding fathers was to get rid of the old regime but continue its anti-Jewish policies.

Copou Park's most famous monument is not Sturdza's obelisk but an old linden tree in the shade of which Romania's most beloved citizen and poet, Mihai Eminescu (1850–1889), liked to sit. Strolling through the park Iorga may have passed the tree if not the poet himself, some twenty-one years his senior. In one of his many journal articles Eminescu observed that to say Jews were persecuted because of their religion was only false clamoring by the Jewish press, the "true causes" being social and economic. Jews had crowded into Romania, he said, as peddlers, tavern keepers, and usurers, exploiters who exhibited a "solidarity of race, interest, and religion," attributes they used "to compete with and ruin Christian commerce." "The tendency to monopolize trade is evident in the race," he wrote, and their wealth came "without work, without production, only through speculation and through cheating." "It is . . . a truth that Jews have a disastrous effect on the moral and material conditions of our people, a truth that they are a foreign race, immigrants of the past 40 years, a truth that corruption and immorality accompany their immigration, a truth that—except for those among them who can be assimilated—they must be removed from villages, must be forbidden from peddling in cities, must bend to the need to work."[11]

Like Eminescu, Iorga was a prodigious and diverse writer, especially concerning Romania and its history. Both studied in the West. Eminescu took up philosophy in Berlin and Vienna; Iorga concentrated on history in Berlin and Paris, earning a doctorate in Leipzig. One is the nation's first poet, the other its greatest historian, two stars in a constellation of anti-Jewish artists, scholars, and politicians who flourished from the mid-nineteenth century to the 1940s, poisoning the ground between Gentile and Jew, adding skillful discourse to the anti-Jewish arsenal of mindless crudities and violence.

Iron Guard founder Corneliu Codreanu praised Alecsandri, Kogălniceanu,

Eminescu, and others who brought Romania into statehood and fought against citizenship for Jews. He claimed to have discovered in the writings of professors Iorga and A. C. Cuza the three essential "ideals of life for the Romanian people": unity, economic and political elevation of the peasantry, and "solution of the Jewish problem." For Codreanu and Iorga, the city of Iași was itself a national monument, "the eternal city of Romania," wrote Codreanu, "great by virtue of its great past and great by its present tragedy—for the city of the forty churches dies daily forgotten under the merciless Jewish invasion."[12] Iorga, the intellectual and antisemitic dean of Romanian nationalism, described Iași as "the church of churches of our past." Those who had not seen the city, he urged, could not be fully conscious of their Romanian nationality. Soon after the turn of the century he wrote nostalgically about its clean and decent past, lamenting its loss of political and economic vigor following unification and independence and the attractions of Bucharest, the country's political center. But what weighed most on his mind were the city's Jews who, "though they had no means whatsoever of bettering their circumstances, multiplied all the more" so that "Iași became a miserable ghetto." Here is Iorga's proposal for the city's resurrection: "Jews must either leave or starve to death. With its vital powers reduced, Iași will have to trim its unproductive branches, be reduced to a smaller circle. And inside this ring, which encompasses the schools and great monuments, it will be essential to establish order and absolute purity."[13]

"Purification" became part of Romania's antisemitic jargon, meaning the removal of Jews from teaching at or attending public schools, from the legal or medical professions, the military, the ownership of rural property, or from the entire economy, or the country, or from life itself. Iorga's meaning is clear; to restore Iași to its rightful place as the spiritual heart of the country, Jews living there must be cleaned out. Indeed, "purification" or "ethnic purification" or "cleansing the ground" are words and phrases government leaders used in June–July 1941 to identify the mass murder of Jews in or their deportation from Bessarabia and Northern Bucovina, the soon-to-be conquered and Romania-ruled territories of the Soviet Union. On June 17, 1941, Mihai Antonescu, dictator Ion Antonescu's second in command, spoke about these territories to the Romanian Council of Ministers: "We must take advantage of this moment, to purify the population."[14] On July 3, 1941, the first full day of Operation München, the Axis invasion across the Prut River into Soviet territory by Army Group South (primarily the German 11th and Romanian 3rd and 4th armies), he spoke again on the same subject, this time at the Ministry of Interior whose gendarmerie were to be a major force in deporting and killing Jews. The speech was an outline of administrative procedures to be used by civil and military officials who would govern the two provinces. Article 10 was titled "Purificarea Etnică şi Politică" (Ethnic and Political Purification). It began: "We find ourselves at a most favorable moment in history, for a complete ethnic liberation, for a national revision, and for the purification of our nation from all those elements alien to its soul."[15]

During his visit to Iaşi in 1991, Elie Wiesel, besides speaking at the National Theater, visited the city's Jewish cemetery and the mass graves of those murdered during the pogrom. Not far from these graves is another mass burial site, a field of stones arranged in neat rows and columns, marking the remains of soldiers killed, fighting for Romania in World War I. The twenty-four years (more or less) that separate these two burials saw antisemitism in Romania become increasingly strident and violent. A major cause of this particular upwelling of hatred and an issue that linked those buried at the two sites was the citizenship question. During the First World War Romanian Jews were encouraged by promises of citizenship to join the country's military. At the time the vast majority of Romanian Jews were prevented from becoming citizens, not by their country's constitution, which had been revised in their favor in 1879 (to satisfy demands of other countries), but because Romanian officials had put up procedural barricades that effectively neutralized the law. Finally, after the war and following many months of determined opposition by top political figures, the government did grant citizenship to Romanian Jews. However, this was not done to reward military service, or from a sense of long-delayed justice. It was done because the victorious allies demanded it (this time secured by international treaty, statute, and revision of Romania's constitution) and coupled that demand with an extraordinarily large gift of territory, one that should have satisfied even the most ardent nationalist's dream of a Greater Romania. Jews were elated, but for the government and Christian public in general the political emancipation of Jews was bitter medicine forced on them by outsiders. To make matters worse naturalization was dragged out for months; not until March 28, 1923, did a new constitution with the necessary revisions become law. Meanwhile, hate mongers used the contentious issue to stoke the public's antisemitic passions.

On March 4, 1923, Corneliu Codreanu and his mentor, Professor A. C. Cuza, held a mass meeting in Iaşi to protest the upcoming constitutional change. Participants from forty-two Romanian districts first gathered at the Metropolitan Church, across the street from the National Theater, for religious services and to have their identical forty-two flags blessed:

The cloth of these flags was black—a sign of mourning; in the center a round white spot, signifying our hopes surrounded by the darkness they will have to conquer; in the center of the white, a swastika, the symbol of anti-Semitic struggle throughout the world; and all around the flag, a band of the Romanian tricolor—red, yellow, and blue.

All 42 flags at the moment they were to be blessed were unfurled before the altar. . . .

From the Cathedral, thousands of people, banners unfurled, formed a procession through Union Square, Lăpușneanu and Carol Sts., headed for the University. There, in a gesture of homage and veneration, wreaths were placed for Mihail Kogălniceanu, Simion Bărnuțiu and Gheorghe Mârzescu, the last defender of article 7 of the Constitution of 1879 and, ironically, father of the liberal minister George Mârzescu, defender of the Jews.[16]

"From the Cathedral . . . headed for the University." The Romanian Orthodox Church, like the universities and government, was a pillar of antisemitism. In the nineteenth century Christians in Romania were alarmed by what they perceived as a flood of Jews invading their country. Then, after the First World War, adding to the injury of numbers, these offspring of Satan and murderers of Jesus became Romanian citizens. On the streets young priests who joined in the antisemitic demonstrations of Christian university students and legionnaires carried out the Orthodox war against Jews. At the highest political level church officials stood behind their government's draconian anti-Jewish policies. Early in the war against the Soviet Union and at a time when the Romanian government had begun its campaign of genocide, Patriarch Nicodim added Bolshevism to the Jewish crimes of Satanism and deicide, and Moldavian Metropolitan Irineu identified Hitler, Antonescu, and Mannerheim (Finland's military commander during World War II) as God's archangels who, "with the sign of the cross on their chests and in their hearts" led their armies "in a war against the Great Dragon, red as fire, and . . . the synagogue of Satan."[17]

CHAPTER 2

Unification and the Jewish Question

The creation of Romania was advanced in 1859 when parliaments in the principalities of Moldavia and Wallachia each elected Alexandru I. Cuza its prince. Independence came with the defeat of the Ottoman Empire in 1877 and recognition of statehood by European powers was conferred in the 1878 Treaty of Berlin. The hopes of Jews for citizenship were elevated or beaten down at various stages in this process. Their hopes were dampened as a result of anti-Jewish measures taken by Prince Cuza's government, consisting of economic restrictions and the levying of extraordinary taxes. They and their allies abroad, including the Alliance Israélite Universelle (established in Paris in 1860), objected to these actions and demanded civil and political rights for Jews. As a result of this pressure, or a real desire to extend political rights, or because he needed foreign support to become permanent head of state, Prince Cuza changed course on the "Jewish question."[1] He adopted legislation that advanced the civil and political rights of Jews and tried to persuade assemblies in the two principalities to accept a provision in his Statut (Law Code) of 1864–65 granting citizenship to all those born in Romania and to others by act of parliament after ten years' residency. Although the code only pointed toward citizenship, the Jewish community of Iași informed Cuza of its "unlimited devotion" and "profound homage for the work that your government has done to hasten the emancipation of the Jews of Romania."[2]

Jewish rights were still unresolved in 1866, however, when Cuza and his code were replaced by Carol of Hohenzollern-Sigmaringen (r. 1866–1914) and a new constitution. Article 6 of its preliminary draft stated that "religion is no obstacle to naturalization," but it was left to a "special law" to establish procedures for naturalizing Jews. Although citizenship was not promised, the draft-article so infuriated antisemites that they plundered the houses and shops of Jews in Bucharest and destroyed their main house of worship, the Choir Temple. Lawmakers got the message; when the matter came before the parliament Kogălniceanu urged opposition, claiming that within two days of enactment Jews in Iași would be murdered. But the safety of Jews was not his main concern; he also emphasized how different Jews were from Romanians, pointing not only to their peculiar dress and manners but also accusing them of moral corruption, urging delegates to see the poet-playwright Vasile Alecsandri's play, *The Village Bloodsuckers* (*Lipitorile Satelor*), in which a Jewish innkeeper is one of the villains.[3] In the end the Romanian parliament replaced draft-article 6 with article 7; it ruled that among foreigners in Romania only Christians might become citizens.[4] This lost opportunity and the bitter words and vicious actions that surrounded the debate had grave consequences for Romanian Jews. Even those whose families had lived in Moldavia and Wallachia for generations were fixed, at the beginning of the new state, as undesirable aliens. Another failure of the founding fathers, which indirectly affected Jews, was the agrarian reform of August 1864 that emancipated Romania's peasants but left them impoverished and oppressed.[5] Jews (some of them moneylenders, middlemen, estate managers, innkeepers, merchants) were convenient targets for angry peasants or politicians and officials who wanted someone to blame for problems they could not or would not fix.

Early in 1868, Delaporte, the French consul in Iași, expressed his thoughts about anti-Jewish feelings in Romania in a letter to the French foreign ministry. He was prompted to do this by efforts of Moldavian interior minister Ion Brătianu (1821–1891) to expel Jews from the countryside, which tended to stir up local anti-Jewish violence, and by efforts of the Iași mayor to drum up support for draconian anti-Jewish legislation before the chamber of deputies. Delaporte addresses a basic question: what generates the popular support that underlies the government's anti-Jewish campaign? Jews, he said, use their mental quickness to excel in commerce, finance, and industry, while Romanians continue to be contemptuous of such work and seek only careers in public service. By default, then, Jews gain control of trade, finance, and most small industry so that financial or commercial transactions must be mediated through them. As a result Romanians either envy and hate Jews or fear them because of their economic power. Delaporte also pointed out that Brătianu's alleged campaign against so-called vagabonds was really intended to destroy the economies of prosperous Jews and then drive them out of the country.[6]

European states formally recognized Romania's independence in article 43 of the Treaty of Berlin (1878), providing it accept article 44, the main intent of which was to force leaders of the new state to naturalize its Jews.[7] The Romanian government did in fact sign the treaty and revise its constitution to accord with article 44. However, while the government was working on ways to change its law to give the appearance of compliance, the Romanian press laid down a barrage of antisemitic slander. Editors warned the Berlin signatories that should they try to force Romania to grant citizenship to the diseased, child-stabbing, "blood sucking charlatans," and turn the country into another Palestine, the Romanian people themselves would see the Jews hanged and buried.[8] In the end Romanian officials made a show of compliance, won Europe's endorsement of statehood, and granted citizenship to a few Jews. According to article 7 of the revised 1879 constitution, Jews, grouped under the designation "foreigners," could not be denied citizenship. At the same time the law set out procedures that were intended to do just that, most applicants needing individual approval by an act of parliament followed by a ten-year probationary period. To convince skeptical European powers of its good intentions parliament naturalized en bloc 1,075 Jews, including 883 who had fought against the Ottoman Empire in the 1877 War of Independence. By 1913, of the thousands of Jews who had applied (not counting veterans of 1877) those naturalized numbered (living and dead) only a few hundred.[9] So the issue continued to burn because Romania's Jews (with growing support from outside the country) regarded naturalization as the only way toward full participation in the country's life, and that is precisely what antisemites feared.

Clearly, the constitutional promise of political rights for Jews in article 7 was a ruse. One provision of the article, however, was undoubtedly sincere; it denied rural land to noncitizens, that is, to all but the few hundred Jews noted above. In fact, one characteristic of the new state's legislative history is its anti-Jewish measures, laws prohibiting or limiting their owning, renting, or leasing land; being innkeepers or tax collectors; selling spirits in the countryside; owning pharmacies; being stock or money brokers or commission merchants; obtaining work as agents and forwarders; selling lottery tickets; or peddling in towns. Jewish lawyers and doctors were severely restricted in their practices by law in the 1880s and 1890s. Jews paid state taxes on kosher meat and, as "foreigners," needed special permission to move from one part of Romania to another.[10]

Legal barriers denied Jews the full benefits of public education and health care. Jewish children were admitted free of charge to public schools in the 1860s, but two decades later, as their number grew, accounting for a third or more of the elementary pupils in some places, principals began to deny them entry and were encouraged in this practice by the government. In 1892 a law regulating primary schools assessed school taxes on "foreigners" (mostly Jews) and gave first preference to "Romanians" should schoolroom space be limited. Similar legislation over the next decade aimed at reducing or eliminating altogether the admission of Jews to any level of public schooling. Schools founded by Jews to meet the educational needs of their communities were harassed by state officials, requiring, for example, that they be open on Jewish, but closed on Christian, holy days.[11] Regarding access to public hospitals, Dr. Wilhelm Filderman, who headed the Romanian Jewish community in the 1920s and 1930s, recorded in his memoirs the regulations of February 18, 1895, for St. Spiridon Hospital in Iași: "clinical service will admit Jews only when their sickness presents a special interest to the medical students, and even then only if the number of such patients does not rise above a third of the unoccupied beds."[12] Besides laws, officials issued rulings to local authorities, like the anti-Jewish circulars sent out by Brătianu and Kogălniceanu.[13] The administrative and legal war against Jews was compounded by private actions. Christian citizens organized boycotts of Jewish businesses in Iași in the 1880s. In September 1886 an Antisemitic Romano-European Congress was held in Bucharest; out of it was born the Anti-Jewish Universal Alliance. Alliance member Ioan Polihroniade, who edited the journal *Deșteptarea (Awakening)*, printed and distributed thousands of lithographs in 1897 depicting the alleged ritual murder of a Christian girl in 1882 by Jews of Tiszaeszlar, Hungary. The Hungarian press had managed to draw the whole country's attention to the yearlong trial. Acquittal only added to the outpouring of hatred, setting off a number of violent anti-Jewish actions. Fifteen years later, the notorious case was still useful for firing up antisemitism in neighboring Romania.[14]

The twentieth anniversary of Romanian independence was in 1897. A proposed law that year to exclude Jews from military service drew protests from Jewish army veterans. In response the antisemitic Cultural League, directed by N. Iorga and A. C. Cuza, held a public meeting in Bucharest in November to defend the measure and speak out against Jews. The meeting spurred groups of students to rampage through the Jewish quarter of the capital, singing the patriotic hymn "Awake Romania!" as police stood aside.[15] Among those who came under attack were members of the General Association of Romanian-Born Jews (created in 1890), which had initiated the protest against excluding Jews from military service. As a result the association was disbanded. The violence in Bucharest spawned outbreaks elsewhere in the country over the next several months. The Jewish community of Iași was attacked on May 28, 1899, a Sunday. The action occurred after members of the National Committee of Students of Iași posted an incendiary anti-Jewish manifesto around the city and held a public assembly to decide on the best way to defend the nation against Jews. When people came out of the meeting in an angry mood they first attacked policemen sent there to keep order and then turned on Jewish stores and homes, breaking out windows. The French vice-consul reported two or three persons killed in the melee.[16]

More ominous for the Romanian Jewish community, perhaps, was the great Kishinev pogrom of 1903. Kishinev, about 62 miles (100 kilometers) straight east of Iași, was then capital of the Russian province of Bessarabia. Like Iași, its Jewish population at the turn of the century was about half the total (approximately 50,000 out of 108,000 in 1897). The pogrom began on the afternoon of Easter Sunday, April 6, 1903, and lasted until the next evening. Forty-nine Jews were killed, women and girls raped, shops and homes plundered. As in the 1941 Iași pogrom, the action was not spontaneously ignited, and authorities did little to prevent violence. Some even supported it. Both disasters grew out of old official policies of encouraging or ignoring crimes against Jews. Furthermore, the presence of state security or intelligence agencies, the *okhrana* (Okhrannoe Otdelenie) at Kishinev and SSI (Serviciul Special de Informații) at Iași, before and during the violence, indicates government complicity in both massacres.[17]

In the 1890s and early 1900s tens of thousands of Romanian Jews emigrated in an attempt to escape severe economic hardship and persecution. Some groups of mostly young men and boys walked to Western Europe. Many of these *fussgayer* made their way to Hamburg and there embarked for the United States or other countries. Some of those who remained tried to organize in order to provide their communities with basic services, present a united voice on the question of political rights, and defend against antisemites who were themselves becoming organized. After the demise of the General Association of Romanian-Born Jews in 1897 and various failed attempts at reestablishing a national association, Romanian Jews in December 1909 established, at the suggestion of B'nai B'rith, a lasting (until 1948) Union of Native Jews (Uniunea Evreilor Pământeni [UEP]), renamed Union of Romanian Jews (Uniunea Evreilor Români) in 1923. The UEP appealed to King Carol I and the government to give Jews the political rights that had been promised them since the revolution of 1848 and on a regular basis took their concerns directly to members of parliament. In 1910 *Curierul Israelit* (*Israelite Courier*) became the official journal of the Union. In the Balkan

Wars UEP pledged its support of Romania and was encouraged by some leaders to believe Jewish veterans would be rewarded with citizenship for their patriotism.[18]

Neither emigration, military service, nor the dire poverty of most Romanian Jews around the turn of the century diffused antisemitism. During these years, journals called *The Antisemite* (*Antisemitul*) began publication in each of several cities. In 1906 N. Iorga founded a national journal, *The Romanian People* (*Neamul Românesc*), in which the so-called Jewish question was ever present. Iorga himself contributed numerous anti-Jewish articles. Even after his break with A. C. Cuza in 1919, he continued to insist that Jews were dangerous to Romania, more so than other minorities because they had their own alien political agenda that threatened national interests and because they were so prominent in certain professions. Whether, or to what extent, anti-Jewish opinions from prominent figures like Iorga or Cuza reached into the ranks of peasants is not clear. Carol Iancu claims that Iorga and his journal were partly responsible for the "antisemitic diversion" that occurred at the outset of the peasant revolt of 1907. Jewish shops and houses were especially targeted for plundering in the first days, but then peasants turned on big tenant farmers and absentee landlords as they moved south, threatening Bucharest itself. Wilhelm Filderman claimed the relationship between peasants and Jews was friendly, that peasants in 1907 were not after Jewish blood but wanted to bring down the government. He did not deny that Jews and their property were attacked but emphasized that peasants did not kill any Jews. "Anti-Semitism comes from higher up," he wrote, "from politicians and semi-intellectuals, never from deep roots in the heart of the population." Still, destruction of Jewish property at the beginning of the rebellion hardly suggests friendship. Nationalist-antisemites, encouraged by the Peasant Revolt, held a large meeting in Iași in November 1907. Professors railed against the Jewish menace and called for the exclusion of Jews from the army and journalism. Dr. Ghelerter, a Jew and leading socialist agitator among workers in Iași, was singled out for special abuse. A. C. Cuza called for exclusions or expulsions, and Iorga urged that Jews be denied political expression. The beliefs that drew Iorga and Cuza together in Iași for the 1907 "reunion" led, two years later, to their formation of the National-Democratic Party. Leaders of existing political parties, conservative or liberal, by and large held views and supported laws hostile toward Jews, but the Iorga-Cuza party was fundamentally antisemitic in its origins, ideology, and platform. Basically the party advocated a double-harnessed national program: on the one side, promotion of the native-Romanian economy through subsidies, protectionism, cooperatives, and education, on the other, systematic elimination of Jews from villages, army, press, administration, and finally from the country.[19]

In 1913 Iorga delivered a paper, "The History of Jews in Our Country," to a session of the Romanian Academy. In it he described Jews as recently arrived, despicable, poisonous aliens: greedy doctors and merchants, money forgers, bribers, murderers, spies, cowards, thieves, friends of the Turk, and loathsome shopkeepers.[20] Iorga pictured the "ugly Jew with a well-oiled tongue" against the "majestic rolling hills" of Romania's countryside. He described fields rich with harvested grain "leased . . . to Jews"[21] and contrasted the filthy present with a golden age when the suburbs of Iași were "peaceful and clean" before Jews "swamped even this Christian island, rich in orchards and gardens."[22] Such talk appealed to a growing number of Christian nationalists whose opinions were not softened by the general economic misery of Jews or by the fact that their number was slowly declining. Nor did antisemitism abate as a result of the patriotic military service of Romanian Jews in World War I. Neither the Jewish soldiers who survived nor those who were killed got much recognition for their service. The government either denied or minimized their sacrifices.

Following the war Romania's victorious allies rewarded her with roughly a doubling of population and territory, but to the dismay of antisemites and nationalists (usually one and the same) the gift included a half-million Jews and the demand that Romania do what it had promised and extend to them basic political rights.[23] At the Paris Peace Conference, Premier Ionel Brătianu, leader of the Romanian delegation, was reminded that his country had not naturalized its Jews as required by the 1878 Treaty of Berlin. For his part Brătianu opposed that treaty or any other obliging his government to extend political rights to Jews. The resulting impasse was only resolved after the premier and then his successor resigned and King Ferdinand (r. 1914–27) formed a new cabinet. In December 1919 the new delegation agreed to a Minorities Treaty, which required that persons who met reasonable tests for claiming Romanian nationality be made citizens. This rule (article 7) specifically applied to Jews who had no other nationality, including residents of the annexed territories.[24] The government appeared, at last, ready to abandon the cynical strategy of granting citizenship tied to conditions that virtually denied the same, and bound itself constitutionally (article 133 of the March 1923 constitution) and by statute (Citizenship Law of February 1924), as well as by the Minorities Treaty, to naturalize Romanian Jews who claimed no other citizenship. Still, even as some were constructing the legal means for naturalization, others began the undermining, and in the end Romania's government fell short of delivering, in the citizenship law, all it had promised constitutionally and by treaty. In newly annexed territories, for example, Jews, even those who had been citizens of these territories, were frustrated by legal barricades to Romanian citizenship.[25]

No one, I think, anticipated the surge of an already pronounced antisemitism in postwar Romania. Hostile words and violent actions rained down on Jews. Jewish soldiers were accused of having betrayed their country during the war. Jews escaping westward into Romania from civil war in Ukraine were accused of importing communism.[26] In 1919 the Union of Romanian Jews first advised Jews to vote for parties sympathetic to them but, having discovered none, recommended they not vote.[27] Government, the Orthodox Church, and universities joined together in a loose partnership aimed at reducing or eliminating the Jewish presence. Patriarchs, ministers, professors, editors, artists, and students spearheaded the movement.[28]

What set off this extraordinarily strident and volatile campaign was the uprising of Christian university students in 1922 against the granting of citizenship to Jews and their unrestricted admission to the universities. Irina Livezeanu adds that the student movement gave rise to Romanian fascism, a militant, Christian, racist, nationalism.[29] The process of citizenship was dragged out for four years, from the Minorities Treaty of 1919 to the constitutional revision of 1923 and Citizenship Law of 1924, time enough for antisemities to stir up all the old racist slanders. The standard formulation—Jews were an ever-expanding population of malignant alien invaders—had been around since the 1831–32 rules (Règlements) governing Wallachia and Moldavia: "the Jews . . . are everywhere in Moldavia . . . and increase daily . . . mainly at the expense of the natives."[30] What made the issue especially acute for nationalists and antisemites after World War I was the fact that the number of Romanian Jews had more than tripled, from about 240,000 (3.3 percent of the total population) in 1912 to about 780,000 in 1920 (4.8 percent) due to the expansion of the country's territory. Not only were these Jews now citizens, but they were represented in the cities and universities in disproportionately large numbers, accounting for roughly 14 percent of all Romanian city dwellers and university students by the late 1920s. Livezeanu contends that for nationalists, especially intellectuals among them, this represented a significant barrier to the formation of a modern Romanian state that they believed had to be fashioned by ethnic Romanians in the country's cities and universities, where Romanian blood must triumph, over Jews in particular, in order to bring this ethnic modernization about.[31]

The University of Iași was especially important in the antisemitic war. It was home base for Professor A. C. Cuza and Corneliu Codreanu. The latter began his law studies there in 1919. Both men became leaders of the extreme nationalist movements of the 1920s and '30s. Cuza had been campaigning against Jews for years when he was made professor of political economy in 1901. He joined Iorga in publishing *Neamul Românesc* (*Romanian People*) and in founding, in 1910, the National-Democratic Party. In 1919, however, Iorga abandoned Cuza and his obsessive racism, accepting Romania's treaty obligation to grant rights to minorities. Codreanu considered Iorga's departure a significant loss and a betrayal.[32] In fact, though Professor Iorga was a highly respected intellectual, writer, and editor (in contrast to Cuza, whose credentials were tarnished by the credible charge of plagiarism),[33] his departure seems to have had no effect in slowing the nationalist-racist movement he helped bring into being.

On December 10, 1922, student delegates from the country's four major universities met in Bucharest and threatened to strike if their demands, including *numerus clausus*, allowing only a limited number of Jews into public schools, were not accepted by the government. Codreanu, in Jena at the time, got news of the student meeting and subsequent demonstrations and returned home where he called for another, bigger, rally and urged students to broaden their program into one that was national and anti-Jewish.[34] For their part Codreanu and Cuza organized a mass demonstration in Iași on March 4, 1923, to praise past leaders who prevented the naturalization of Jews and to oppose the upcoming constitutional change (March 26–28, 1923) that would grant citizenship.[35] Out of these events came a new party, the Christian National Defense League (Liga Apărării Național-Creștine, or LANC), with Codreanu as organizer and headed by Professor Cuza. *The National Defense* (*Apărarea Națională*), a newspaper that Cuza had begun publishing with physiology professor Nicolae Paulescu (1869–1931) the previous year, became the official organ of LANC.[36] Formation of the party occurred three weeks before the constitutional change that replaced article 7 with article 133, granting citizenship and political rights to Romanian Jews. Codreanu, who was so distressed by the action that he could not think of a worthy condemnation,[37] should have taken comfort in the government's record of failed promises.[38]

In October 1923 Codreanu and five other students, still angry about article 133, decided to avenge themselves by killing cabinet ministers most responsible for it, "treacherous Romanians who for Judas' silver pieces betrayed their people" and then "Jews . . . our enemies," rabbis first, the "real chiefs of the Judaic attack on Romania," then bankers and then journalists. The conspirators got to Bucharest but were betrayed and arrested before they could act. At Văcărești prison, awaiting trial, Codreanu began planning a national youth organization to be named after the Archangel Michael, whose icon hung in the prison chapel. Before the trial, scheduled to begin at the end of March 1924, the six would-be assassins, charged with "conspiracy against state security," decided that upon release they would meet in Iași and make it the center of their new movement. On the morning of the trial (March 29, 1924) one of the accused, Ion Moța, from the University of Cluj, shot and killed another student defendant suspected of having been a police informant. Because of the shooting the trial was rescheduled for the next day. Codreanu wrote that by 10:00 a.m. the following morning, "thousands of students and citizens" were gathered around the court. Speaking for the defendants were several notables, including Paulescu, described by Codreanu as a "connoisseur . . . of Judeo-Masonic manipulations." In less than twenty-four hours the trial was over. At 6:00 a.m. the next morning jurors began deliberating and within the hour had decided. The crowd, wrote Codreanu, "upon learning we were acquitted broke into 'hurrahs.'" The defendants returned to the prison to gather their belongings and bid farewell to Moța and an accomplice who had smuggled him the revolver. The trial of these two came at the end of September 1924. Moța defended himself on the grounds "that treason must be punished." Codreanu wrote that students "at all universities held huge demonstrations for his acquittal" and thousands gathered at the trial demanding Moța's freedom. Again, exoneration came the morning after the trial began.[39]

A month later, on October 25, 1924, Codreanu shot and killed Iași prefect of police C. G. Manciu and wounded two other policemen. Codreanu claimed he acted out of vengeance and to prevent further police violence against students. Any policeman, he wrote, who wanted "to increase his sources of revenue from the Jews or to get promoted, grabbed a student by the throat [and] beat him to a pulp." Within days of the shooting right wing newspapers were condemning the brutality of Prefect Manciu. Growing support for Codreanu resulted in the trial being delayed and relocated twice. It finally took place in May 1925 in the southwestern town of Turnu Severin. The National Theater building housing the proceedings was filled with spectators; thousands gathered outside. The trial of Codreanu and five other defendants lasted six days. He described the final scene as the six awaited the verdict: "we heard a thunderous applause. . . . The doors opened and the crowd took us into the meeting hall. . . . Everybody stood in acclaim. . . . The jurors were all in their places, this time wearing tricolor lapel ribbons with swastikas." The crowd outside rousingly added their approval. The return by train to Iași was a hero's homecoming for Codreanu; many of his schoolmates were on the train, and sympathetic crowds greeted him at each stop. "The Captain" (*Căpitanul*), as he was called, gained national attention and growing support for his violent exploits and acquittals.⁴⁰

In 1927 Codreanu broke with Professor Cuza over doubts about his mentor's ability to lead and his dream of creating a militant youth organization. On June 27 that year he assembled his Văcărești prison mates and a few other students in Iași to form the Legion of Archangel Michael.⁴¹ Early in 1930 he set up a new organization within the Legion, for combating communism, called the Iron Guard. Almost from the beginning Legion and Iron Guard came to mean the same thing. Like other contemporary fascist movements it was nationalistic and hostile toward mainstream reform ideologies (democracy, liberalism, socialism) engendered or advanced in western political and economic revolutions over the previous three hundred years. At the beginning of the movement legionnaires were, on average, in their mid-twenties, had joined as university students, were Romanian Orthodox, militantly patriotic, fervently antisemitic, generally disciplined and loyal, came to regard death in the line of duty as the noblest sacrifice, and demonstrated zealous adoration for dead comrade-heroes, like Codreanu himself following his assassination in 1938. Their uniform included a green shirt, black leather trappings, and a blue swastika on a yellow patch. They were revolutionaries driven by hateful and noble motives, nationalists, racists, and assassins determined to erase two grievous and enduring features of Romanian society: official corruption and rural depression that was among the worst in Europe in the 1920s and '30s.

What made the Iron Guard a major threat to Romania's Jews, besides the members' fanatic antisemitism, was the possibility that it would become the nation's political master. Cuza was no less an antisemite than Codreanu, but even when he became a government leader in December 1937 there was little chance he might actually wield much power. Codreanu appealed widely to a public frustrated by the chronic failures of the interwar Liberal and National-Peasant governments and caught up in strong currents of nationalism and racism. As the Legion grew into an effective political organization and began to show evidence of broad popular support, it also attracted the attention and opposition of other political parties. "The Captain" was in and out of Văcărești prison twice in 1930–31, and the government dissolved his party in 1931 and again in 1933. But the Legion refused to fold and, under different names, began to record modest election successes. In the general election of July 1932 the Guard received 70,674 votes and five delegate seats.⁴² The Romanian government, besides outlawing the Legion, tried to force it out of existence. But after each of the beatings and killings the Guard came back stronger. Still, fearing the Legion would do even better in the 1933 elections than it had done the year before, Carol and Prime Minister Ion Duca decided again to use force.

Duca, chief of the National Liberal Party, had publicly declared in Paris that the Iron Guard was in the pay of Nazis and assured the French of his determination to destroy the movement. As prime minister, he tried to accomplish this by outlawing Codreanu's party and having several thousand legionnaires arrested. This occurred on December 9, only eleven days before the scheduled election. As a result, Duca's National Liberals got a parliamentary majority. But Iron Guardists gunned down the prime minister himself on December 29. The three assassins were tried by a military court in Bucharest and defended by a team of prominent political figures, including sometime prime ministers Iuliu Maniu and Alexandru Vaida-Voevod. The murderers were given life sentences; their alleged confederates, including Codreanu, were acquitted.[43]

Codreanu changed the name of his party in March 1934 to "All for the Fatherland" (Totul Pentru Țară) and selected a stand-in leader so the Iron Guard could operate legally. In the December 1937 election it received an impressive 478,378 votes (15.6 percent of the total) and sixty-six seats in parliament. Now the third largest party and connected by a "non-aggression pact" to the National Peasant Party, which had won 20.4 percent of the vote and eighty-six seats, it was ready to play a major role in government. However, King Carol II, his power threatened by the Legion's success, intervened, first setting up a government quite at odds with the election and then casting aside even the pretense of a republic.[44]

CHAPTER 3

Romanian Jews

Jews have lived in the region now called Romania for centuries. Some were there before and others came during and following the Roman conquest of the early second century: from the Jewish Khazar state centered on the lower Volga from the eighth to the late tenth centuries and after being expelled from Hungary in 1367 and Spain in 1492. From the fourteenth to eighteenth centuries Moldavian and Wallachian princes occasionally invited Jews into their lands to advance commerce and sometimes treated them well. By the 1600s Jewish merchants, competing with Poles, Greeks, Armenians, and Turks, crisscrossed the region moving hides, livestock, wine, foods, and finished leather and textile products. The occupations of Jews who settled there ranged from inn keeping and money lending to serving princes as diplomats or physicians. In 1564 the capital of Moldavia was shifted from Suceava to Iași, a stopping place for tradesmen moving goods between Poland and Ottoman lands through ports on the lower Danube and Black Sea. Seventeenth-century documents clearly show the making of a Jewish community in the city.[1]

Fighting in 1648–49 between Poland and the Cossack-peasant armies of Bogdan Khmelnitsky, with his Crimean Tatar allies, in the western Ukraine and southeastern Poland, was a great disaster for Jews. Many were driven from these areas of conflict into Moldavia. In August 1650 Cossacks and Tatars invaded Moldavia itself and plundered Iași. The Jewish community was especially hard hit and remained in the cross fire of different rapacious factions for several months.[2] Among Jews who fled Poland when it came under attack from Khmelnitsky's troops was Nathan Hannover, a teacher and

CHAPTER 3

kabbalist (mystic). After some years of traveling in the west, Hannover settled for a time in Iași where he became a community leader, president of the local rabbinic law court, and head of the yeshiva (school devoted to studying the Talmud). He also published various works, among them a polyglot lexicon, prayer book, and *Yeven Metzulah* (*Abyss of Despair*), a chronicle of the Khmelnitsky pogroms.[3] Two documents of the 1690s mention a "Jewish school" (*școală jidovilor,* i.e., a synagogue or prayer house, *shul* in Yiddish) in the "saddlers' quarter" of Iași. The presence and importance of Jews is also reflected in three mid-seventeenth-century Orthodox religious codes; one such set of rules was included in a general code (*Pravilele împărătești*) published in Iași at the Three Hierarchs Monastery in 1646 for Prince Vasile Lupu. Christians in Wallachia and Moldavia were prohibited by these codes, under threat of excommunication, from having contacts with Jews or heretics.[4]

In 1714 three lay elders, representing the city's Jews, successfully petitioned Prince Nicolae Mavrocordat for a ruling in a dispute with a monastery over land near the synagogue. The elders produced evidence that the land had been purchased by and remained in the hands of Jews since 1670. The synagogue or *școală* mentioned in the prince's decision is almost certainly the city's "Great Synagogue" (Sinagoga Mare), first built no later than 1670.[5] In 1741 Prince Grigore Ghica authorized the three elders of Iași to collect a tax "for the use and assistance and administration of the whole community, as is their custom." The Breasla jidovilor, Jewish guild or corporation, supervised by lay elders appointed to one-year terms,[6] was chartered to conduct business freely, maintain members' good behavior, establish places of worship, and, as indicated above, tax members and allocate funds. The Community Council was concerned with health, education, and religion and supported synagogues, a Talmud-Torah school, shelter for transients, and a cemetery, with tax monies from kosher meat.

The most prestigious office among Jews in the Moldavian capital was *hahambasha* (or *hakham bashi,* chief rabbi). In 1719 the Ottoman sultan conferred that office on Naftali Cohen. Because Naftali died before he could take the post it was awarded sometime later, apparently to his son and then his grandson, Bețăl, who held it from about 1724 to 1743. From his residence in Iași the *hahambasha* had authority, it seems, over the entire Jewish population of Moldavia and Wallachia. One of his responsibilities was to recommend, for the Moldavian prince's selection, persons to fill the three offices of Jewish elder, one of them holding the elevated office of Great Elder and Regional Chief.[7] Between 1755 and 1774 the number of registered Jewish heads of households in Iași grew from 65 to 171 (from about 5 to 9 percent of the total). About half the households were concentrated in two districts; in one of them (Tîrgu Cucului) were located the Great Synagogue and residence of the *hahambasha*.[8] Commercial enterprise, the economic backbone of the community, ranged from a monopoly on the sale of wine and brandy and a large share in the marketing of manufactured goods, especially cloth, imported clothing, cattle, grain, honey, wool, and cheese, to small shops or peddlers selling tobacco, rice, kitchen utensils, boots, salt, and other such items. Among Jewish craftsmen or artisans were jewelers, metalworkers, glassmakers, clockmakers, lace makers, hatters, shoemakers, masons, furriers, and tailors. Members of particular crafts and trade, including butchers and junk dealers, often formed their own guilds and had their own prayer houses.[9] Makers of fur hats and *kamelaukions* (special hats for Orthodox priests and monks) established their guild in 1797 with the approval of the *hahambasha* and other community notables. Full and candidate members of the guild comprised a general assembly, elected elders, and made annual donations for the feast of Passover and festival of Sukkot, the Holy Land (Țara Sfântă), the "Society for helping the sick," and Torah study.[10]

Periodically the Jewish population was rocked in murderous attacks—by Cossacks in 1650 and Russians and Turks during their wars of the 1870s and '80s. In the atrocity-filled conflict between rebel Greeks and Ottoman Janissaries in 1821–22, rebels robbed and murdered the Jews of Iași, despite protection money paid to rebel leader Alexander Ypsilanti, then the Turks pillaged and burned the community. Documents from the early eighteenth century report accusations of blood libel (ritual murder of a child, usually Christian) followed by violence against Jews, often in the springtime and in towns and cities of northern Moldavia. In Tîrgu-Neamț such an accusation in April 1710 was followed by a pogrom in which five Jews were murdered and some survivors viciously beaten. Property was stolen or destroyed and twenty-two persons were put in chains and imprisoned. Although Prince Cantemir (r. 1710–11) found the charges to be false, a similar action occurred in 1714 in the town of Roman where two Jews were hanged and others had their houses plundered.[11]

In 1726 four Jews of the Moldavian town of Onițcani (Onișcani?) were accused of ritual murder and beaten to force them to confess. The one who allegedly disposed of the body was broken first. He said two others in the house of an accomplice committed the murder. The four were sent, with their families, to Moldavian Prince Mihai Racoviță in Iași where the prince himself imprisoned and interrogated them. Only the house owner persisted in denying the crime. On the morning after their arrival in the capital the prince questioned the accused before an assembly of Jews, Turks, and noblemen. The three who had confessed did so again, saying they had killed the child and taken its blood to be used in making the unleavened Passover bread. "The prince then said to the assembled Jews: 'You have seen and heard!' And the Jews responded: 'Let them be punished according to their deed.'" Although their execution seemed imminent, the four were kept imprisoned until a platform was built near their synagogue and there they were publicly and nakedly displayed. Then a boy of five, near in age to the alleged victim, was brought from the house where the alleged crime had occurred to the prisoners, one being his father. They were ordered to wash the child in preparation for slaughter following which the father was given a knife and ordered to kill his son. He refused, was threatened with death and beaten, and still refused.

Now the prince's base motive was revealed. The accused were informed that their fate depended on how much money they were willing to pay the prince and his agents. When a large sum was promised the threats against them ceased, though they were kept imprisoned while the money was being collected. Meanwhile, the community sent one of its members to Istanbul to seek relief from the grand vizier through his chief business agent, a Jewish merchant. Not only did the Porte order the prince to free his prisoners without them paying him, it was further ordered, when the accused found their houses looted, that the stolen property be returned. Not willing to drop the matter, Prince Mihai wrote to Istanbul, claiming the Porte had not treated him impartially because eleven years before the then grand vizier himself had hung three Jews accused of the ritual murder of a Turkish child and that in the current case a fine of "a thousand purses" would be just punishment. The Porte responded by deposing the prince. The author describing these events closes his account laconically, pointing out that the prince's troubles arose from his own greed, his disrespect for God's laws, and (what could be said of many rulers just before their fall) his ill-considered final actions. In Istanbul the French ambassador saw the matter thus: the prince of Moldavia had revived an old lie in order to extort money from the Jews. "This prince," the ambassador wrote, "cannot be ignorant of the fact that today the accusation of ritual murder is no longer believed by anyone in the civilized world."[12] Civilized or not, in the world of eastern Europe the myth of blood libel persisted into the twentieth century, if not always believed, then as a pretext for slandering or attacking Jews, as in the Kishinev pogrom of 1903 and the trial of Mendel Beilis in Kiev in 1913.

Not long after the Janissaries withdrew from Iași in August 1822, having wrecked the Jewish community, the city was occupied by Russians (1826–34) who defeated Turkey in 1828–29 and made Moldavia and Wallachia their protectorates. As noted earlier, in each principality they established a new governing code (Règlement organique) that identified Jews as foreign parasites.

Russian military occupation ended in 1834, but the reign of Prince Mihai Sturdza in Moldavia (1834–49) under Russian protection continued to be unfriendly. The prince tried to force Jews to rid themselves of hair curls, beards, felt hats, and sandals and extorted money from them in various ways.[13] Furthermore, he no longer recognized the Jewish community as a semiautonomous corporation. The guild (*breasla*) and offices of *hahambasha* and elder were abolished, though the chief rabbi kept his title of *hahambasha* and some of its functions while elders were replaced by a commission of ten *epitropi* (administrators) elected by the community. In Iași some guild or council functions fell to individual groups, members of certain prayer houses, for example, or those belonging to one of the trades or to the burial society. Furthermore, administrators of the Jewish hospital (established in 1772) undertook to provide various services paid for, as before, out of taxes on kosher meat. However, authority to collect that tax was denied to community leaders after 1863, and as their tax revenue and authority declined, internal divisions became more pronounced, especially between traditionalists, or Hasidim, and modernists. Particularly heated was the controversy over the establishment of modern Jewish Romanian schools.[14]

Despite unfriendly regimes, violence and poverty, the appearance of antisemitic publications,[15] and denial of citizenship, the Jewish population in Iași and Moldavia grew steadily in the nineteenth century, from several thousand in 1800 to about 267,000 at the end of the century. In Iași over these hundred years the number of Jews increased from about 2,420 (in 1803) to 39,441, according to the census of 1899, approximately half the city's population.[16] Between 1830 and 1860 Jews came to dominate small businesses in the cities of northern Moldavia. Already in 1831 Jewish commercial guilds outnumbered their Christian counterparts in secondhand, wine-spirit, and tailoring enterprises, and Jews completely or nearly dominated as money changers and peddlers. Overall, however, Christian guilds still outnumbered their Jewish counterparts. Based on data from twelve Moldavian cities in 1831 there were 5,784 Christian and 3,342 Jewish corporations. In Iași that year merchants and artisans numbered 2,540 Christians and 1,897 Jews. By 1839, however, the number of Jewish merchants and artisans in the city had more than doubled, to 4,528, while the number of Christian tradesmen declined, and by 1860 merchants and artisans numbered 1,962 Christians and 6,933 Jews.[17]

Alongside this remarkable economic transformation there occurred a cultural flowering, both religious and secular. Hasidism, Talmudic learning, and the enlightenment movement (*haskalah*) each had its spirited teachers and followers. Hebrew books were first published in the city in 1842; the first journal, *Korot Haitim* (*Current Events*), a Yiddish biweekly, began appearing in 1855 and ran irregularly to 1871. Other journals or newspapers followed, though most had short runs of weeks or months.[18] The first modern Jewish school in Iași (for boys) was founded in the fall of 1852 under the direction of banker and insurer Benjamin Schwarzfeld (1822–1897). He came to Iași as a boy from Galicia and rose to prominence as a reformer, writer, and educator, and was among the first in the city to promote the ideas of Jewish *haskalah:* more secular and language studies for schoolchildren, accommodations with the dominant native culture and political regime, and increased interest in industry and farming. His main opponents were Hasidic and Orthodox Jews who made common cause against haskalah and forced the school to close in 1857. Benjamin himself continued to promote Jewish schools and modern curricula and to support other causes as a member of various community groups in Iași. He was one of a number of vigorous, intelligent, and reform-minded leaders who came to consider themselves Romanian and aimed to translate their allegiance to the nascent state into citizenship. In 1858 another attempt was made to replace traditional Jewish schools with one (for girls) designed to broaden the curriculum and promote acculturation; this too failed to stand against traditionalist or Hasidic opposition. New schools were opened once more and once more closed in the 1860s. Not until 1893 were modern Jewish schools again established in Iași in response to the expulsion of the relatively small number of Jewish children from public schools.

Sons of Benjamin Schwarzfeld (Elias, Wilhelm, and Moses) made their own contributions to the culture of Iași and its Jewish community. Elias published several studies on the history of Romanian Jews, founded *Revistă Izraelita* (1874–75) and edited the political weekly *Fraternitatea* (Bucharest, 1879–85). *Fraternitatea* ceased publication, except for a short run in 1889–90, when Elias and its other editor, Isaac Auerbach, were expelled from Romania, along with noted scholar Moses Gaster (1856–1939), for voicing opposition to the antisemitic policies of the government. Wilhelm also published historical studies on the education of Jews in Iași and on the city's Jewish writers and scholars.[19] Another benefactor of the community and, like Benjamin, a financier, was Iacob Neuschatz (1809–1888) who founded a temple and an orphanage, both of which the community continued to maintain as late as the Second World War. Neuschatz and the Daniel brothers (Chaim, Leon, and Albert) gave substantial gifts of money to the Romanian Academy to be used for scholarships and the purchase of historical artifacts.[20]

One of the community's most prominent Zionists, a man honored at the Basel Congress of 1897, was Dr. Karpel Lippe (1830–1915). Some said of him that he opposed dancing and refused to make sick calls in homes that displayed no picture of Theodor Herzl. Zionists and anti-Zionists, despite their differences, came together in the Barasch Society to study the history of Romanian Jews. Its membership included Moses Gaster, Elias and Moses Schwarzfeld, Jacob Psanter, and Lozar Saineanu. Saineanu, a Romanian linguist and philologist, emigrated after being refused citizenship. Psanter (1820–1902), for some thirty years a traveling musician, began gathering documents on the Jewish past in Romania, including tombstone inscriptions from Jewish cemeteries, many of which no longer exist. He came to this work in reaction to allegation that Jews were rootless recent immigrants.[21]

Much of the organized intellectual life of the city was centered on a group of energetic professionals, businessmen, artists, and writers, many of them attracted to Zionism, men like Dr. Marcu Bercovici, who became head of the community's cultural section after the murder of Ghetzel Buchmann in one of the death trains.[22] In the 1860s and '70s, years before the Basel Congress, Dr. Lippe started up activities and organizations in Iași to advance Jewish culture, especially the study of Hebrew, promote the settlement of Jews in Palestine, and advance interest in and understanding of modern literature and science. The first Zionist Hebrew newspaper in Romania, *Emek Israel,* came out in Iași in 1882, and at the turn of the century at least three Zionist journals were published there. A Cultural Association of Jewish Women served in such areas as child care, schooling, and fund raising. There were Zionist sports clubs, reading and discussion groups, university student associations, and a *Fermă de Hachshara,* a "preparation farm," where youngsters made ready for living in Palestine. Most of these societies were joined in 1910 into a single Zionist organization (Organizație sionistă).[23] A library was built from funds collected by the student association, Hasmonaea. Its holdings included Hebrew, Yiddish, and Romanian books with special emphasis on Zionism and Judaica. Zionism was not, of course, the only focus of Jewish culture in Iași. The library served other interests as well, as did two of the longest-running cultural institutions in the city: the Ohalei Șem society (1878–98), created by Lippe and others to advance interest in and understanding of modern literature and science, and Toynbee House, hosting social and cultural events on a weekly basis (irregularly from 1906 to the 1930s), drawing Jews from around the country to its sessions.[24]

In 1919 Jewish leaders in Iași expanded community organization from one centered on the Israelite Hospital (Spitalul Israelit) staff to an elected Communal Council that took on broad responsibilities in the areas of education, including religious instruction, and social services.[25] Among the leaders who assisted in the reorganization and directed the community over the next several years were Dr. Ghelerter, Ilie Mendelsohn, and Dr. Herman Solomovici. Ghelerter was prominent in the Socialist Workers' Party (established in 1925) and was a contributor to its paper, *The Proletarian* (*Proletarul*), and various other journals. He was known as an orator and an agitator among workers. Codreanu singled him out as "leader of the communist movement in Iași." Before World War II Ghelerter moved to Bucharest where, after a split in the socialist movement, he became president of one faction, the Unitary Socialist Party of Romania.[26] Solomovici, murdered by a German soldier during the Iași pogrom, was a widely respected medical doctor who learned Hebrew in his seventies.[27] Mendelsohn, a manufacturer of mirrors and, like Solomovici, a Zionist leader, was president of the Communal Council from its founding in 1919. Iosef Iacob succeeded him as president in 1939.

During the community's most perilous years (1940–44) the council passed millions of lei in protection money to various police and other officials: chief inspector Chirilovici, inspector Leahu, police secretary Stînciulescu, and Iron Guard leader Alexandru Ventonic. There is no way to measure the effectiveness of these payoffs, but community leaders had some confidence in the practice. In his account of events, Iacob takes credit for the fact "that during the whole of the legionnaire government [September 1940–January 1941] . . . there was in Iași not one human victim," not even "when in Bucharest . . . many Jews were slaughtered." However, payoffs secured no warnings to Jewish leaders of the great pogrom of June 28–30, 1941. Iacob believed the pogrom was planned "well in advance," leaving ample time for such a warning.[28] Had the council been forewarned perhaps it might have done something to deflect its cruelest effects. Unannounced, the violence broke suddenly on the uninformed and was carried forward with powerful feelings of hatred, fear, and greed by private citizens, soldiers, and policemen.

The social assistance section of the community, like its parent council, had an executive committee made up of rabbis, physicians, and businessmen. It took over or created or assisted a number of operations: an old-age home, two orphanages, two canteens (one for scholars and one for the very needy), a night shelter, ritual baths, medical dispensaries, and the Israelite and Dr. Ghelerter hospitals. The latter was a children's hospital built between 1915 and 1920 with help from the Joint Distribution Committee and was, between the wars, a modern and expanding institution under the vigorous leadership of Moshe Moscovici. Moscovici worked for a wholesaler of glass and household articles, was a member of the Iași Chamber of Commerce, edited the socialist journal *Der Veker* (*The Alarm Clock*) in 1915–16, was a member of the Community Council, and directed a number of other social services. During dedication ceremonies for the children's hospital Moscovici announced that it would treat the sick whatever their religion and whether or not they had money.[29]

In the late 1930s and during the war the council was constantly defending the community against hostile government actions and trying to answer the basic needs of a population growing ever poorer and dependent. When the government demanded land on which was located one of the two Jewish cemeteries in Iași, the council put Rabbi Wahrmann, director of the yeshiva, in charge of evacuating the buried remains.[30] When the number of orphans and other needy children increased dramatically as a result of the pogrom and death trains and the forced unpaid labor of parents, Aron Stievel, head of the social assistance section, organized a boarding school for them and, because the state had confiscated community buildings, installed the school in one of the synagogues. Stievel also organized canteens that served at least one hot meal each day to thousands of persons and a meal with meat almost every day to primary schoolchildren.[31] The dentist David Gruenberg-Moldvan, who had headed the section until 1939, and Stievel so effectively organized relief for Jewish beggars that they virtually disappeared from city streets. During the war, besides the very difficult tasks of supplying the community with food, clothing, firewood, and the like, it was able to accommodate hundreds of Jewish refugees, including several hundred children from the Transnistria labor-death camps.

Primary responsibility for education had first belonged to private persons or institutions but eventually was shifted to the community. Before the Goga-Cuza government (December 1937–February 1938) inaugurated a relentless and ruthless official antisemitism that was carried forward by successive dictatorships, there existed in Iași a variety of so-called Jewish Romanian schools: three primary schools for boys and one for girls and a primary and professional girls' school called Stars. These independent schools were always short of funds and had constantly to struggle against poor attendance and fight the government to get official recognition for their diplomas. In order to improve education for Jewish children and obtain state accreditation, the various school committees and directors got together with the Community Council and decided to put their schools under the direction of its cultural section. The section faced a host of difficulties, as when the state decreed the expulsion of Jewish teachers and students from public schools or when it denied to Jewish schools the right to advertise, that is, to publish the names of graduates and so demonstrate publicly that the state officially accepted those students as having graduated from accredited schools. Work had to be found for the expelled teachers. The problem was made especially difficult because at about the same time others (doctors, lawyers, pharmacists, and journalists) were being barred from their professions and also looked to the community for help.

The cultural section's main concern was to provide continued schooling so children would be prepared to step back into the stream of life when better times returned. The community set out to expand building space and educational materials in existing schools, employ teachers from the ranks of the various unemployed professionals, and create new learning institutions. So a comprehensive program of primary schools, lycées for boys and girls, commercial and trade schools, and a music conservatory replaced the old financially troubled parochial system. The new organization, which aimed to make places for all Jewish children, including refugees, was better than the old at surviving severe financial and material shortages and resisting hostile official actions, which continued unabated. Financial support and classroom space were never adequate, and the cultural section always had to be ready to find alternative places when the police or military requisitioned community buildings. The greatest shock to the system came as a result of the June 28–30 pogrom and death trains. Students, teachers, parents, school taxpayers, and community leaders like Ghetzel Buchmann himself were among the victims. As a result many families joined the list of those dependent on the hard-pressed community for food, shelter, and clothing as well as education.[32]

The Jewish economy up to the eve of World War II was, by and large, in the hands of small merchants, tradesmen, and artisans. At the beginning of the twentieth century Jews outnumbered their Christian competitors in these areas by three to one. Jewish tailors (the single largest artisan group by far), shoemakers, dressmakers, engravers, tinsmiths, watchmakers, and bookbinders dominated their crafts.[33] Different from the past were the number of bankers, professionals (doctors and lawyers especially), and industrialists, particularly in textile production.[34] This economic base and education made possible the comprehensive, if thinly stretched, social and educational programs. For the community as a whole was not affluent. In a 1929 report, the American Committee on the Rights of Religious Minorities pointed out that contrary to the general view Romanian Jews were not wealthy. The Iași Jewish population, numbering about 35,000 at the time, is described as having "400 to 500 that are well-to-do and a few of them wealthy," while "the rest are in abject poverty such as it is difficult to describe. We went through street after street into the miserable hovels which display to the eye the misery and poverty of . . . the Jewish inhabitants, many of whom are kept alive only by relief from America and the contributions sent home by relatives."[35]

The general economic misery was made worse between the wars by private and official efforts to end the professional and intellectual work of Jewish lawyers, doctors, journalists, professors, teachers, and students. For example: following attacks by Christian students against their Jewish classmates at the University of Iași in December 1927, the Faculty Senate first announced that the guilty ones would be expelled but later ruled that the punishment would be applied only to those who repeated the offences.[36] And when Jewish lawyers were expelled from the Iași Bar in 1939 by their Christian colleagues but received a favorable ruling from the High Court of Appeals, these colleagues ignored that decision.[37]

In the realm of politics Romanian Jews had little influence. During the Balkan Wars and World War I the Union of Native Jews (Uniunea Evreilor Pământeni) pledged its support of Romania. After these wars the union tried to establish a national strategy, not an easy task given the great diversity of Jewish cultures (Yiddish speaking, Orthodox, Hasidic, Magyarized, Austro-Germanized, Russified, or Romanianized) in the newly expanded state. In January 1922 the union told its local chapters to recommend to their members political candidates who would work to reverse discriminatory laws, most certainly article 7 of the constitution, denying citizenship to Jews. It also aimed to support any political party that sympathized with this goal. Although the union did not plan to become a party in the 1922 elections, Jewish parties in Transylvania and Bessarabia were organized and put up candidates. Dr. Filderman, vice president of the Jewish Union, was himself a candidate who was first informed he had won his election and three days later that he had lost it.[38]

The doors of political opportunity appeared to open wide for Jews after the war and especially after the constitution was changed (March 1923), granting them citizenship. Momentarily gripped by optimism, Jewish leaders changed the name Union of Native Jews (UEP) to Union of Romanian Jews (Uniunea Evreilor Români, or UER). To mark itself as politically cooperative and Romanian the UER supported, and encouraged individual members to support, one or another of the Romanian parties. UER continued to oppose both the creation of a Jewish party and the political activity of Zionist organizations and, in an attempt to deflect the charge that Jews in Romania represented a separate and alien nation, predicted its own dissolution once Jews definitely became citizens. UER tried to ally itself with one or another national party: the Liberal Peasants, National Peasants, and even (in 1931) the "national union" led by the antisemitic prime minister

N. Iorga. These efforts failed utterly to move political emancipation forward. Romanian political parties either had little concern for or opposed the citizenship of Jews.[39]

Thus, in the late 1920s, while UER continued to reach "understandings" with established parties, a Jewish political party began taking shape under Zionist initiatives in Transylvania and Bucovina. Four Jewish deputies were elected in 1928 and they founded in 1930–31 a Jewish Parliamentary Club that became the nucleus for the National Jewish Party (Partidul Național Evreiesc). In the elections of 1931–32 UER fared badly, while the new party elected four and then five members to parliament. This was, however, a Pyrrhic victory; in 1933 the National Jewish Party failed to get 2 percent of the votes in the general election, the minimum required to have any seats in parliament. Political failures and, as one observer put it, the "rumble" of antisemitism brought the Jewish party and the UER finally together in 1936 to create the Central Council of Jews in Romania (Consiliul Central al Evreilor din România).[40]

Iași Jews were active in political agencies and parties, in various Zionist organizations, and served locally, two or three at a time, on the city council. Some of the most active leaders of the community were also attracted to the socialist movement. Besides Dr. Ghelerter, there were the Marxist theorist Max Wechsler, who was killed at the front in World War I, and Leon Geller, known, as was Ghelerter, for his fine oratory. Utopian socialism appeared in the principalities in the 1830s, and Marxist ideas may have come in with Russian immigrants as early as the 1870s when the ideas of Marx and Engels first began to be discussed by Russian populists. These newcomers established the first socialist circle in Iași and then the movement spread, spawning other groups and the publication, beginning in 1879, of several socialist newspapers, including *The Worker* (*Muncitorul*, established in Iași in 1918 and Bucharest in 1919). At the turn of the century Jewish workers had a socialist lecture club and published the Yiddish journal *Der Veker*, which twice failed and was twice resuscitated under the editorship of Moshe Moscovici.[41]

The Social Democratic Party (SDP), established in 1893, appealed to some Romanian Jews because it called for their full political emancipation. The general congress of the party in 1910 specifically advocated "the emancipation of Jewish nationals." The Social Democrats (SDs) also appealed to Jews because of the party's emphasis on social justice. Regarding abandoned children, for example, they demanded full rights, free and compulsory public education (for all children), canteens in schools, free food, clothing, school supplies for children without means, and so on. At the time, however, neither the SDs nor any other socialist party could have advanced the political rights of Romanian Jews. The ineffectiveness of the Romanian SDP is indicated by the fact that some of its earliest leaders, after twenty years of party work, and little to show for it, joined the National Liberals.[42] Defections, divisions, factional fighting, and hostile government actions stifled the socialist movement in Romania.

The fact that Romanian Zionists were prominent in the formation of a national party in 1930–31 and the Union of Native Jews, having changed its name to Union of Romanian Jews in 1923, renewed efforts to gain full political rights, indicates that Jews had not given up hope in the 1920s and '30s of being recognized as Romanians. The coming together of the Jewish National Party, the UER, and top religious leaders in the spring of 1936 to form the Central Council of Romanian Jews, under Dr. Filderman's presidency, represents a further effort in this direction. However, in the spring and summer of 1936 the goal of full political rights began to give way to the community's need to defend itself against a wave of extreme anti-Jewish actions.

CHAPTER 4

Fascism and Antisemitism in the 1930s

Between the world wars public institutions to which Romanian Jews had appealed for relief from persecution or support in their struggle for political rights declined or disappeared, or, like the government, church, law courts, and press had become united against them. Beneficial influences from the west, which had brought some advantages to Romanian Jews in the past, faded as Romania moved into the economic and political orbit of Nazi Germany. The underlying cause of this growing hostility was a volatile mixture of the old Christian mythologies, emerging pseudoscientific racism, militant nationalism, and a multitude of economic woes. In the rising tide of discontent, fascist antisemitic political parties flourished. A key event in the success of this movement in Romania was, as Livezeanu points out, the energetic and sometime violent response, especially of Christian university students, to the granting of citizenship to Jews after the First World War.

The two most effective postwar antisemitic parties were the Christian National Defense League (Liga Apărării Național-Creștine, or LANC), founded by A. C. Cuza and Corneliu Codreanu in 1923, and the Legion of the Archangel Michael created by Codreanu in 1927. Success of the Legion (also known from 1930 as the Iron Guard) encouraged the formation of other such militant-nationalist groups, such as the Svastica de Foc (Swastika of Fire), founded in 1933 by Colonel Emanuel Tătărescu, whose brother Gheorghe was prime minister in the 1930s, Frontul Românesc (The Romanian Front), founded in 1935 by former Interior and Prime Minister Alexandru Vaida-Voevod, a staunch supporter of the Legion, and Straja Țării (Guards of the Fatherland), established by King Carol II in October 1937.[1]

CHAPTER 4

A key issue for these and other militant nationalist parties was "the Jewish problem": that Jews were a plague on Romania and their participation in the life of the country had to be reduced or eliminated. Their offenses ranged from "peculiar" noxious habits of speech and dress to having murdered God. They were accused of poisoning peasants with alcohol, practicing usury and tax evasion, and taking control of the legal and medical professions, newspapers, classrooms, banks, industry, commerce, and even some cities. They were described as parasites, seditious agents of international Jewry or Bolshevism or both, destroyers of morality, wandering-vagabond exploiters, an alien epidemic, and hostile toward good, honest, hard-working Christian folk. Typically, the mythical venomous Jew was contrasted with the mythically virtuous Romanian peasant. There were differing opinions about how to solve "the Jewish problem," but all major parties called for limiting Jewish participation in the economy, culture, and governance of the country. Christian lawyers in 1935 called for *numerus nullus,* eliminating Jews from the legal profession; Christian university students demanded *numerus clausus,* sharply cutting the number of university places available to Jews. The University of Iași admitted only five Jews for the 1939–40 academic year.[2] Vaida-Voevod's Romanian Front favored *numerus Valahicus,* a general limitation on minorities, claiming for native Romanians (Valahi, Wallachians) a share in the economy and culture "proportional with their ethnic number." By the late 1930s, however, fascist parties generally favored a statewide *numerus nullus,* eliminating Jews from Romania.[3]

Codreanu's green-shirted Legion survived King Carol II's determined efforts to destroy it and continued to widen its public support. In September 1936 British envoy Sir Reginald Hoare was assured by Prime Minister Tătărescu that he "had undressed the wearers of the green, blue and other coloured shirts." Hoare replied that General Cantacuzino (Codreanu's stand-in leader of the Iron Guard) had recently received *Times* correspondent Mr. Reed at green-shirt headquarters in Bucharest itself and "declaimed for about half an hour on the necessity of exterminating the 1 million [Romanian] Jews." Hoare also reported that during the general's harangue young men in green shirts were entering and leaving the building.[4] The blue shirts, mentioned by Tătărescu, belonged to the National Christian Party, created in 1935 when Professor Cuza's LANC merged with poet Octavian Goga's National Agrarian Party. The symbol of the National Christians was the swastika. The party's storm trooper and Jew basher was the revolver-toting, black-trousered, blue-shirted, Lance Bearer (Lăncier).[5] Each fascist party was supported by its own and other publications. *Apărarea Națională (The National Defense)* belonged to A. C. Cuza's LANC and was one of the papers that repeatedly charged Jews with ritual murder. *Țara Noastră* (*Our Country*), which appeared with a swastika immediately before and after the title, became a Bucharest daily in 1923. It supported Goga's National Agrarian Party and after Goga and Cuza merged their parties into the National Christian Party, became its official newspaper. *Universul* (*The Universe*), owned and edited by legion supporter Stelian Popescu, was the leading daily on the right. One of its features was a series of antisemitic cartoons. The Iron Guard published *Buna Vestire* (*Good News*) and had the attention and sympathy of a growing number of young and influential writers and editors, especially after the remarkable election success of 1932 (73,135 votes and five deputies).[6]

In the summer of 1936 *Universul* intensified its campaign against democratic papers, claiming Jews dominated or unduly influenced them. In concert with the press attack, fascist shirts destroyed offices and machinery belonging to such papers and beat up so-called Judeo-Bolshevik journalists. Socialist and Jewish newspapers were eliminated, as were the major democratic papers. *Adevărul* (*The Truth*), which supported land reform and citizenship for Jews, and *Dimineața* (*Morning*) managed to keep going for several months but were finally shut down in January 1938, despite large donations of money from the Union of Romanian Jews.[7]

Violence against the opposition came to characterize the tactics of both the government and right-wing parties in the 1930s. Even the National Peasant Party, unable to get adequate government protection for its supporters and candidates from fascist thugs, created its own "Peasant Guard." In 1933 the government used extraordinary force against striking railroad workers. In December of the same year it outlawed the Iron Guard and then launched a massive, brutal roundup of its members, killing several legionnaires in the process. As I noted earlier, legionnaires retaliated, assassinating Prime Minister Ion Duca. The shooters were tried and convicted, but Codreanu was acquitted (of planning the murder), and his and the Legion's popularity continued to grow.[8]

In a 1936 report home Sir Reginald Hoare described "the spread of extremist 'right' doctrines amongst the youth" and the widely held view "that so far as the Nazi organizations are concerned no serious attempt will be made [by government] to put an end to their activities." An exception to his otherwise pessimistic dispatches came on April 27, 1936. In this report Hoare said that Foreign Minister Titulescu had spoken "very emphatically to the King about the folly of encouraging Hitlerist tendencies," about his unwillingness to serve a fascist despot, and his intention to "resign rather than condone an internal policy which conflicted with Romania's affiliations in Western Europe." Titulescu told Hoare that the king appeared to have taken his warnings to heart and, writes Hoare, "if M. Titulescu is right, the crisis is over." However, Hoare's subsequent reports are again, in the main, "gloomy." Carol apparently heeded none of his minister's warnings and in August 1936 fired him.[9]

The right celebrated its ascendency in grand style. In October 1936 a large banquet was held in the capital to mark the twentieth anniversary of the newspaper *Universul,* but also to bring together leaders of the antisemitic right to show their "unity of purpose." Miron Cristea, patriarch of the Romanian Orthodox Church since 1925 and an outspoken Jew-hater, led off the event, and Octavian Goga praised the paper's director, Popescu, for acting to stop the incoming "tide of 'parasites.'" In November the National Christian Party held a huge demonstration in Bucharest. Tens of thousands of peasants were brought in; blue shirts and swastikas appeared in large numbers. A main purpose of the gathering was to attack Jews, who were described by Goga as lepers and eczema. Another massive demonstration took place in February 1937 to honor two Iron Guard leaders, Ion Moța and Vasile Marin, who had been killed fighting for Franco in the Spanish Civil War. Legionnaire Mihail Sturdza, who became foreign minister in 1940, described the event as a profound spiritual revelation of the "virtues of the nation," a "deep and silent communion before the sacrifice of the valiants." Patriarch Cristea and other church officers gave their blessings. Policemen were absent while green shirts, despite a government ban, and swastikas, were everywhere to be seen. Sturdza saw the massive funeral as "the beginning of an acute crisis between ... Codreanu and King Carol."

Carol tried to advance his own popularity and limit or reverse the advancing fortunes of the Legion by moving to the right: extending support of the Liberal Party government of Gheorghe Tătărescu to the rival National Christians in some 1936 by-elections, dismissing Minister Titulescu, creating his own right-wing youth group, considering the removal of some Jews from Romania, promoting closer economic ties with Germany, and, following the practice among Romanian political leaders, visiting Hitler, as had Goga and Cuza in 1935 and Gheorghe Brătianu in 1936.[10] After the December 1937 general elections, in which the Iron Guard won a remarkable 16 percent of the vote and sixty-six seats in parliament, the king formed a new government headed by Goga and Cuza whose National Christians had received 9 percent of the vote. The new leaders dissolved parliament without its having met and called for another general election early in 1938.

The general election of December 1937 and subsequent formation of the Goga-Cuza government shocked the Jewish community. The new leaders had promised to confiscate Jewish property, Romanianize enterprises, and expel half a million Jews from the country. When Carol actually put them in charge of the government some Jews took their money out of banks for fear it would be confiscated and quickly sold business property fearing takeovers by Christian commissioners. Economic problems, occasioned by these events, worsened as the new government began shutting down opposition newspapers, prohibiting housemaids under forty from working in Jewish homes, and revoking liquor licenses Jews held. Thousands of persons (Christians and Jews) were either put out of work or threatened with unemployment. The decision to prohibit the employment of maids, made by labor minister Gheorghe Cuza (A. C. Cuza's son), had such an immediate and strong negative effect that the cabinet overruled the order. The event revealed a split over policy between A. C. Cuza, who wanted to take drastic action at once against Jews, and Goga, who wanted ministers to follow the law and have their decisions reviewed by the cabinet. The division was a serious one for the party but hardly a comfort for Jews. The number of blue shirts multiplied. Peasants, eager to move on the National Christian promise to drive Jews from the countryside, pressured Jewish farmers and innkeepers to leave their rural holdings and occupations. The party had also made election promises to limit or eliminate Jews from the professions.[11]

The heaviest blow the six-week Goga-Cuza government delivered to the Jewish community was the "Citizenship Revision Law" decreed on January 21, 1938. One of Cuza's campaign promises had been to overturn the effects of article 133 of the 1923 constitution, which naturalized Romanian Jews, and the 1938 decree was a sharp turn in that direction. According to its provisions Jewish citizens had to produce, personally, within a twenty-day period, in towns where they had been naturalized, documents proving their rights to citizenship. Minor discrepancies in the records or lost documents meant revocation of citizenship even for veterans or war widows. Of the 203,424 adults examined, 73,253 persons (and their 151,969 dependents) were denaturalized. Another decree of March 9, 1938, which required officials of territories acquired after World War I to identify Jews without naturalization records, added another 44,848 persons to the category of stateless Jews (altogether more than 270,000). The Citizenship Revision Law went far in removing legal barriers that prevented enterprises from dismissing Jews, encouraging local officials and professional organizations to begin or continue efforts to Romanianize businesses. Zealous officials had interpreted a *numerus clausus* law of July 16, 1934, requiring that most employees of private firms be Romanian citizens, to exclude Jewish citizens on ethnic or racial grounds. The 1938 "Revision" made that deceit unnecessary for approximately one-third of the Jewish population and did nothing to discourage exclusion of citizen Jews, based on "blood." For Christian lawyers and doctors the new law was a green light to move ahead with efforts to exclude Jewish colleagues. Stripped of citizenship, new "stateless Jews" became vulnerable to all sorts of legal disabilities, including special taxes assessed on "foreigners."[12] For Romanian Jews these laws meant the eventual destruction of their economic means and the loss of any sense of security that had come with citizenship.

On February 9–10, 1938, forty-four days after appointing the Goga-Cuza cabinet, King Carol dismissed it and established a royal dictatorship. The change seemed to favor Jews, shifting power from a singularly antisemitic cabinet to the king who, though no philo-Semite, opposed the Iron Guard. Carol chose Patriarch Cristea, who likened Jews to parasites that sucked the very life out of their Christian victims, as the new prime minister.[13] Armand Călinescu and Ion Antonescu became, respectively, ministers of interior and defense, posts each held in the Goga government. Carol asked past presidents to become ministers without portfolio, expecting thereby to gain their support for the dictatorship and its constitution of February 21, 1938. In a plebiscite on these changes, the public gave its overwhelming support. Encouraged, Carol imagined he could sweep aside political opposition and the day following the vote outlawed all political parties except his own. Codreanu immediately announced the disbanding of the Iron Guard and his intention of exiling himself to Italy. However, on Călinescu's orders, he was arrested and tried twice on trumped-up charges, once in April and again in May. In the second trial he was convicted of treason and sentenced to ten years in prison, despite Defense Minister Antonescu's testimony as a character witness on his behalf. Codreanu's end came on the night-morning of November 29–30, 1938, when he and thirteen other legionnaires were taken from prison, securely bound and strangled, and finally shot in the back to give the appearance of having been killed while attempting to escape. Horia Sima, who succeeded "The Captain" as chief of the Iron Guard, ordered the revenge assassination of Călinescu, who almost certainly arranged the mass murder with the king's approval. Interior Minister Călinescu was killed on September 21, 1939. The government responded with a massive roundup, executions, and the public display of executed legionnaires. Iron Guard leaders who were not killed or imprisoned tried to hide or flee the country.[14]

Carol continued the anti-Jewish work of the Goga cabinet, which, in its last days, had shifted away from an unbridled attack to a no less determined but more deliberate approach to racist lawmaking—namely, the implementation of a nationwide *numerus clausus* or *numerus nullus*. At the time of his dismissal Goga was reported to say, "Israel you have won."[15] In fact, Carol's government delivered a second legal blow to the Jewish community (the first being revision of citizenship in January 1938) in decrees of August 8 and 9, 1940, similar to the Reich citizenship laws of 1935, making further drastic reductions in the status of Jews. Among many prohibitions, they could no longer marry Romanians. The laws defined three categories of Jews; only those belonging to the smallest group, numbering a few thousand, retained a substantial portion of their rights. These had obtained Romanian citizenship before December 30, 1918, or had fought in World War I or were the descendants of either of these two groups. Religion was the main, but no longer only, criterion determining who was a Jew. Some converts to Christianity, children who lived with unbaptized parents, and women baptized after June 21, 1939, even though married to Christians, remained legally Jews. Framers of the laws explained why it was necessary to separate Jews from Christians, there being

> a moral, spiritual and organic incompatibility between the Romanian by blood and the Mosaic religion; we have extended this idea [of who is a Jew] to those born of parents of the Mosaic religion, carrying in their blood the destiny of a spiritual and organic incompatibility, worsened through succeeding generations; we bar the way into the confines of the national community to those who, at birth, received the blessing of the Christian religion, if the parents, of the Mosaic religion, never having been baptized, considering this commitment of their child, to the Christian religion, an opportunistic act from a political point of view, because their implacable ancestry cannot be blotted out, even if the mother of this Christian [child] is of the Christian religion, and the father of the Mosaic religion, considering the father's religious opposition a sign of the child's future.[16]

The decrees prohibited all Jews from being employed in public work, such as teaching in public schools, or from holding rural property, participating in government administration, or having military careers. In addition, all but the few thousand "privileged" Jews were prohibited from engaging in any specialized or professional work (medical or legal, for example) linked to public service; membership on administrative councils of private enterprises; rural trade; the tutoring or caretaking of disabled Christians; any sort of business connected with cinema; the writing, editing, or selling of Romanian books, journals, or reviews; participating in any national sports associations; or the exercise of parental authority over Christian children. Jews also were prohibited from taking Romanian names, closing stores on Saturdays, and the ritual slaughter of animals. The law required Jews to divest themselves of rural land but empowered the state to prevent private sales so it could expropriate such property.[17]

The framers of the law claimed that "Romanian realities defined Romanian dictates," and that "the Romanian reality, in substance, boils down to a 10% population of Jews in the national total." Overstating the number of Jews in the country was always part of the fear-mongering tactics of Romanian antisemites. For them any number of Jews was too many, but 10 percent was a gross exaggeration. In the relatively thorough census of 1930 Jews accounted for 4.2 percent of the total (756,930 of 18,057,028) and probably never exceeded that proportion during the next decade because of low birth rates and emigration. For August 1940, when the laws were promulgated, even 4.2 percent is a much too high estimate because of Romania's loss to Russia the previous June of Bessarabia and Northern Bucovina, territories that had relatively large populations of Jews. By the end of August 1940, after the further loss of part of Transylvania to Hungary, the Jewish population of what was now approximately the Old Kingdom or *Regat* accounted for about 2.4 percent of the whole.[18] Of all exaggerated numbering, however, the most remarkable comes not from a Romanian but from the noted British historian R. W. Seton-Watson, who published his *History of the Roumanians* in 1934. In his book he repeats the prejudices of his Romanian friends and admirers, identifying Jews as newcomers, usurers, and exploiters of peasants and landlords. He claims that in some towns in northern Moldavia, Jews were in the majority but "tended to remain apart in distinct communities, as aliens." He does not state the obvious, that not all Jews were ruthless exploiters or cheats, nor wished to live in isolation, and while it is true that in some northern Moldavian cities Jews were in the majority, in most Romanian cities the Orthodox greatly outnumbered them. Even in cities like Iași or Botoșani their relatively large number did not translate into comparable political power or social status. Some Jews preferred to live apart and resisted assimilation, but the same could be said about Orthodox Christians. Jews and Christians alike shared in the high birth and death rates and the high incidence of infant mortality, tuberculosis, cholera, poor housing, and all that follows from deep poverty. But when it came to violence between them it was seldom Jews who murdered and plundered Christians. Seton-Watson wrote that in the 1850s and '60s Jews "speedily acquired a virtual economic hegemony in Moldavia." Anticipating the objection that in such a short time and in relatively small numbers Jews could not have gained such power, he argues that their number at the turn of the century (4.5 percent in 1899) does not reflect their dominant place in the cities. He put it this way, "as late as 1900 the total urban population in Romania was 700,000 and of this 300–400,000, or more than half, were Jews." This is pure nonsense. Seton-Watson knew that the 1899 census registered 266,652 Jews in the country. Thus, according to him, of the approximately 267,000 Jews living in Romania in 1900 some 350,000 of them lived in cities—about four of every three![19]

A significant event in the campaign against Jewish professionals was the election in December 1935 of Istrate Micescu to the presidency of the Bucharest Bar Association, from which Jewish candidates were henceforth refused membership.[20] Not long before his election Micescu had opposed the persecution of Jews and favored proportionality, but now as president he became a willing persecutor and advocated *numerus nullus,* accepting no Jews into the legal profession. In 1936 he joined the Goga-Cuza National Christian Party. As foreign minister in the Goga-Cuza government, he explained to Sir Reginald Hoare that the antisemitism of his party was an expedient for attracting support away from the Iron Guard, as though the National Christians were not themselves committed antisemites.[21] In 1936 some other local bar associations followed the lead of Bucharest in refusing to register Jewish applicants. In 1937 the Romanian Bar Association and Union of Romanian Lawyers also decided to exclude Jews. Opponents to such exclusions failed to reverse matters.[22]

In January 1939 Ionel Teodoreanu, Iași Bar Association vice president, called Christian members together and proposed they expel their Jewish colleagues, which they did. The following day some of the debarred lawyers, like Filip Dauer and Iancu Leib who had survived beatings in the halls of the university to get degrees, took their complaint to the Iași Palace of Justice. Their Christian colleagues had clearly broken their own rules, since dismissal of members was for the bar's disciplinary council to determine. At the court building thugs attacked Jews who tried to enter. When Dauer and some of his colleagues managed to fight their way in, taking blows and spilling blood, they found only an unsympathetic judge. Unable to get satisfaction in Iași, a delegation of Jewish attorneys went to Bucharest and put their case before the High Court of Appeals. The case was accepted and the court promptly decided for them, declaring the expulsions null and void. But there was no way for the Jews to bring this decision into the court in Iași, and the government refused to enforce the high court's ruling.[23]

Expelled lawyers got some support from relatives; military conscription solved Dauer's immediate problem though he was soon again unemployed when Jews were dismissed from the military in August 1940. A number of lawyers were immediately picked up by the community's legal assistance section, which, at the time, was feverishly helping residents of the city and region gather the documents needed to save their citizenship. From the time of the 1938 Citizenship Revision Law the legal section had been occupied in a losing effort to overcome it and other discriminatory measures. When Klara Scheinfeld's husband was expelled from the bar and began working for the community she decided to do the same. Her main task was helping Jews get their papers ready so that when they reported to the district police to be verified, as the law required, they could present evidence of their parents' Romanian birth, of military service, or other information establishing length of residence, loyalty, service, and so on. Especially troublesome were those who, in years past, had failed to document themselves and now poured into the community center by the hundreds seeking help in drawing up petitions. Because Commissar Georgescu, who oversaw the process, expected to profit by charging petitioners a fee, Clara had the additional work of preparing "certificates of poverty" for the very poor. This particular issue was finally resolved, she writes, "by means of a monthly salary which the Community paid Georgescu to emphasize its good will in resolving the petitions."[24]

Some Christians opposed measures that closed Jews off from their livelihood or resulted in their expulsion from school or loss of citizenship. Among them were members of the small Radical Peasants Party, formed in 1932–33 by defectors from the National Peasant Party. In the December 1933 election Radical Peasants won six seats in the chamber of deputies. They argued that the well being of minorities benefited the state, while militant nationalism was divisive and otherwise harmful.[25] Some intellectuals and political figures occasionally spoke out against antisemitism as well as fascism, Nazism, and jingo-nationalism. Jews were sometimes even praised for their good work. Among twenty-seven Jews the king honored in July 1936, five physicians were decorated for their "exceptional" patriotism. Jewish doctors were again praised in November 1937 at a meeting of Iorga's Romanian Cultural League. Health minister Constantinescu credited these doctors for their willingness to work in remote villages, while other Romanian doctors, who were pleased to be rid of their Jewish colleagues, would not. Acting against the prevailing hatred, a group of peasants saved a Jew from a blue-shirt beating, and a group of invalid war veterans contributed money to help victims of an attack in the Moldavian town of Panciu.[26]

These were remarkable instances of praise, assistance, and sympathy, but they did not signal a large reserve of public goodwill on the part of non-Jews. At the time Carol honored the Jewish doctors there was an explosion of right-wing politics, violence, and antisemitism, encouraged by Carol himself and his government. Nor had the political situation changed for the better when Constantinescu delivered his praises of Jewish doctors the following November. At that time Carol was only weeks away from replacing the moderate Tătărescu with the rabidly antisemitic Goga-Cuza cabinet. Although the short life of that government, followed by a retreat from some of its decrees and a decree of August 1938, guaranteeing the rights of minorities, seemed promising, the fact is there was no change of course. The minorities decree did not include Jews, and the devastating Citizenship Revision Law remained after Goga and Cuza were dumped. The new prime minister, Patriarch Miron Cristea was clearly in step with the fascist antisemitic right. His government began to move against Jewish culture since its schools, languages, and religion were not protected by the new minorities law. Sunday classes were forbidden and the use of Yiddish restricted. Some shop owners who could not speak Romanian, many of them elderly, were forced to close their businesses. Others had to stay open on Saturdays. Then in the fall of 1938 the Cristea government began to plan the forced removal of "denationalized" Jews from Romania, 43,000 according to an official count. Some were to leave within three months, others in a year's time. The government treated the problem of where the Jews would be sent indifferently—someplace in the British Empire, perhaps, or to the French island colony of Madagascar. That was a problem, it seems, for the international community to figure out. At first Romanian Jews were in a panic and then somewhat relieved to learn that the process of forced emigration would actually take many months. In the meantime the government decreed (December 3, 1938) a graduated tax of from 500 to 10,000 lei on those who had lost their citizenship. Nonpayers could lose their jobs and be conscripted for forced labor.[27]

Bad as it was, the domestic situation for Romanian Jews in the late 1930s got worse in 1940 due to mounting violence, including mass murders and the creation of a thoroughly fascist antisemitic National-Legionnaire government. At the same time Romania and Nazi Germany were being drawn closer together by shared economic, political, and ideological interests. Fascists in both countries were generally eager to join forces; the Germans were also attracted to Romanian raw materials, especially oil. What King Carol's government hoped to gain by an accord with Germany was protection against the growing power of the Soviet Union and prevention of Romania being dismembered. For King Carol himself his only hope of retaining power was Hitler's blessing.

CHAPTER 5

The Rumble of Violence

For Romanian Jews the turn of the century was a time of deepening economic hardships and unsettling news from abroad. In nearby Russia the nineteenth century went out and twentieth came in on waves of violence that swept across the Pale of Settlement leaving many Jews murdered and much property destroyed: in pogroms following Tsar Alexander II's assassination in 1881, in the Kishinev pogrom of Easter 1903, and during the revolution of 1905. Wilhelm Filderman was shaken, not only by events in Russia but also by news of the Dreyfus trial (1894), which he described as casting a "shadow on the life of the Romanian Jewish community." From inside Romania Filderman sensed "a rumbling anti-Semitism"; in particular he had in mind a student-led pogrom in Bucharest in November 1897, one sparked by a public meeting in the capital organized by professors N. Iorga and A. C. Cuza to celebrate Romania's twenty years of independence and to vilify Jews. After the meeting Christian students set about beating up Jews and trashing their property. Some Romanians spoke out against these actions but to no avail.[1]

Moshe Moscovici, an unstinting activist in the Iași community, surmised that "the first manifestation of anti-Semitism" in his city occurred on May 16, 1899. University of Iași students had issued a general invitation to Christians to meet at the university on that day for the purpose of dealing with the Jewish menace. After the meeting students and others took to the streets targeting Jews and their property: breaking windows, plundering stores, invading homes, beating up residents, and wrecking some synagogues. Only in one district of the city were Jews able to drive the mob back.

CHAPTER 5

When the matter was heard in court almost three years later Professor Cuza defended those accused of destroying property. He argued that Jews themselves were responsible for what happened. The Christian perpetrators were mildly reprimanded; the court sentenced a Jew accused of provocation to three months in prison.[2] As a result of such threats and the severe economic hardships of the time, thousands of Jews from Iași and other Moldavian cities and towns emigrated westward, some "on foot," writes Moscovici, "a long journey, to the place of departure, [then] in steamships to America."[3]

The granting of citizenship to Romanian Jews after World War I, regarded by many non-Jews as forced on them by outsiders, stirred up an antisemitic storm. In the vanguard were University of Iași professor A. C. Cuza and his student Corneliu Codreanu. Cuza had the title of University Professor, earned in part by the publication of *Poporația*, a book that E. Socor alleged included plagiarized passages. Socor, besides publishing a book on the matter, *Shame of the University: The Plagiarism of A. C. Cuza* (1922), wrote in *Adevărul* (February 8, 1923), one of two democratic newspapers he published, that "Mr. Cuza has hoodwinked the Academy by extracting from it a prize for a plagiarized book; he has hoodwinked the University from which he obtained a professorship for the same work. He has fooled . . . Mr. Iorga, who raised him to a position of which he is unworthy." The courts rejected Cuza's accusation of slander against Socor and Iorga responded to the scandal by ending his political association with Cuza and resigning his professorship at the university.[4] As for Codreanu, he was a fanatic committed to what he believed were basic principles of patriotism and justice, a Christian fascist who despised Jews and was willing to kill and die for his convictions. He believed political murder was perfectly justified, but nothing in his reprehensible actions suggests that, like his professor Cuza, he was a charlatan.

Between the wars antisemites claimed the "Jewish problem" had become more threatening. They pointed out that territories added to Romania after World War I included half a million allegedly Russified and Bolshevized Jews and thousands of other thoroughly destitute Jews who had escaped to Bessarabia (now part of Romania), fleeing gangs of White terrorists who roamed the Ukraine during Russia's Civil War (1918–21).[5] Efforts of the Romanian Union of Native Jews to help the refugees was complicated by the fact that the Romanian government, willing at first to issue passports, reversed itself when the US consul refused to issue them visas. Thousands of refugees were thus stranded in internment camps in Bessarabia. Embarrassed by the camps' deplorable conditions, the government finally accepted the union's offer to evacuate them and find them places to stay, on condition it bear the full cost of resettlement and prevent refugees from spreading communist propaganda. Over the next six years some 45,000 were settled, the union providing funds to localities that gave them shelter. Iași received support to establish a home for orphans. One of the charges against the operation was that the Jewish Union and Bolsheviks were conspiring to flood Bessarabia with hundreds of thousands of Judeo-Bolsheviks.[6]

The year 1922 was filled with antisemitic student demonstrations. To the sound of breaking glass, gangs looted stores and shouted out "death to Jews!" or slogans in praise of Corneliu Codreanu and his father. Christian students and school officials verbally assaulted Jewish students. At the University of Iași, Codreanu and his close student friends formed the Association of Christian Students on May 20, 1922, dedicating themselves to defend the nation against the "Jewish invasion." The following December, days after the government ordered posters put up in all schools prohibiting insults against Jewish students, Christian students took to the streets in university towns across the country. In Bucharest they demonstrated against democratic and Jewish papers, parading their contempt before the offices of *Dimineața* and *Adevărul,* smashing windows of the daily *Lupta,* and destroying the whole printing operation of *Mântuirea*. On the morning of December 6, Jews were attacked on the streets of the capital and a large gang demolished the equipment of both *Opinia* and *Lumea*.[7] Government appeals for an end to the violence were ineffective. On December 10 students from across Romania gathered in Bucharest demanding *numerus clausus* in the schools and calling for a general strike at all universities. That same day in Iași Christian students expressed amazement that a program organized by "Maccabi," a Jewish student sports association, did not include the national anthem and began to demonstrate in front of the meeting place. After the Maccabis called off their festivities the Christian students moved to a hall in the university's main building and, because the rector had the lights shut off, pledged in torchlight to fight for Cuza's ideas; then they went out smashing windows and beating up Jews.[8]

Student activists who participated in these events came to be called "the generation of 1922." Most came of age between the wars in a climate of militant-nationalism, anticommunism, and antisemitism. Codreanu described leaders among them as romantic outlaws (*haiduci*), "muzzle-loaders on their backs heading up the mountain paths carrying with them honor and the spark of freedom" to "conquer or die." Their populism, antisemitism, and patriotism identified them as the spiritual or ideological children of the most honored national political and intellectual figures: patriarchs, statesmen, historians, poets, playwrights. They were encouraged by the triumph of fascism in the west and both celebrated and mourned, in massive fashion, those in their number who died fighting for Franco in the Spanish Civil War. In Iași they greeted the constitutional changes of March 1923, granting political rights to Jews, by attacking the community. They staggered the times and places of attack to prevent police and soldiers from focusing their efforts. Areas of Jewish concentration were the main targets. "We did our duty," wrote Codreanu, "toppling everything that stood in our path and showing the Jews that Iași, Moldavia's ancient capital, was still Romanian." Student riots and vilification of any who approved granting political rights to Jews doubtless encouraged members of parliament to begin the process of subverting the revised constitution even before the ink on it was dry. "The Captain" and his companions failed in their attempt to murder those responsible for changing the law, but their acquittal of conspiring to do so and Codreanu's acquittal in 1925 for murdering the Iași prefect, demonstrate strong public sympathy for their violent brand of antisemitism. Following the murder trial, high school students across the country handed out photographs of their "Hero of the Nation."[9]

Student demonstrations of December 1922 and March 1923 were the beginning of a nearly constant antisemitic "rumble," to use Filderman's word. Swastikas were painted on walls everywhere, the journal *Swastika* was published in Iași, Jewish students were prevented from taking classes or examinations, Jews were thrown off moving trains, and pogroms occurred in 1925 in the Moldavian towns of Piatra Neamț and Focșani. The Jewish deity was characterized as a god of brothels and pimps, and rabbis as agents of Satan. Epithets against Jews came in an endless stream: poisoners, swindlers, perverts, snakes, spiders, eczema. In December 1925 the government shut down Jewish Normal schools. Students at the universities of Iași and Bucharest threatened to strike if Jewish students were not further restricted from admission and altogether excluded from student organizations.

In the fall of 1926 a controversy over university admission examinations rigged against Jewish and other non-Romanian students in Cernăuți (Northern Bucovina) got the attention of the antisemitic press. Some of the failed applicants, many if not most of whom were Jews, set off a lively protest against the examiners, who, among other things, refused to let applicants see their graded test papers. During their trial for allegedly threatening these examiners, one of the dissident students, David Fallick, a Jew, was shot to death by Nicolae Totu, a University of Iași student and colleague of Codreanu. Prominent Romanian antisemites, including A. C. Cuza, Octavian Goga, and Codreanu, defended Totu, praising him as a national patriot-martyr while characterizing Fallick as an enemy of the state who had brought the crime upon himself. Totu's trial took place on February 21, 1927, but

THE RUMBLE OF VIOLENCE

not in Cernăuți, which had a large nonethnic Romanian population, including a substantial number of Jews. Instead, it was held in the (more Romanian) Southern Bucovina city of Câmpulung, a place likely to favor the defendant. Cuza himself testified for the defense. As the trial drew to a close, Totu's lawyer advised jurors to make their decision quickly, and they did so, acquitting his client in a matter of a few minutes. For presenting the affair with an "energetic attitude," the government confiscated *Curiierul Israelit*, the journal of the Jewish Union.[10]

In the late 1920s at meetings of the two main antisemitic organizations in Iași, Cuza's LANC and the National Romanian Christian Student Union, members called for harsh measures against Jews: reversal of naturalization, elimination of rights to own rural property, confiscation of other properties, deportation of recent arrivals, and so on. Meetings such as these sometimes set off anti-Jewish violence. A congress of Christian students meeting in Oradea in December 1927 was followed by the burning of synagogues and Torahs in the city. This action sparked similar violence in other places, including Iași. Protests from church and government officials against these attacks had little effect.

Hardships borne by Jews in Romania between the wars were reported in 1929 by the American Committee on the Rights of Religious Minorities. Especially telling are the comments of the French delegate, Pastor Jules Jezequel, who represented himself as trying to understand minority issues from a Romanian, as well as from a critical and independent, point of view. To put the matter in a nutshell, he concluded that Romania's constitution, although democratic, liberal, and admirable, "is nothing . . . but a scrap of paper"; elections are orchestrated by those in power, bypassing "the people"; antisemitism, which at times causes violence, has nothing to do with the peasants and is condemned by the educated class "as a whole"; "the Government is not strictly speaking anti-Semitic, but it tolerates the anti-Semitic manifestations of a small group . . . and it has a . . . policy toward the Jews which seems to be activated by a spirit of anti-Semitism"; that Jews, despite citizenship guarantees, even those whose ancestors had lived in Romania for two or more generations, may very well be denied their political rights; and that public office, officer ranking in the military, judgeships, and teaching are professions closed to Jews. Regarding education, Jezequel reported that in public schools Orthodoxy is taught and the official assertion that the non-Orthodox are free to follow their own religions "is perfectly gratuitous"; "it was perfectly evident that actually only Roumanian and Orthodox pupils attend public schools"; where there are relatively many Jews they have set up their own schools, but these are besieged by hostile government actions, requiring them to gain official approval each year and each year facing the prospect of being rejected and not receiving government subsidies to which they are entitled by law; efforts to restore the outlawed Normal schools have failed, which means that new teachers will be scarce; Jews who want to go to state gymnasia, Jewish secondary schools having been shut down, face severe numerical restrictions; though *numerus clausus* is not in the law it has been applied since 1922 as though it were; "Universities, particularly that of Iaşi, have at times been the theatre of bloody scenes, of which the Jews have been the constant victims"; although the complaint that Jewish medical students will only dissect the bodies of non-Jews has some merit, the Cuzists avow publicly that they are "against the Jews . . . for the sole reason that they are Jews"; for that reason alone, "students have been insulted and beaten unmercifully"; "authorities have not tried, or have tried only feebly, to stop these outrages," which draw attention away from official incompetency; Christian students find it easier to force Jews out of the university "than to surpass them in examinations"; neither academic excellence nor even superior knowledge are the essential groundings for positions of prestige and leadership; and finally, "Romanian intellectuals have a very pronounced tendency to believe that all positions and honors are theirs by right of birth."[11]

The American Committee arrived in Bucharest on the morning of June 12, 1927. That day's newspapers described attacks against Jewish students at the University of Bucharest Medical Faculty. These students had been prevented from taking their examination in physics and some were badly beaten. The committee was "shocked and astonished to discover the number of such demonstrations which had occurred," but took some comfort in the fact that "thirty-six members of the faculty of the University of Iaşi drafted and sent to the Ministry of Education a . . . protest against this student movement for which their colleague, Professor Cuza, was responsible."[12]

In 1930 Codreanu promised to ship Jews out of Romania in cattle cars as soon as he had power to do so. The following year, in which Codreanu was elected to parliament, *Patriotul Strămoşesc* (*The Ancestral Patriot*) announced approvingly that Hitler would murder two million Jews and communists to save Germany.[13] Murder became, as it did in other fascist states, a way of getting rid of opponents. Political assassinations even included mass murder, of Codreanu and thirteen other legionnaires in 1938, "attempting to escape from prison," and of sixty-four former government officials by vengeful legionnaires two years later. An acquiescent or approving Christian public encouraged crimes against Jews. Police ignored such crimes or juries acquitted perpetrators or judges handed them light sentences, and they were sometimes hailed as martyrs and heroes. In 1927 the council of ministers ignored a complaint Filderman submitted on behalf of sixty-five Jews who had been attacked on trains. Gangs of "shirts" openly terrorized Jews with their fists and bloody rhetoric. In 1928 an Antisemitic League met in Iași and drew up a program advocating the burning of synagogues and wrecking of Jewish homes. In 1931 *Strălucitorul* (*The Shining One*) pointed out that the best time to burn down synagogues was the Jewish New Year when they would be filled. Besides their worry over verbal and physical assaults, community leaders were especially concerned about government passivity toward or support of university student organizations that were largely responsible for the attacks.[14] That antisemites contemplated extreme measures is clear. "Before my death," said Professor Cuza, "I want to see the blood of Jews *mêlé à la boue*" (smeared in the mud).[15]

Most remarkable of these events were the mass demonstrations of 1922–23 and the crimes and trials of Codreanu and his companions. Out of these and other student efforts emerged a number of antisemitic organizations, most notably Codreanu's Legion of the Archangel Michael. By the mid-1930s, however, student firebrands of the 1920s had joined the ranks of professionals, intellectuals, publishers, government officials, political figures, Orthodox clergy, and others who marched in step on the "Jewish problem." Each of them was driven, more or less, by political considerations, the advantage going to those who professed love for country, its peasantry and church, and hatred for Jews and communism. In 1937 British minister to Romania Sir Reginald Hoare reported that except for right-wingers, "nearly all prominent officials and politicians . . . were prepared to admit privately the unfortunate effects of anti-Semitism, but professed themselves unable, public opinion being what it was, to take any active measure."[16]

King Carol, as sensitive to the changing political climate as anyone else and just as cynical, shifted further to the fascist right after the German-Soviet conquest of Poland in 1939. Beginning in December 1939 and over the next few months, he moved toward securing political alliances with Berlin and the Iron Guard. Cutting ties with England and France (both countries had promised to support Romania's independence after Germany took over Czechoslovakia in March 1939) and accommodating Germany appeared necessary, not only because of its growing economic and political importance in Romania but also to dissuade Hitler from partitioning Romania among its Axis-friendly neighbors. Carol even made overtures to the Legion. In June 1940, less than two years after he had "the Captain" and other leading Iron Guardists assassinated, he interviewed Codreanu's successor Horia Sima, publicly called for reconciliation, released imprisoned legionnaires, and invited the Legion to join his Parti de la Nația, renamed from Frontul

CHAPTER 5

Renașterii Naționale (Renaissance National Front), which was associated with the assassination. These efforts won for the king a public declaration of obedience from Sima and praise in the fascist papers of Italy and Germany. During the first two weeks of July 1940, Carol withdrew Romania from a British guarantee of independence, made his government more Nazi friendly (replacing Tătărescu with the pro-German Ion Gigurtu and including Iron Guardists), abandoned the League of Nations, sought to become an Axis partner, and in August enacted racist laws patterned after those the Nazis decreed in 1935 at Nuremburg.[17] But all this availed Carol nothing. Even as he rushed to change course, his country was being partitioned. On June 26, 1940, the Soviet Union, based on its pact with Germany the previous August, ordered Romania to withdraw from Bessarabia and Northern Bucovina and began occupying the territories almost immediately.

Now occurred the first of many mass killings of Jews by Romanians. During their retreat from the two territories, Romanian military units carried out a number of such killings. The first action took place on June 29 near Mihoreni, a town close to the border between Moldavia and Northern Bucovina, where eleven Jews, including five children, were shot down by soldiers under the command of Major Goilav. Isac Moscovici, whose wife and two daughters were among those executed, was captured apart from the others and beaten to death. Next day soldiers of the 16th Infantry Regiment, under Major Valeriu Carp, retreating through Northern Bucovina, entered the village of Ciudei, and shot to death seven or eight Jews.[18]

At Dorohoi, in northern Moldavia, at least fifty Jews were murdered. Shortly after noon on July 1 an honor guard of several Jewish soldiers entered the city's Jewish cemetery accompanying the body of Iancu Solomon, a soldier who had been shot during a border incident in his unsuccessful attempt to save the life of a Christian officer. As Solomon's body was being lowered into his grave, those attending heard shooting. At first they thought the gunfire was a salvo honoring that officer in the nearby Christian cemetery, but the firing continued. The frightened civilians hid themselves in a mausoleum and the honor guard moved out. At or near the cemetery gate the guard was met by Christian soldiers whose commander ordered his men to disarm and shoot the Jews. Afterward these soldiers searched the cemetery, found those who were hiding, and killed them. Meanwhile, several more Jews were murdered in the city, some having first been mutilated. The mass killings might have continued had they not been interrupted by a severe thunderstorm. Only Jews were killed in the cemetery: eleven women, thirty-four men, including Sergeant Emil Bercovici's honor guard, six other soldiers, and five children. An official account suggests the killing had been planned by Christian soldiers and called it "significant" that some houses in the city had icons in their windows or crosses marked on their walls at the time of the massacre, evidence that residents of these houses had been forewarned. The same report offered the exculpatory explanation that military units responsible for the shooting, the "3rd Frontier and 8th Artillery," had been "humiliated and ridiculed by the Jews of [the town of] Herța" during their retreat through Northern Bucovina.[19] Thus victims became perpetrators and the retreat—not the murders—came to be regarded as a national "humiliation."

On the day of the Dorohoi killings soldiers rounded up thirty-four Jews from several communities and assembled them in the village of Zaharești and then murdered them. The killers were soldiers of the same 16th Infantry Regiment, commanded by Major Carp, who were responsible for the killing a few days before in the village of Ciudei. In both cases some of the victims were tortured before being executed. Four Jews were shot to death on the evening of July 1 in the village of Șerbăuți. Soldiers shot seven more persons outside of Dolhasca near the railroad tracks that run through the town. Next day a number of Jews were thrown from a moving train between Dolhasca and Pașcani; four were killed and thirteen survivors were badly injured. At each of several other places between July 2 and 6 as many as eight persons were murdered.[20] On June 30 at Galați, a border city in southeast Romania, Romanian soldiers fired on and killed a large number of evacuees who had been pulled out of Bessarabia, many of them Jews. A full reckoning of all Jews murdered during the retreat is not known, but probably number well over one hundred.[21]

Two months after this rash of killings, King Carol II, having failed to prevent further annexations of Romanian territory by Hungary (northwestern Transylvania) and Bulgaria (southern Dobrogea), lacking German or Romanian public support, and threatened by an Iron Guard assault, prudently decided to run. Before doing so he abdicated in favor of his son Michael (September 5–6, 1940) but relinquished political power to General Ion Antonescu (1882–1946). Royal dictatorship was formally replaced a week later by the National-Legionnaire State (September 14, 1940 to January 27, 1941). The Leader (*Conducătorul*) Antonescu was a politically experienced distinguished military careerist who had been on good terms with Codreanu. Coleader and vice president of the Council of Ministers was Iron Guard chief Horia Sima. The decree that established the government named Antonescu "chief of the Legionnaire Regime" and Sima "Commander of the Legionnaire Movement."[22] Antonescu commanded the Romanian military and Sima's legionnaires had almost unrestricted police power. German officials, planning the invasion of the Soviet Union when the Carol government collapsed, lost no time contacting the new leadership. On September 8 Admiral Wilhelm Canaris, head of German military intelligence (*Abwehr*), arrived in Bucharest to meet with Antonescu and receive assurances that Romanian oil would continue to flow to Germany and to mend ties between his agency and Romania's secret service (SSI), broken during the change of government. Antonescu proved to be a willing partner, appointing the pro-Nazi Eugen Cristescu to head SSI.

For Sima and Minister of Interior General Petrovicescu the moment was right to unleash Legion police against Romania's Jews. One focus of the attack was Iași, where the campaign, directed by Ilie Sturdza, Legion commander of Moldavia and son of the foreign minister, had the support of local authorities. Jews were regularly pulled from their homes and taken to the municipal police station (*chestură*) or Legion headquarters (Casă Verde, Green House), where they were beaten until they confessed to being communists and revealed the names of coconspirators. Wealthy Jews were favorite targets. Some were kept for hours or days and then released; others were summarily tried and imprisoned. Herman Auerbach, a prosperous co-owner of a mill, was arrested on November 11, 1940 (the same night a sizeable earthquake shook Romania). Two policemen took him to Legion headquarters where he was severely beaten and forced to confess that he and nephews of his were working together as communist subversives. The nephews were now, of course, new and "identified" suspects. Because his wife Rebeca convinced Italian consul Augusto Santorio to intervene on her husband's behalf, he was let go the following day, but over the next several weeks Herman and Rebeca were repeatedly threatened by legionnaires at their home or mill.[23]

Extortion usually accompanied threats and beatings. The higher the police rank the bigger the payout. Policeman Bălan got less than Inspector Gheorghe Leahu, his uncle, who was so proficient at eliciting bribes that he managed to wring a monthly salary out of the Iași community. The largest bribes went to Legion boss Ilie Sturdza, who Soloman Cries (or Cristian), a prominent Jewish merchant in Iași, described as having no compassion for the victims of torture, neither the children whose limbs were broken nor parents who cried out for mercy. Sturdza proposed to the Iași community that it pay him 12 million lei for halting the terror. It agreed finally to pay him half that sum in three equal monthly installments.[24] Still, armed thugs continued to rob residences or places of business and arrest occupants who were tortured into denouncing others who were themselves dragged out of their homes and put through the same wringer. Synagogues were usual targets of Legion malice. Mayor Poliacu ordered two of them, located near Iron Guard headquarters in Iași, destroyed. Aurel Golimas, director of the National Lycée, supervised the work. Abraham Hahamu described how lycée students and others tore down the two buildings while "Jews, overcome with grief, stood helplessly by." Demolition proceeded without regard for religious objects except that some salvaged things were distributed to the workers.[25]

Bucharest Jews suffered similar acts of Legion brutality, but the worst incident occurred in Ploiești. On November 10 Legion police took some fifty Jews from a synagogue there. Four days later Horia Sima and state security director Alexandru Ghica, who had come to the city, ordered legionnaires to release the Jews. At first they refused, but at Sima's insistence, six of eleven prisoners who had been murdered were returned, bodies riddled with bullets, to their families. The other five, however, were not recovered. Twenty-four others, taken from the synagogue, were held and tortured for eighteen days before being released.[26]

Besides violence and thievery, the National-Legionnaire State brought down on Jews a number of laws that continued the process of destroying their economy. The racist foundations for these measures were established by the Gigurtu government during the last month of Carol II's reign, in the decrees of August 8–9, 1940. Explaining the reasons behind and sources for the August 9 decree, regulating "the legal situation of the Jews," Justice Minister Gruia repeatedly cited Nazi precedence. This law, wrote Filderman, "wiped out all our rights so painfully gained since 1880," not only political rights but also, for many Jews, the right to gainful employment.[27] Particularly Nazi-like are the prohibitions against intermarriage or the taking of Romanian names. These August decrees served the Legion and Antonescu, as the Nuremberg laws of September 1935 (Reich Citizenship Law and Law for the Protection of German Blood and German Honor) served the Nazis, as foundations for additional extreme anti-Jewish laws and policies. Under Antonescu the legal sanctions of August 9 were applied to the few formerly exempted "privileged" Jews. Practically all Jews were excluded from public education; authoring, publishing, or trading scholarly or school texts; theatrical and musical performances (Gypsies but not Jews could perform in Jewish restaurants); membership in professional artistic associations; practicing medicine in public institutions, and so on. The Jewish religion was no longer protected by law, and Antonescu ignored a pledge by the Gigurtu government to rescind a rule that prohibited the closing of Jewish stores on Saturdays. On the contrary, he required they be open on the Jewish New Year and Yom Kippur. By prohibiting ritual slaughter, as had Gigurtu, and promoting the destruction of Jewish cemeteries, Antonescu further weakened Jewish communities that relied on these institutions as a source of funding for social services. Especially noteworthy among the array of anti-Jewish measures were those concerning the expropriation of rural property (October 5, 1940) and those extending prohibitions into the areas of commerce and industry. The August 9 decree forbade Jews from owning rural property but permitted its sale to Romanians. The October 5 law prohibited such sales and ordered that land and other rural property (including crops, harvested or standing) be taken over immediately by the state. By expanding the Gigurtu restrictions to commerce and industry, the Antonescu government finished off a number of Jewish enterprises.[28] Finally, bad as the Antonescu-Legionnaire regime was for the Iași community, it suffered less than some, perhaps most, other large communities, despite the fact that the Moldavian capital was, after Bucharest, the center of Legion power. Damage to synagogues was less extensive in Iași than in many other places, and neither of the city's two Jewish cemeteries (in the districts of Păcurari and Ciurchi) was destroyed, although the community was evicted from its Ciurchi cemetery during the war.

Compared to the Legion, Antonescu's prewar anti-Jewish actions appear conservative and methodical. His solution to "the Jewish question" was a "step-by-step" process of having Romanians take over vital economic operations from Jews who would eventually be driven from the country. Careful consideration was not part of the Legion's modus operandi; it intended to quickly wipe out the old order, Antonescu as well as Jews. One of its acts of uncontrolled rage occurred on November 26, 1940, the day legionnaires were exhuming the bodies of Codreanu and thirteen other Iron Guard leaders who had been murdered two years before by order of the king and buried at Jilava Prison. The bodies were to be paraded through the capital on November 30 in a giant second anniversary memorial service. In prison, at the time of the exhumation, were former government officials who had been responsible for the murders or other anti-Legion actions. Word that Antonescu intended to replace Legion prison guards with soldiers and suspicion that he was backing away from executing the former officials enraged the diggers who turned on the prisoners, slaughtering sixty-four of them.[29] Over the next two days legionnaires began rounding up other former officials while a death squad murdered eighty-year-old Nicolae Iorga and the well-known economist and former minister Virgil Madgearu. Only the intervention of Hermann Neubacher, minister-overseer of German economic interests in Romania, persuaded Antonescu to retreat from his demand that Sima turn control of the Legion over to him. Thus Legion police continued their acts of destruction and theft beyond the reach of the general.

That same November, however, Hitler was contemplating the invasion of the Soviet Union and wanted, for that reason, a productive and stable regime in Romania and sent an invitation to Antonescu to meet with him. The general came away from the meeting (November 21–24, 1940) with no assurances regarding the Legion but with a sense that the Führer was on his side and was sensitive to Romania's national aspirations. During a second visit on January 12, 1941, Hitler assured him of Germany's backing in putting down Iron Guard disorders. So, on his return Antonescu began to dismantle the legionary apparatus in government, expelling from government various Legion ministers and police officials.[30] The Legion responded with a demonstration on the night of January 20, protesting the dismissal of Interior Minister Constantin Petrovicescu, attacking soldiers and occupying government buildings the next morning. General Antonescu answered by bringing in troops to reinforce units already in the capital; he also asked German ambassador Wilhelm Fabrizius to inform the German foreign ministry of these events and request the Führer's advice. Hitler recommended he take decisive action against the rebels. On their side, legionnaires had barricaded several buildings, set up machine guns around the city, and ignorant of Hitler's decision to back the general acted with confidence that it was they who had Nazi support. On the evening of the twenty-first, Antonescu requested panzer support from Wehrmacht General Hansen. The next day German tanks rolled through the city and were welcomed by both sides. Finally, Antonescu ordered his troops to fire on Legion positions early on the morning of the twenty-third. Shortly before the attack Neubacher again intervened, this time meeting Sima at Iron Guard headquarters and pointing out that besides having superior forces, Antonescu was backed by the highest German authority. He then persuaded Sima to sign an order to take down the barricades in return for a guarantee that legionnaires would be allowed to withdraw safely. Knowing of this agreement or not, Antonescu ordered an assault that crushed the rebels in a few hours. Sima and several other top Legion officers were saved by Otto von Bolschwing, chief of the SS Security Service (SD) in Romania, who got them out of the country disguised as German corpsmen. Altogether some three hundred legionnaires escaped to Germany. Hitler, who was not pleased with the rescue operation, sent his new ambassador, Manfred von Killinger, to Bucharest with a message of firm support for Antonescu.[31] The National-Legionnaire State was abolished officially on February 15 and replaced by a military dictatorship.

It was during the rebellion that another mass killing of Jews occurred. While the Legion was in control of a large part of Bucharest, from the evening of January 20th to the early morning of the 23rd, legionnaires attacked the capital's main Jewish district. At least one hundred and twenty Jews were murdered. Some of the victims were decorated war heroes. Leon Rosenthal, veteran of World War I, his wife Rebecca, son Henry, and son-in-law Lazar Bălan were murdered, as was Isidor Goldstein, secretary of the Jewish Community of Bucharest and a highly decorated veteran of the wars of 1913 and 1916–18. The cantor Osias Kopstuck was killed and the Coral Temple in which he sang destroyed, one of twenty-five synagogues that were plundered and wrecked. Legionnaires moved, unhindered by military or police units under Antonescu's command, through Jewish neighborhoods, raping, plundering, burning, and killing. Most of those murdered were beaten and then shot. At the municipal slaughterhouse thirteen Jews were butchered; some were hung on meat hooks and labeled "kosher meat"; some had their stomachs cut open and intestines wrapped around their necks.[32] Hundreds of shops and homes lay in ruins. Emil Dorian, a resident of Bucharest at the time, recorded this in his diary, "the list of beaten and tortured people is endless, and the crimes cover the complete range of a demented imagination.... All this has not prevented [editor] Ilie Radulescu from stating authoritatively, in the first issue of *Porunca Vremii* to appear after the bloodbath of these three days, that "the kikes have fired on the army!"[33]

Dr. Filderman, president of the Federation of Jewish Communities, sent General Antonescu a list of 120 Jews who had been murdered in the rebellion and enumerated the synagogues that had been burned down or otherwise wrecked and pillaged and the hundreds of stores, homes, and other buildings that had been ransacked. A number of victims were savagely beaten during the night-morning of the twenty-first–twenty-second and then taken by truck to a wooded area south of the city, near the village of Jilava and the Sabar River, and shot.[34]

Thousands of rebels were captured and eventually tried. Some who participated in the Jilava massacre of November 1940 and the murder of Iorga were sentenced to die, but for the most part crimes against Jews were not punished. The Legion's defeat meant a reduction in violence against Jews but no easing of anti-Jewish legislation. The deliberate legal destruction of the Jewish community had frustrated legionnaires who wanted immediate solutions and personal involvement and whose methods were often disruptive and bloody, but it suited Ion Antonescu and his idea of an official, orderly process. One of his most severe measures was the decree of March 27, 1941, which provided "for the transfer of the urban property of Jews into the patrimony of the state."[35] Vice president of the Council of Ministers, Mihai Antonescu, described the law as a major step toward recovering Romania's Christian heritage. About a month later, on May 2, 1941, the government established the National Center for Romanianization, which had as its main task expropriating Jewish properties and distributing them to Romanians.[36]

Some property-owning Jews tried to protect themselves from losing everything by taking on Christian partners. Ghetzel Buchmann took Iași mayor Bogdan Petricu as an associate in some woodland he had inherited. "It was an association in name only," wrote Ghetzel's wife Roza, "Bogdan . . . profited from the situation, exploited us until we bled."[37]

When Romanian Jews considered which would do them less harm, the Legion or Antonescu, they clearly favored the latter. After nearly four months of Legion government, Filderman was so convinced of this that he sent the general a treatise praising his ideas for solving the Jewish question in Romania. These ideas, he wrote, were "perfectly identical" to the systematic and nation-serving approaches of Hitler, Mussolini, and Horthy. By contrast, he argued, Iron Guard leaders, out to destroy the general's authority, had succeeded in having their own disruptive methods put into practice and thus exposed the country to grave misfortune.[38] Given a choice, in January 1941, any Jewish leader would have taken Antonescu over the Legion. Besides legal sanctions he contemplated isolating Jews in ghettos and eventually forcing their emigration, but his course appeared to be nonlethal.

CHAPTER 6

War and the Mass Execution at Stânca Rosnovanu

Max Gaer, a trade-school graduate and active Zionist, born in Iași in 1911, recalled the spring of 1941 as a time of growing tensions in the Jewish community. Engineer Moșe Herșcovici recalled that in the months before the war "we were soon afraid to go out on the streets, especially after the retreat of troops from Bessarabia, and even more after the abdication of Carol II and the ceding of a large part of Transylvania."[1] Provisions grew scarce; eventually, only the black market had the most essential things. Street predators taunted, robbed, and beat Jews. Soldiers and military equipment began moving into the city and its environs to make ready for the invasion of the Soviet Union. "Night after night we heard the clatter of tracks on the cobblestone streets," recalled Gaer, and then "suddenly German regiments began coming in."[2] Max Volovici was thirteen at the time. What stands out in his memory, besides the appearance of German troops, was a disappointment at his school's awards-granting ceremony: "I knew I was first in the class and waited for my reward. But instead of the school principal giving out awards another person led the ceremony and awards were given only to Christians. They didn't give me my prize! After this, someone . . . came and began talking about the war situation and there was great silence in the room and he said, 'the holy war has begun!' It was like electricity. Some Jewish students started to leave. I was with mother and we left together because the atmosphere became threatening."[3]

The danger was real. Legal persecutions, which stripped Jews of employment, money, and property, did not end as the war drew near but were eclipsed by a greater threat, anticipated in the government's campaign vilify-

CHAPTER 6

ing Jews as dangerous aliens, communists, and allies of the Soviet Union. Accusations of treasonous behavior and warnings of vengeful remedies began appearing in official reports, speeches, and orders. Addressing his cabinet of ministers on April 4, 1941, General Antonescu said he had instructed Interior Minister General Popescu to summon all Jewish leaders in order to remind them how he had saved their lives in January and to warn them that if they attempted to sabotage the economy of Romania, there would be violence in the streets and, he said, "I will leave them unprotected . . . and let them be massacred."[4] The January event he spoke of was the Legion uprising in Bucharest of January 21–23, 1941 when he held his troops back, allowing legionnaires two days to pillage and murder Jews before he crushed the rebellion.

In a report of June 7, 1941, the propaganda ministry, summarizing the activity of its secret service the previous April and May, identified Jews and communists as the main (practically the only) internal enemies of the state. All areas the mission investigated were described as being "infested with Communist propaganda." Although Iaşi was not the only target of the investigation, the ministry gave it special attention, sending twenty-two agents there. It was the largest city in the northeast, had the largest Jewish population in the region, was minutes away from the Soviet border, and, according to the ministry, was a hotbed of subversive activity. The report claimed that "the most active Communist agents are Jews who exercise a strong influence over all local authorities," and "Jewish coffee houses are the focus of Communist activity."[5]

The first Jewish community the Antonescu dictatorship victimized in a mass action occurred at Dorohoi. Like Iaşi, Dorohoi had a relatively large Jewish population and was located in northeastern Romania near the Soviet border. Since the pogrom of July 1, 1940, that took the lives of more than fifty members of its community, Dorohoi Jews had kept to themselves and off the streets as much as they could, fearful of more violence. Dr. Brăilescu-Gotlieb described his feeling of "being hunted" in the months after the massacre. His fears were realized on the night of May 28–29, 1941, when 150 "suspicious Jews" were arrested and interrogated. Next day, with small packets of food and clothes, the prisoners were loaded into cattle or freight cars and sent off to the main camp for political prisoners at Tîrgu Jiu in the southwest of the country. Prisoners received no food or water during their three-day journey. After six months of hard labor there, Gotlieb was allowed to return home.[6]

In the days before the invasion of Soviet Russia, Ion and Mihai Antonescu began to speak about taking drastic, even deadly measures against Jews. At a June 17, 1941, meeting of the council of ministers, Mihai, a professor of law, spoke about actions necessary for the reconstruction of the soon-to-be reincorporated territories of Bucovina and Bessarabia. Chief among the difficulties that had to be overcome, he said, was the problem of population. "We must take advantage of this moment, to purify the population. That is why Bessarabia and Bucovina should remember the policy of Titus insofar as it concerns certain populations of ethnic origin—and I assure you not only regarding Jews, but regarding all nationalities—we will come to practice a policy of total and violent elimination of foreign elements ... a policy of purification and unification of the race through a process of emigration."[7] Titus had commanded the Roman legions that destroyed the Jews of Jerusalem, their city, and their temple in 70 CE. "No destruction," wrote Josephus, "ever wrought by God or man approached the wholesale carnage of this war"; in the end "there was no one left for the soldiers to kill."[8]

On June 19, three days before the invasion of the Soviet Union, Ion Antonescu ordered "all Jewish communist coffee houses in Moldavia" closed and instructed the propaganda ministry to provide information collected by its secret service on "all Jews, Communist agents or sympathizers" to the ministry of interior so it could "prevent their movement and be in a position to do whatever may be ordered, when the opportune moment arrives."[9] On the twenty-first he ordered prefects (district police chiefs) to begin the immediate evacuation of all Jews (ages eighteen to sixty) from villages between the Siret and Prut rivers to the camp at Tîrgu Jiu and its nearby settlements. The remaining Jews in this broad eastern strip of Romania bordering the Soviet Union and in other villages of Moldavia were to be evacuated into cities. Forty-eight hours were given for the task. All Jewish families living in villages elsewhere in the country would also be evacuated to cities; four days were allotted to this work. Even Jews married to Christians had to leave. Evacuees were not to return; their homes and other property were to be confiscated by the state. Those who should try to destroy or recover property, said General Antonescu, "will be submitted to a Military Tribunal and will be punished with death."[10] The interior ministry ordered prefects to exclude certain groups, such as industrial managers and in some places doctors and pharmacists. But on June 28 General Antonescu ordered a total evacuation; prefects were not to make any exceptions. Furthermore, all moving expenses were to be borne by Jewish communities.[11]

Germany attacked the Soviet Union on Sunday, June 22 and rapidly advanced along the whole front except in the south. Here the invasion was delayed, but radio broadcasts and newspapers made clear that Antonescu supported the invasion and Romanian troops would soon cross the Prut

CHAPTER 6

River into Soviet territory beside their German ally. In Iași, on this first day of war on the eastern front, Jewish neighborhood streets and courtyards were generally empty, doors shut, and curtains pulled. Jews were apprehensive and watchful; one recalled thinking they might be evacuated from the city and should have a small pack of necessities ready to go.[12] None it seems (based on survivor accounts I have heard or read) feared mass murder. In an interview with Max Volovici's mother, she was asked:

Q: Did you feel something was going to happen in the days immediately before [the pogrom]?
A: It was hard to tell because German troops were passing through and everyone was interested in that.
Q: Did the Germans do anything to you?
A: No, only passing, many on horseback; we were only watching them.[13]

On June 23 Mihai Antonescu again informed the council of ministers of the great ethnic struggle that lay ahead, of General Antonescu's measures to expel Jews from rural Moldavia, and the need to begin immediately reconstituting the businesses, formerly operated by Jews, to prevent the area's commercial life being paralyzed. The only distinction he made between Moldavia and the territories of Bucovina and Bessarabia in the matter of removing Jews was that the process had already begun in Moldavia.[14] That same day at Tobias Zwieback's tailor shop, the policeman Bălan ordered two uniforms, to be finished in two days, one for him and the other for Inspector Leahu. Tobias, working long hours with one of his best tailors, finished the job on time and had his wife, accompanied by an apprentice, deliver them free of charge. That was done because Bălan had earned a "favor" from the owner some weeks earlier. It went like this: having arrested Tobias's son for possessing a book by a Soviet author and "slapping him around some" at the police station, Bălan let him go. It was, the son wrote, "typical of the way of life in Romania."[15]

Rabbi Wahrmann recalled that on June 21 and 22 the police arrested a number of Jews (to be held as hostages perhaps) and that in the days immediately following the declaration of war, harassment of Jews on the city's streets intensified. Moise Ben Aaron, forty-eight in June 1941, remembered troops and the roar of tanks and transports, which kept him awake at night, and "face slapping, being spit on, broken windows." As much as they could, Jews remained in their homes and shelters.[16] Articles in Iași newspapers welcomed the chance to take back Northern Bucovina and Bessarabia and to get revenge for those who had been humiliated by Jews during the retreat from those areas in 1940. Placards appeared around the city blaming Jews for starting the war.[17] Rumors and official reports claimed Jews were armed and were putting lights in their chimneys to avoid being bombed and to help Soviet pilots find their targets.[18] Alarming news also circulated in the Jewish community. According to Marius Mircu, Henry Staerman, boss of a compulsory labor crew of 110 young Jews, was ordered on the twentieth to prepare two large ditches in the Păcurari Jewish cemetery, one thirty and the other fifteen meters in length, both of them two meters wide and deep. General Constantin Ionescu remembered seeing Jewish boys taken to the cemetery on the twenty-third and being told by them on their return that they had dug large graves. General Ionesco also claims he was informed that "in the train station some cars had been made ready to evacuate the Jewish population from the city." Some Jews were encouraged by Christian friends to leave Iași. Roza Buchmann remembered being warned on the twenty-fifth that rail cars were ready for a June 29 evacuation, and she also heard about graves being prepared in the Jewish cemetery. Marcel Braunstein reported that on the twenty-fifth police were advising Christians to mark their homes with crosses.[19]

Romania declared war on the Soviet Union on Tuesday, June 24, and that same day Soviet planes bombed Iași. Little damage was done but residents were terrified. Some Christians connected the bombing with Jews, persuaded by rumors, propaganda, and long-held prejudices that they were conniving with the enemy. Not only did some say that they had signaled Soviet pilots to their targets but that some pilots were themselves Jews who had once lived in the city.[20] Another bombing occurred on Thursday, June 26, beginning about 10:00 a.m., this time with greater effect. Dozens of people were killed. Telephone and electrical services were temporarily knocked out and 14th Infantry Division Headquarters and St. Spiridon Hospital were damaged. Frightened citizens crowded into the municipal police station wanting authorization to buy train tickets out of the city. Israel Schleier remembered people complaining about the lack of antiaircraft defense and Romanian military incompetence and even talking about defeats of German-Romanian forces along the Prut, unaware that the invasion of Soviet Ukraine from Romania, code named "Operation München," was not to begin until July 2.[21] In the afternoon of June 26 Herșcu Wolf, who had been wounded in the leg and neck during the morning air raid, along with Iosub Cojocaru and Leon Schachter were pulled from their residence on Strada Vasile Lupu by soldiers who alleged that signals had been seen coming from their building. Sergeant Mircea Manoliu and Corporal Stefan Nicolau took the three up Copou

Street to 14th Division Headquarters in Exposition Park. Two captains questioned the three, found no reason to hold them, and returned them to their escort to be taken home. Instead Manoliu and Nicolau took them toward a military firing range. It was night and the city was blacked out; suddenly the sergeant drew his pistol and began shooting. One bullet grazed Wolf's head and another struck him in the back. As he fell he heard Manoliu yelling at the others to stop. Before fainting he remembered looking up from the ground to see Manoliu pointing his revolver at him and firing, and shouting at him to keep his head still. Wolf awoke in the Păcurari cemetery near daybreak Friday. Although unable to get to his feet he could see Cojocaru several yards away. He was dead, but Schachter had escaped.[22] A second murder occurred on Thursday night when thugs forced their way into the house of Mose Kaufman and shot him dead. The killers said they were paying him back because shots had come from his house.[23]

Friday, June 27: around noon Police Chief Constantin Chirilovici called community leaders to the police station to deliver accusations from General Gheorghe Stavrescu, commander of the 14th Infantry Division, that Jews had not only signaled Soviet pilots but planned the attack and flew some of the bombers. Chirilovici told the leaders that only Christians had suffered in the raid and threatened death to Jews, "even children at their mothers' breasts," who brought harm to German and Romanian soldiers.[24] President Iacob, Vice President Hahamu, and ten other community leaders told Chirilovici and Inspector Leahu that Jews, as well as Christians, had suffered in the bombing and flatly rejected the charge of collaboration, guaranteeing with their own lives the loyalty of the community. They were given twenty-four hours to make inquiries and the following day presented the police chief with an affidavit identifying thirty-eight Jews killed and one hundred Jewish homes destroyed in the bombing. According to Roza Buchmann, whose husband Ghetzel attended the meetings, Jewish leaders suspected that some kind of action against Jews was being prepared, a clear sign of danger were crosses going up in front of Christian residences, but apparently none of them anticipated a massacre.[25] Friday afternoon General Stavrescu reported in the daily *Prutul* that thirty-eight enemy planes had been shot down and threatened quick discovery and death for anyone who helped the enemy.[26] Because of their supposed complicity in the bombing, five Jews were sent to the rail yard of the 13th Infantry Regiment to mark locations of unexploded bombs. Then they were arrested for being in a restricted area and handed over to Sergeant Manoliu and Corporal Nicolau to be escorted to a regimental office for questioning. Instead, Manoliu took them to the garrison firing range and shot them dead.[27]

WAR AND THE MASS EXECUTION AT STÂNCA ROSNOVANU

A much larger mass execution occurred that same Friday at a place called Stânca Rosnovanu about 5 miles (8 kilometers) north of Iași. Events leading up to the killing began four days earlier (on June 23) when soldiers of a German regiment and troops of the Romanian 6th Cavalry Regiment crossed the Prut River and established a bridgehead in Soviet territory at the Bessarabian border town of Sculeni. When Red Army units forced them back into Romania three or four days later they took with them the Christian and Jewish townspeople they could gather up. Among Romanian officers who participated in this action were Captain Ion Stihi and Second Lieutenant Eugen Mihailescu. These two were among Romanian soldiers who had been forced out of Bessarabia in June 1940 and saw the captive Sculeni Jews as a target of revenge for that alleged humiliation. They apparently had permission to execute the Jews from the German commander of the joint operation, Colonel Buck, as well as orders to do the same from their own 6th Cavalry commander, Colonel Matieș. Gheorghe Cîmpoeș, a former mayor of Sculeni, was borrowed from a nearby artillery unit to assist in separating Jews from Christians.

Ioan Petraru, nineteen when he witnessed the massacre, gave an account of it after the war. He saw the Jews, after they had been sorted out, grouped together except for some who were put to digging graves. A number of soldiers and people from local villages were also standing nearby watching. One of the soldiers told Petraru that the gravediggers had been promised they would be saved. Petraru observed, however, that "they did not want to dig because they probably understood the reason for the promise." "The graves," he said, "had the shape of long trenches and I think they dug four or five." Petraru named Stihi and Mihailescu as directing "the operations." After the graves were dug, Stihi ordered mounted soldiers to chase the civilians away, but Petraru remained close by hidden in a cornfield. He saw "captain Stihi say something to the Jews who were standing in front of the graves, to which they threw up their arms and shrieked." Then, "at a distance of about 50 to 60 meters two machine guns were set up." When Mihailescu appeared to give instructions to those manning the guns they left their posts but were replaced by others; a "sergeant Cîmpoieșul" took over one machine gun and "officer M . . ." got behind the other, each assisted by other soldiers. Petraru recalled that "when all was ready captain Stihi turned his back, probably so he would not see what he had hardened himself to. . . . The shooting lasted 5 to 6 minutes during which time all the Jews fell to the ground except one woman who remained standing." According to Petraru, Stihi ordered that she be allowed to live. Soldiers covered the bodies with dirt and returned to their units. "After a week I passed along the same road and saw a rigid pole mark-

CHAPTER 6

ing the place of the massacre."[28] In the postwar deposition of another witness to the execution, Lieutenant Colonel Andronic Pripoliță said Captain Stihi and Sergeant Major Vasile Mihailov manned the machine guns and Lieutenant Mihailescu used a machine pistol to execute the Jews who were lined up, mixed together (men, women, and children), along three ditches. Before they were murdered, said Pripoliță, Stihi and Mihailescu searched them "for all they had of value," and after the shooting they were "buried like dogs."

A month later Colonel Matieș received an inquiry about the mass execution from the 14th Infantry Division. In his response he said he gave the order to execute the Jews because they took up arms and carried out acts of sabotage against the Romanian army: "Capt. Stihi, by my orders and in conformity with superior orders precisely given on this matter, executed these scoundrels, for which no consideration is necessary." In other reports on the massacre Matieș again states that he gave the order and had superior orders to do so. If there was such an order, it likely came from Matieș's superior, General Stavrescu, commander of the 14th Infantry Division. Pripoliță claims that during the fight to secure the Sculeni bridgehead Matieș received "orders . . . from Division that any partisan caught was to be shot on the spot," and having received this order immediately put Stihi and Mihailescu to work organizing the evacuation and execution.[29] In all, the bodies of 311 men, women, and children, fifty-three of them under the age of eighteen, were exhumed by the Iași community in 1945, some children among the dead still clinging to their mothers' necks.[30] In the war against European Jews it was one of the first mass executions to include women and children.

Like other Romanian officials and military officers who murdered Jews or were complicit in such crimes during the war and afterward stood accused of them, Matieș defended his actions by revising his wartime record and reports. In one report, dated July 20, 1941, concerning the actions of his 6th Cavalry Regiment, he recounts his orders: (1) to Captain Stihi "to arrest and to execute all the Jewish suspects from Sculeni," (2) for the execution of "50–60" armed Jews near the village of Gura Căinari, and (3) for the execution "in mass" of "400 Jewish men and women [at the town of Mărculești] . . . [who] attacked us without being in uniform." He concluded that these actions (which included the murder of women and children) "are motivated by and in conformity with superior orders."[31] In his postwar account of the execution of Sculeni Jews, however, Matieș claims he had nothing to do with the evacuation of the town's residents or with the execution of the Jews among them. Nor did he give orders to anyone under his command regarding the evacuation and execution. Orders were given, he writes, "solely by the German Division Commander without in any way involving the undersigned [Matieș]." He claims not to know if his officers, Stihi and Mihailescu, took part in the execution but does not rule out the possibility they did so "presuming they received direct orders from the German Division Commander." Regarding the massacre of a large number of Jews at Mărculești, in his postwar account Matieș claims he had no knowledge of the incident until he read about it in the newspapers.[32]

Besides the massacre at Stânca Rosnovanu there is evidence of two other mass killings of Jews in the same area around the same time. Colonel Captaru, prefect of Iași District reported the shooting of six Jews (four men and two women) on June 29, 1941, about noon in woods near the village of Cîrlig near the northern outskirts of the city of Iași. According to the prefect's report these six came from the city escorted by four soldiers, three Romanian and one German. These soldiers, and perhaps some men of the Romanian 41st Artillery Regiment who were stationed in the area, shot the Jews and then invited civilian onlookers to strip the dead of their clothing. However, reports Captaru, when money was found on the bodies the soldiers "swooped down" and took it.[33] Evidence of another killing of Jews in the same area was discovered in November 2010—namely, a mass grave of persons killed in 1941 in a forested area near the village of Popricani, a few miles from Stânca Rosnovanu and Cîrlig. Remains of some forty persons from this site were buried in the Iași Jewish cemetery in April 2011 near the mass graves of victims of the Iași pogrom.[34]

CHAPTER 7

Duminica ceea *(That Sunday)*

Saturday, June 28, signs of trouble in Iași: Aron Stievel, part owner of a textile factory with an office on Stradă Stefan cel Mare, described the Sabbath morning as "heavy with silence." Ordinarily he would have gone to the factory in order to pay workers but decided to have two of his Christian employees take and distribute the money. These two had told Stievel he should leave the city and stay away until the following Wednesday, that "great disorders," which Christians but not Jews were prepared for, were about to take place. On the same day Stievel's partner was advised by a policeman, who he paid for information, that the two owners should stay off the streets and keep hidden. Engineer Israel Schleier said that from the day war began (June 22, 1941) Jews felt an impending but undefined threat, a feeling that intensified with each bombing and the rumors that followed: of Jews flying Soviet bombers or directing pilots to their targets from the ground with lanterns or red sheets or assisting enemy agents who had parachuted into the city. Schleier recalled feeling extremely anxious on Saturday, the more so as the day's events unfolded: word that several Jews had been murdered; the arrest of prominent intellectuals, activists, and communist sympathizers; and the appearance of signs posted on houses and public buildings calling for blood: "Romanians! With each Jew you kill you kill a communist. The time for revenge has come!" and "Kill the yids! Every yid is a communist! Liquidate forever those who threaten us!"[1]

On Saturday afternoon Jewish residences in the slaughterhouse district came under attack. Leading the action was Sergeant Manoliu with soldiers from the 13th Infantry and 24th Artillery regiments, joined by some civilians and German troops whose commander was told by Manoliu that Jews in the area were signaling enemy planes with their radios. The violence, which district police would not or could not stop, was only brought to an end after the arrival of Chief Chirilovici, Garrison Commander Lupu with a platoon of gendarmes, and Major Scriban, praetor (chief legal officer) of the 14th Infantry Division. Some of the perpetrators were arrested but Scriban soon released them, including Sergeant Manoliu who had already murdered six Jews with the assistance of Corporal Nicolau. In a report dated four days later, Romania's director general of police Emanoil Leoveanu expressed astonishment at the release of "this assassin."[2] The general's report is probably the second (i.e., later) of two quite different reports Leoveanu drew up, both with the same date (July 2, 1941), number (58), and his signature. It belongs to a class of documents intended by officials who created them to show, should they later be called on to answer for their actions, that they had acted responsibly.[3]

The general assault against Jews was set off about 9:30 Saturday evening by flares or rockets launched over Iași by one or more planes followed by real and/or simulated gunfire that erupted throughout the city. Top municipal and regional police officers and representatives of the two major Romanian military units headquartered in the area, 3rd Army and 14th Infantry Division, were at the municipal police station (*chestură*) at that time. The gathering of these officials at this time and place indicates they knew what was about to happen and were prepared to exact some level of control over the action. In response to reports that began coming in from district police posts that Romanian and German troops in the city were being shot at, these officials sent out teams of police and gendarmes to protect military units and search out and arrest the alleged shooters. General Stavrescu, 14th Infantry division commander, and von Salmuth, German 30th Army Corps commander, also sent out patrols. General Antonescu responded to the action late Saturday night by making Garrison Commander Constantin Lupu military commander of Iași, an authority he assumed the next morning. In addition he ordered that all residents living in places from which shots had been fired be arrested (except children), summarily investigated, the guilty immediately executed, and those harboring such criminals punished in the same way. He further commanded that all Jews of Iași (including women and children) be evacuated from the city, "package by package" ("*pe pachete, pachete*"), first to the town of Roman and then to the prison camps at Tîrgu Jiu.[4]

Sunday, June 29: Police Chief Chirilovici reported that about 3:00 a.m. on Sunday columns of soldiers being escorted by teams of gendarmes and

DUMINICA CEEA (THAT SUNDAY)

police were attacked with "violent automatic weapons fire and grenades" on Stradă Lăpușneanu from buildings "occupied by communist jews." Teams of municipal and military police, soldiers, and gendarmes carried out a punitive search of the area. German units also participated in this operation, he reported, "in a very determined manner." Jews were pulled from shelters; some were executed on the spot, others while being herded to the chestură with arms raised. Chirilovici also said a Romanian military column, moving along Stradă Lascăr Catargiu, received a burst of gunfire. Some soldiers panicked; some returned fire, but a search by soldiers and police turned up no shooters. He also reported that some Romanian and German soldiers and private citizens, on their own, began bringing Jews to the chestură while most of his policemen remained in their homes, at least during the hours of darkness. Chirilovici indicated they did so to protect their families, but one of the city's district police commanders testified after the war that he had been ordered during the day of the twenty-eighth by Leahu, Chirilovici's deputy chief, not to interfere in the action the army was about to undertake.[5]

General Stavrescu ordered continued and expanded searches and arrests at first light on Sunday. In a telegram to the interior ministry that day he reported his suspicion that Soviet parachutists and Judeo-communists were responsible for terrorizing the city. He pointed out that Jews, including women and children, who had been pulled from buildings suspected of harboring shooters, were sent off to the chestură, except that "those found guilty have been executed on the spot by the German and Romanian soldiers who arrested them," this in spite of the fact that, as Stavrescu himself put it, the shooting at troops was "without . . . any visible effect."[6] Regional Police Inspector Giosanu reported to Director General of Police and State Security Emanoil Leoveanu that military units, despite being targets of intense automatic fire, suffered no casualties nor had police and soldiers who searched areas where shooting had occurred "been able to catch even one of the jewish shooters." Nor were any weapons found when a systematic search of Jewish residences began at daybreak Sunday.[7]

Chirilovici, in a July 2 report, gave a similar account: no one was caught firing on the troops, and he found it "extraordinary" that intense automatic weapons' fire and grenades had produced but a single casualty, a slightly injured policeman. "'Jude' was the word which met each soldier and policeman," he said, resulting in massive and senseless arrests of Jews, including women and children, and their imprisonment at the chestură. Soldiers from both camps, "civilians recruited from the dregs," and his own policemen robbed and viciously beat the Jews. Some German soldiers, he said, having killed a woman, amused themselves by throwing her body around. Rather than subversive agents, the Jews are now seen by the police chief, in this second report, as victims of incendiary rumors, a scheme "instigated by certain agents" to fire up the anti-Jewish rage in the Romanian population. Chirilovici's findings are supported by General Leoveanu, who came to Iași on July 1 to investigate the massacre. Assisted by Chirilovici, the general found neither wounded nor dead Romanian soldiers nor evidence, in the way of broken windows or scarred walls, of bullets having been fired. A German captain told him twenty of his troops had been killed or wounded, but he would not show him the evidence, not even the place where these soldiers had allegedly been attacked. Leoveanu and Chirilovici investigated the matter further, but in the end the general was convinced no Germans had been killed or wounded and the shooting had been staged, firecrackers used to simulate automatic weapons' fire. The feigned attack was, he believed, the work of "some interested party" and carried out by "legionnaires and thieves" for the purpose of creating a panic and at the same time provoking German soldiers into "devastating" the Jewish community.[8]

Jews were forced from their homes and shelters that Sunday morning and marched off, men and some women and children, hands raised, to various locations, the largest number to the chestură. Those who held back were beaten or shot. Oscar Marcovici saw men in plain clothes, accompanied by soldiers, enter Jewish residences and order the men out. He himself successfully hid from the first searches but was later found and arrested. In the basement of the Auerbach home some twenty persons found shelter on the night of the twenty-eighth. At first light Rebeca Auerbach left the cellar and entered her house where she was arrested by German soldiers brought there by the Auerbachs' maid and her husband. The others were also arrested, told "your time has come," and all, including Rebeca's two young daughters, marched off with hands raised to the chestură. From his house on Stradă Vasile Lupu, Beniamin Rabinovici heard shots and screams from the street and looking out saw a convoy of Jews surrounded by Romanians and Germans. Some prisoners were killed as he watched, "the wounded crying out their pain," he remembered, "to a god that did not exist. I stood dumbfounded . . . shaking without understanding why. I was with my wife and four children."[9] Max Volovici's home and his father's blacksmith shop had been destroyed in the Soviet bombing of June 26, and the family had taken refuge in an aunt's home. Through her curtained window he watched the convoys, impressed that the prisoners kept their hands raised, even children and old people. An old man fell. For a moment it seemed he might be left behind, but one of the guards, a Romanian soldier, returned and shot him several times. Max, recalling these events of forty-five years before, said, "af-

DUMINICA CEEA (THAT SUNDAY)

ter half an hour the old man moved again and we could see this through the curtains. But the soldier shot him again; that soldier was released from the convoy to shoot him. I don't know what happened but for half an hour or one year that soldier kept shooting."[10]

Max Gaer was badly beaten by Gypsies as they drove him and others toward the police station. At one point Germans joined in and began giving commands. Both groups shouted as they moved from one residence to the next: "Jews live here! Jews live here!" Bystanders spat on and clubbed Jews as their convoys passed by. Clubbing increased as they moved through the crowded streets and Piața Unirii in the city center, especially on Stradă Vasile Alecsandri that fronted the police station. At the gate opening into the chestură courtyard Gaer remembered Romanians and Germans lined up "on either side of the entrance using clubs or other blunt objects to hit those passing through." Some prisoners got through unharmed; others were seriously injured. Among those killed or mortally wounded by the blows were Herș Gherner, secretary general of the Community Council, and his fourteen-year-old son.[11]

Ghetzel Buchmann, head of the community's cultural section, had heard shots and screams during the night and was told by a terrified neighbor about the convoys. Around 8:00 a.m. Sunday morning he left the shelter where he and others had hidden during the night to check his residence on Stradă Mârzescu and on the way inspect the community center, which had recently been moved to the same street, near the National Theater. There he escaped the bullets of men who were shooting out windows. At home he gave a note to a Christian woman, employed as a servant by his family, to take to his wife Roza and her brother, still in hiding. When the woman got there she had with her an armed civilian who marched the two off to the chestură. Roza found the police station courtyard so crowded she could hardly move about. Some twenty Romanian and two German soldiers, accompanied by some civilians, appeared at the residence of Israel Schleier around 8:00 a.m. and began shouting that gunfire had come from the garret of his building. Three families were pulled from their dwellings, and as the women and children cried and pleaded, the men were marched away.[12]

During the roundup a meeting of all top city police officials took place in the chestură, beginning about 8:00 a.m. An hour later Police Chief Chirilovici and Deputy Inspector Leahu went to Prefect Captaru's office in the Administrative Palace to meet with other officials: Colonel Captaru, General Stavrescu, Regional Inspector of Police Giosanu, Major Scriban, and a few others. They decided to have all civilians turn in their weapons and be off the streets by 7:00 p.m. and named Garrison Commander Colonel Constantin Lupu chief security officer of the city. The "commission," as Giosanu called the group, also decided to create more patrols of reserves and police and to put troops on battle alert. Giosanu reported by telephone to Director General of Police Leoveanu at 9:30 a.m. that German soldiers threatened to bomb Jewish districts if the gunfire continued, but about this time the shooting generally ceased. After meeting at the prefecture, Inspector Leahu returned to the chestură where he organized squads of soldiers and police to patrol the streets. To these squads he assigned units of police that had been among those the Soviets had forced to retreat from Bucovina and Bessarabia the year before. These policemen, who were extremely hostile toward Jews because of the "humiliating" retreat, were in Iași awaiting the invasion and their return to the same region.[13]

Moșe Herșcovici and his wife watched the convoys from their apartment, men for the most part, with a few women and children, herded along, some not fully dressed, haggard and disheveled, some bruised or bleeding. Silvia Manole, who lived with her husband, a doctor, on the same floor as the Herșcovici family, appeared on the street below. She was a tall blond who wore a cross and spoke perfect German and hoped to persuade the Germans that no Jews lived in her building. Nevertheless, it was invaded and Dr. Manole was dragged outside and shot to death in front of her. As Silvia was being helped into a neighbor's home, Moșe's doorbell rang. To his great relief it was his mother-in-law. In a state of great agitation, she reported that many Jews were already murdered and that the killing continued. She also said orders had been posted around the city requiring Jews to present themselves at the police station to get a permit that would protect them from arrest. Neighbors came in and, having heard about the permits, were at their wits end about going to the chestură or not. Then others entered who actually had received their papers, each about the size of a playing card on which was a police stamp and the word *Liber* (free). Moșe knew if he went he might walk into a trap but decided to take the risk.[14]

One of those who received the *Liber* paper was a tailor who lived in the city center with his wife and daughter Tibia. On Sunday morning his wife had gone out, despite the dangers, to look for food. During her absence Romanian police entered their courtyard and ordered Jews to come outside and then marched them, as Tibia recalled, "like schoolboys," to the chestură, a few minutes away. Recalling these events fifty years later, she said, "My father was very afraid; he was a gentle man. He knows only to sew. . . . I was afraid. I was fifteen. So, I am in a very great emotion in this [present] moment. I don't want to came here [to be interviewed], but it is for my father's memory, if you can understand me. He was only thirty-nine [Tibia thumped the

DUMINICA CEEA (THAT SUNDAY)

table hard with her finger tips to emphasize the words 'only' and 'thirty' and 'nine']." About midday father and daughter were released along with some others and allowed to return home. There Tibia's father proudly showed his fearful wife the slip of paper with the word "Liber" on it, given him at the police station. The reprieve was not a long one. Around four or five in the afternoon Romanian police again entered the courtyard, accompanied by German soldiers. Once more Jews were forced to leave their homes. This time they were separated, women and children on one side of the yard, men on the other. "You don't believe what the mens are, have, in their eyes. They know they will be [statement left unfinished]. . . . It is unbelievable I stay here [remain living in Iași?]. . . . My father was taken but no one coming back from the train knew what happened to him."[15]

About 10 a.m. a gang of three gendarmes, two policemen, and two club-armed civilians entered the courtyard and residence of Tobias Zwieback, owner of a large tailoring firm. They ransacked his home and then drove his family into the courtyard. Among neighbors gathered there was Leon Mayer, owner of a ground floor jewelry store. It was the store that attracted the invaders. They knew Mayer was the owner and, having failed to break open the metal doors, made him hand over his keys. Then they ordered the men (Tobias, his nineteen-year-old son Adrian, and Mayer) into the street, forced them to carry their caps in their hands, and drove them to the chestură. Of the beatings they received along the way those most likely to maim or kill were administered at the police station gates, some soldiers using crowbars and aiming to smash the prisoners' heads. Adrian recalled being pushed forward by others behind him rushing to get through the cordon. Once inside he immediately became aware of intense thirst and oppressive heat, of holding onto his father's hand, and exchanging anxious looks with friends he knew from school. He claims emphatically that he saw German officers and soldiers in uniforms characteristic of the Organization Todt and that it was they who, at the sound of air-raid sirens, began machine-gunning the mass of prisoners jammed into the courtyard. Adrian instinctively dropped to the cobblestones when the shooting began and then scrambled over the wall, one of a few who got over and was not recaptured. At home, in hiding, he heard another patrol enter his courtyard looking for men who had received the "bilet de LIBER." His mother managed to convince the searchers that no men were there and at night stood guard in case other intruders came around and on the lookout for her husband's return. Tobias did come back, but ten weeks later, having survived the courtyard massacre and long death-train journey to Călărași.[16]

Beniamin Rabinovici and his family watched from their apartment the convoys of Jews driven along by German and Romanian soldiers, attacked by civilians, beaten, shot. A neighbor told him about the order requiring Jews to present themselves at the chestură to get the special permit. He decided not to go. About noon Romanian and German soldiers, joined by civilians invaded his home; they began beating him and dragging him out. Beniamin's wife wept and pleaded for him and their four children. His glasses were smashed on his face and pieces of glass lodged in his right eye; his left eardrum was broken. Still on his feet, he was conscious that his wife Etty was screaming and begging hysterically. On the stairs he saw one of the soldiers take out a revolver, point it at her, and fire. As she fell down some steps he lost consciousness.[17]

When police officials ended their morning meeting about 9:00 a.m., the chestură courtyard imprisoned several hundred Jews; Chief Chirilovici estimated eighteen hundred in one report and one thousand in another.[18] Doctors, dentists, women, children, and the elderly were let go. Some women decided to remain with their husbands and some boys were held back. Roza Buchmann saw a boy, she guessed was ten or eleven, who carried a small child in his arms forced to return from the gate and beaten.[19] After the initial release police officials set up tables in the courtyard and began issuing the "Liber" permits. Attorney Gherner was one of two hundred or so who received the paper and was freed, but like a number of the others he was again arrested and returned, this time with his son. Both were killed by blows to the head delivered by Romanians and Germans at the station's gate.[20] Max Volovici was disappointed he was not allowed to get his own permit. He recalled meeting some who had the paper: "All were in good spirits. One let me look at his paper."[21] Max Gaer was issued the permit and released. On his way home he saw convoys of terrified Jews being driven along, as he had been. When he was stopped by the drovers of one such convoy and produced his slip of paper one of the men tore it up, and Gaer found himself again being marched to the police station. Attorney Iancu Leib went to get the permit, not blind to the danger, but desperate. As he drew near the police station he was caught in a stream of frightened people and pulled along between the rows of men with clubs, through the gate. In an instant his head and face were bleeding and his mouth full of blood and broken teeth.[22]

When Prefect Captaru and General Stavrescu visited the chestură about 11:00 a.m. the prefect estimated that some two thousand prisoners were there, "Jews and Christians, as many [brought] by Romanians as by German patrols." Nehama Natansohn, who was in the courtyard at the time, recalled that Stavrescu "said some words of encouragement" to the prisoners.[23] During the noon hour Jews were still being herded in and others were coming

Jews in the chestură courtyard, June 29, 1941. Romanian Information Service. United States Holocaust Memorial Museum.

on their own to get the special permit. Police officials stopped issuing the "Liber" paper about 1:00 p.m., and prisoners were no longer allowed to leave. Rebeca Auerbach remembered seeing a machine gun on the roof of the chestură, trained on the crowded courtyard. The prisoners' clothing was drenched with blood and sweat. She also noted that despite the crush of people, Nazis moved through the crowd, delivering blows left and right. According to her the chestură was taken over about 2:00 p.m. by German soldiers who wore the Death's Head insignia. About this same time women and children still in the courtyard were allowed to go and Rebeca and her daughter left.[24]

In a postwar deposition Prefect Captaru said that around 12:30 or 1:00 p.m. Chirilovici telephoned him that Germans had begun to shoot prisoners in the courtyard and asked him to intervene with General Stavrescu to stop the executions. According to Captaru, as soon as Stavrescu was informed of the action the two of them went to the police station where they saw a few German officers and NCOs with machine pistols and a large number of Jews who had been shot. Captaru recalled that while Stavrescu was trying to persuade the Germans to stop the killing, a German soldier, armed with a shovel, broke open the head of a Jewish woman who had just arrived and began attacking other prisoners in plain view of himself, General Stavrescu, and Chief Chirilovici.[25] Official estimates of the number of Jews in the courtyard about 1:00 p.m. range from thirty-five hundred to five thousand.[26] The question about who was in control of the chestură at the time of the shooting is a vexing one and will be addressed shortly, noting here only that Rebeca Auerbach, who reported the takeover of the police station by Germans, was not in the courtyard when the mass killing occurred and that in their trials after the war it was very much in the interest of responsible Romanian officials to have the Nazis blamed for the mass killing. What Captaru recalled in 1946 (Germans shooting Jewish prisoners at the chestură early Sunday afternoon) does not appear in the prefect's report at the time.

Iancu Leib came to the police station around 2:00 p.m. to pick up his permit and was so badly beaten at the entrance to the courtyard that he became disoriented. Within minutes, however, he was brought to full consciousness by machine gun fire and screaming. It was about 2:30 p.m. The courtyard gates had been closed, an air-raid alarm was sounding, and soldiers and police were firing down into the mass of prisoners from the upper windows and roofs of the police station and other buildings surrounding the courtyard. Leib pushed through the human chaos to the stone wall and with immense effort clambered over, landing near the Sidoli Cinema. He

DUMINICA CEEA (THAT SUNDAY)

found a hiding place nearby and only after several minutes realized he was in the company of two other men, acquaintances of his, who had also scaled the wall. For some three hours he could hear the machine guns and cries of the wounded. Beniamin Rabinovici, seriously injured from blows to the head and face, got over the wall into the grounds of the Grunberg printing house in the cellar of which he and some twenty other escapees hid. He recalled hearing gunfire in the courtyard until late afternoon. Both he and Max Gaer claimed they saw Romanian policemen firing from the upper windows of the chestură building. Gaer, who remembered bullets raining down for about two hours, and a few others found a recess in the courtyard wall where they escaped being hit. Moșe Herșcovici, who had come to get the "Liber" paper, marveled at the great number of people there. From childhood he had been active in "Hasmonea," a Zionist organization, and wondered at the effort necessary to get so many Jews together for a meeting. When the shooting commenced prisoners began falling all around him, screaming and dying. For him, time seemed to stop.[27]

About 3:30 p.m. General Stavrescu again visited the police station, this time accompanied by Corps Commander of the 4th Territory General Carlaonț, and the shooting subsided. Stavrescu told prisoners the shooting was now ended, that the killing had occurred because "some Jews had betrayed their country setting in motion the ax to cut down enemies." But when the generals left, the shooting resumed.[28] Around this same time another meeting of police officials occurred, presided over by Prefect Captaru. Included in this group, which Captaru called "the Council of Collaboration," were Garrison Commander Lupu, regional inspectors of gendarmes Colonel Bădescu and Colonel Barosi, Regional Inspector of Police Giosanu, Commander of the (Iași *Județ* or District) Legion of Gendarmes Major Alexandrescu, Subprefect of Iași Isacovici, and Subinspector of Police Matei Cozma (or Cosma). Captaru reported on the killing of many Jews and the shooting at troops. He also reported his most recent communications with General Stavrescu and Minister of Interior Popescu regarding measures needed to restore order. Then the "council" decided to spread its police and military units throughout the city, setting up mobile units; they fixed posts in especially troubled areas and a reserve company of 135 men at the centrally located telephone building. This meeting of top regional police officials occurred while the brutal roundup and mass killings in and around the police station were going on, a circumstance the "collaborators" did not directly address in their report.[29]

In the vicinity of the chestură, units of police and soldiers searched for escapees. Beniamin Rabinovici and others hiding at the Grunberg printing

CHAPTER 7

house were discovered and forced from their hiding place. At the feet of a German officer he begged for his life, but the officer shoved him away, drew his revolver, and fired. Beniamin was not hit, but he and the others were returned to the courtyard and again battered as they passed through its gates. Only a few of those who had scrambled over the walls into the area of the Sidoli Cinema survived. One was Nathan Goldstein who, after his recapture, was taken to the grounds of the Legion of Gendarmes on Copou Hill, where he and other prisoners had to stand with hands raised and endure beatings for about four hours. In the early evening Nathan was again convoyed to the police station and along the way witnessed the shooting of fellow prisoners by German soldiers.[30] Several Jews who had clambered over the chestură wall into the yard of the auto garage Zarifopol were attacked by men gathered there. When gunfire first erupted in the adjacent courtyard an armed guard stationed at the garage fainted, whereupon Constantin Gavrilovici, a driver-mechanic, took the guard's weapon and began shooting Jews (twelve according to court records) who were just then coming over the wall. One man used a shovel, another a club, to bludgeon escapees. After the killings they scavenged the dead for money and clothing.[31]

Roundups continued during the mass killing at the police station. Israel Schleier, one of those released with a "Liber" permit, was rearrested after a patrol of Romanian soldiers and civilians broke into his building and stood him against a kitchen wall as if they intended to execute him. His wife and young daughters pleaded for his life. What saved him, he thought, was their offer to give up whatever jewelry and money they had. Schleier recalled that soon after the Romanians entered his building, Germans from a Death's Head unit also came in and one or another of them beat him about the head with a gun and then threw him down some stairs and out into the street. There he was forced into a column of prisoners being moved along, hands raised, toward the police station. He was repeatedly knocked down and at other times had to fall to the cobblestones when shots were fired over the prisoners' heads. He recalled seeing prisoners shot when they let their hands down or did not fall to the street quickly enough. He saw corpses on both sides of the streets and heard the wounded screaming for help. He remembered crosses clearly displayed on Christian houses, and on some houses was the notice: "ACI LOCUESC CREȘTINI. NU SUNT JIDANI ÎN CURTE" ("Christians live here. There are no Yids in this courtyard"). At the police station gates Schleier got safely through the cordon of Romanian and German soldiers and civilians, some swinging crowbars or jabbing with bayonets. "Inside the courtyard the sight was terrible. On the ground lay many persons frightful to look at: bloody, eyes out of their sockets, pierced

DUMINICA CEEA (THAT SUNDAY)

Jews cleaning cobblestones in the chestură courtyard after the massacre, July 1, 1941 (?). Romanian information Service. United States Holocaust Memorial Museum.

with bayonets, hands and feet bleeding, bodies on top of one another, crying and groaning horribly. . . . Being unable to move to the back of the courtyard the police commissars ordered us to stack the corpses in order to clear a path for movement."[32]

Rebeca Auerbach and her daughter, like Schleier, had been released from the chestură before the massacre and then rearrested and returned during the afternoon shortly after 6:00 p.m., about the time the shooting had stopped. She and her daughter again survived the murderous cordon. Inside, the courtyard was filled with dead and wounded and "awash in blood." The two were hit a number of times as they searched (unsuccessfully) among the dead and wounded for husband and father. "Towards evening," Rebeca recalled, "the women and children who remained alive were sent home."[33]

Some non-Jews went against the current of violence and death to warn Jews of the coming danger and in some cases risked their lives to prevent the killings. Orthodox priest Răzmeriță and lathe operator Ioan Gheorghiu were among those murdered in such attempts. Some warned friends of the impending danger. A sergeant in the same 13th Infantry Regiment as the murderer Sergeant Manoliu advised his friend Herșcu Ivancu to remain at home on the twenty-ninth because Jews were going to be shot. In a few cases groups of Jews were saved. At gendarme headquarters on Stradă Carol (north of the university) reserve gendarme Captain Richard Filipescu, serving as duty officer and standing outside the large legion of gendarme's compound, witnessed three hundred or four hundred Jews, hands raised, some wounded and bloody, some with their eyes put out, being herded into the Legion grounds by Romanian and German guards and NCOs under the command of three or four Romanian second lieutenants. Jews who let their arms down were shot or beaten with rifle butts. When he asked one of the officers what was going on he was told the prisoners were "Yid spies." Captain Filipescu himself then entered the grounds and saw even old men being kicked or beaten with rifle butts, whereupon he raised his revolver and shouted orders for the beatings and killing to stop. At that moment he was joined by another reserve, Captain Petru Șerban, and the two men together were able to save not all but many of the prisoners. Grigore Profir, manager of the mill Dacia, refused on the twenty-ninth to let gangs enter the mill where dozens of Jewish employees had taken refuge. Profir even managed to obtain provisions for the refugees and bring in some of their family members.[34]

CHAPTER 8

Trenurile mortuare *(The Death Trains)*

Arrangements to carry out General Antonescu's late Saturday night order that all Jews be deported from Iași began to be carried out Sunday afternoon when killing in the chestură courtyard was most intense.[1] Around 2:00 p.m. Prefect (district commander of gendarmes) Colonel Captaru was informed, "on behalf of Gen. Stavrescu," that it was necessary to have Minister of Interior Popescu give orders for the evacuation. Some three hours later, about 5:00 p.m., Captaru got the minister's approval for the transport and however many rail cars were needed. That approval was confirmed the same evening in a call from Vice President Mihai Antonescu, who told Captaru to evacuate all Jews to the nearby towns of Tîrgu Frumos and Podu Iloaiei. In their postwar testimony Romanian officials claimed it was the opposition of one or both German generals, 30th Army Corps Commander Hans von Salmuth and XI Army Commander Ritter von Schobert, to the debarkation of Jews at Tîrgu Frumos that persuaded the interior ministry to change the final destination of that train to Călărași in the far southeast corner of the country. The interior ministry also changed the order to transport all Jews to "all Jewish male suspects."[2]

Between 8:00 and 9:00 Sunday evening survivors of the courtyard massacre were marched to the train station, hands raised, guarded by Romanian police and gendarmes and German soldiers. Two German tanks accompanied the procession of more than 2,500 prisoners. In an open area in front of the station where the Jews were assembled, Moșe Herșcovici recognized among the guards a sergeant he knew from his army days. He offered him money to be set free; the man pulled a bayonet from his belt and thrust it straight at Moșe's face where it entered the jaw through the right cheek, knocking out some teeth. Moșe hardly had time to gather his wits when he heard the command, "get down!" He dropped and stayed down, like other prisoners, kneeling with his forehead on the pavement, making no effort to protect himself from thieves who moved about robbing them. From one of the German tanks, circling the assembly, soldiers broadcast the warning that whoever raised his head would be shot.[3] Schleier recalled the heightened spirits of those who had survived the shooting and been liberated from the courtyard, some expecting to be home soon. A number of the severely wounded, who survived the march of several blocks to the train station, died kneeling among their companions.[4]

The prisoners began boarding the first train around 11:00 p.m. One at a time the Jews were hit with a rod, the signal to get up and run to the cars. Max Gaer recalled being on his knees for three hours, too frightened to move, when he heard people around him being driven out. Finally his turn came and he was directed to one of the freight cars. As he was trying to get in, a railroad worker standing beside the door gave him a powerful blow to the face and side of his head.[5] Not being at a raised platform, the car's deck was about waist high and as a prisoner put his hands down on the floor of the car to pull himself up he was clubbed. Moșe Herșcovici's left hand was smashed. Moise Leib managed to take on his elbow the blow of a crowbar aimed at his son's hand.[6]

This first train had fifty cars when the loading began. Prefect Captaru decided on that number after Chief Chirilovici told him about 2,500 Jews would be evacuated. The train was composed of freight cars, most equipped with small shuttered openings that could be shut or easily boarded up from the outside. The rail yard had between 120 and 180 cars at the prefect's disposal and an additional number of empty well-ventilated cattle cars. Assistant station manager Săvinescu determined there were too few cattle cars to permit their use in transporting Jews.[7] Germans and Romanians, including railroad workers, carried out the loading. They jammed most cars full of prisoners, closed and locked the doors, and boarded up or locked the shutters. Only thirty-five or thirty-six of the fifty cars were used. Passengers numbered 2,530 (2,430 in some reports) men and boys, on average about seventy persons per car. After the prisoners were jammed in, some near death, and the doors shut and vents closed or covered, the train was removed to another line to await departure.[8]

Now a second train was made ready for the hundreds of Jews who had been held in the cellars and other rooms of the police station or at the grounds of the Legion of Gendarmes or had been picked up in the continu-

TRENURILE MORTUARE (THE DEATH TRAINS)

ing raids of Sunday afternoon and evening. From the chestură the second group of prisoners left about 3:00 a.m. Monday and was convoyed by Romanian police and German soldiers to the train station where they were robbed and beaten. Their train of thirty freight cars had already been moved to a loading platform. It was loaded in the same brutal manner as before and shut up tight. Only eighteen cars were used; 1,902 persons were crammed in, on average about 106 per car. This second train was also sent to the marshaling yard, according to Săvinescu, to await official orders from the transportation inspectorate and ministry of transportation and a departure time that would not interfere with military transports.[9]

The longer train left Iași station, guarded by six city policemen, at 4:15 Monday morning, heading toward Tîrgu Frumos, 30 miles (48 kilometers) due west. The motion of his car awakened Leon Haimovici, who had been held standing unconscious by the human pack. Although he passed out on the train, he had a clear recollection of the boarding procedure, kept alert by the danger of being separated from his son. After waiting for two hours or more in front of the station he and his son were, in fact, sent to different cars, but Leon fought his way through blows and bayonet jabs to prevent their separation. "My blood gushed out," he said, "but I didn't care. We were together." The two thought they might be taken someplace to work. "We didn't suspect that we would live to envy those who died in Iași . . . that later we would wish to be shot."

> During the day . . . the heat given off by the insides of the car began to suffocate us. We couldn't breathe. We had been hungry since Sunday morning. . . . At Roman we thought we could get water, but we were not allowed into the station and we were put on a dead line where we were left. Men began to show signs of exhaustion, some had already begun to rave, all of us shouted for water but we were told we would only get salt. The heat was unbearable.[10]

This first train to Călărași, its tightly shut cars growing hotter as the day warmed, meandered westward, stopping at some stations, passing through others: Podu Iloaiei, Tîrgu Frumos (at 7:00 a.m.), Pașcani, Lespezi, Pașcani again, Roman, Trifești, again Roman (where engines were exchanged), Săbăoani, and finally Tîrgu Frumos. It entered this last station—for the second time—about 9:00 Monday evening. Instead of 30 miles (48 kilometers) and one hour, the journey had covered some 125 miles (200 kilometers) and taken about seventeen hours. Moise Leib associated the passage with overwhelming thirst. Even before he, his two sons, and other survivors of the

CHAPTER 8

courtyard massacre had boarded the train they were tortured by thirst, many having gone without water for most of what had been an extremely warm and terrifying day. Then they had been packed together in cars that grew oven-like during their halting journey.

> The heat and stench were unbearable and as soon as the car was shut and sealed men began to collapse so that by morning the car was full of dead. After awhile Gypsies came around to sell water. . . . They organized to bring rags soaked with water, for which they got 100 lei, a bottle of water, 1,000 lei.

Iancu Pascal happened to be right in front of the window and began to collect money and hand out the soaked rags. Anyone who fell, that is, was no longer able to stand, was immediately smothered by someone else and in a few minutes died of suffocation. So the watchword was to remain standing.

> Men began to take their lives, despairing and unable to resist their agonies. They hung themselves with their belts. Many lost their minds. . . . The dead began immediately to swell, reducing the space. Attempting to get a little air, which entered the car through the windows near the roof, we stepped on the bodies which immediately burst.[11]

Attorney David Mittelman described the horrendous conditions in his car: people smashed together, steaming, suffocating, sides of the car like the walls of an oven. Passengers died in the first hours of the journey; the smell of rotting bodies mixed with the stench of sweat, urine, and excrement. Mittelman survived the Călăraşi train to bring to Rebeca Auerbach news that her husband Herman had died on the third day out and to his sister Roza Buchmann news that her husband Ghetzel and their son had also died on the train. Those who fell to the floor did not necessarily perish. Moşe Herşcovici had lost consciousness after climbing into his car in Iaşi and fell to the floor with his face near a small opening along the bottom of the door. A bullet, one of several, fired through the side of the car, struck him in the foot, and he awoke to the pain and bleeding. Then he saw the body of Dr. Max Aizicovici, "riddled with bullets." The random shooting also took another three lives in Herşcovici's car. Like other survivors, Herşcovici told of terrified prisoners, some of them wounded, packed together in their ovens, driven mad by heat and thirst, drinking urine, and killing themselves. At

TRENURILE MORTUARE (THE DEATH TRAINS)

the Tîrgu Frumos station the doors of his car were opened but guards refused to let out the living or permit removal of the dead. Desperate pleas for water went unanswered.[12]

Various officials gave accounts about what happened to the entrained prisoners in Tîrgu Frumos in their reports at the time and in postwar court depositions. In general these officials represent themselves as being aware of the Jews' terrible suffering and wanting, but being unable, to help them—to open the cars, take out the dead, or provide them with bread and water. They take credit for what little aid was given and lay blame for their inaction on lack of authority or interference from the Germans or other Romanians. Apologists Karețki and Covaci, in their *Bloody Days in Iași (28–30 June 1941)*, create a fiction in which the people of Tîrgu Frumos are "profoundly revolted by the measures taken against the Jews," Mayor Aurel Totoiescu challenges the offending soldiers and "fascist elements" by distributing "to the victims water to drink and hundreds of loaves of bread," and Praetor Teodorescu brings "water to the wounded," saving the lives of many Jews but being prevented from doing more by "Hitlerist opponents."[13]

What follows is a summary of official reports and postwar depositions regarding the Călărași train and events in Tîrgu Frumos, including claims of helping or wanting to help the victims. Local officials at Tîrgu Frumos had been informed about the train well before it arrived, but did not know on Monday evening that the final destination for the train had been changed from their town to Călărași, in the southeastern corner of the country. The city's police chief, Ionescu, and mayor, Totoiescu, claim that Iași Prefect Colonel Captaru had instructed them by telephone, at 9:00 and again at 11:00 Monday morning, to assist the Jews with the help of other officials, including the garrison commander, and to arrange with the Jewish community for their housing. Totoiescu relayed these instructions to community president Soloman Freitag and then he and Chief Ionescu went to find Garrison Commander Colonel Perju to arrange for guarding the train. In his place, however, they found Captain Danubiu Marinescu, who had come from Iași the day before, commanding a battalion of some four hundred railroad men. In the train station that afternoon, Marinescu, in the presence of the stationmaster and police chief, described Jews on the Iași train as criminals and communists and wanted them turned over to him for "extermination." The mayor then telephoned Captaru and, with Marinescu listening to the prefect's instructions, confirmed the order to assist the Jews. Marinescu left the meeting in a rage, vowing to give no assistance.

When the train finally arrived on Monday evening, Mayor Totoiescu,

CHAPTER 8

Chief Ionescu, city physician Dr. Constantin Gheorghiu, and Praetor Dumitru Griție were there. They could hear passengers pleading for water and removal of the dead and began opening cars. However, with only three or four opened, Marinescu appeared with his armed railroad workers and a German officer (probably Captain Walter Kosak, commander of the local German garrison) who ordered the unloading stopped "to ensure the security of German troops in Tîrgu Frumos."[14] Totoiescu again called Colonel Captaru, informing him that he had been prevented from unloading the train and that some of the passengers were dead. This time the prefect said he could order nothing without informing the minister of interior. Captaru came back on the line around midnight (Monday June 30) to inform the mayor that those taken out of their cars were to be returned and the train sent on to Călărași within the next few hours, and that a unit of gendarmes from Iași was being sent to guard the train for the rest of its journey. Totoiescu testified that Captaru also instructed him "to do everything possible to give food and water to the men," an instruction that, he said, he attempted to carry out.[15]

Those taken down from the opened cars numbered some 240 persons. They were led to a nearby synagogue and systematically robbed and beaten by assistant police commissioner Ion Botez and his men, Ioan Vătăjanu in particular, and Reserve Lieutenant Dumitru Atudorei, a teacher and school inspector, and men under him. Guards compiled a list of some of the confiscated property to give prisoners the impression they would get their things back. Mendel David saw a sergeant assistant of Atudorei shoot his two sons to death because they refused to hand over a watch and ring.[16] Mayor Totoiescu and Praetor Griție went to the synagogue about 4:30 a.m. Tuesday, learning on the way that guards had badly beaten community president Freitag for his efforts to bring water to the prisoners. Totoiescu testified that he ordered the return of confiscated money but said nothing about the killing and torture and did not actually see the money and other things given back.

At first light the mayor returned to the station where all top city officials, but not Captain Marinescu, were gathered. About this same time, 5:00 or 6:00 a.m., the gendarmes Prefect Captaru had promised arrived, thirty of them commanded by Second Lieutenant Aurel Triandaf. Now, after a delay of nine hours and in the absence of Marinescu and the German officer, the cars were opened with some urgency, given the great number of cadavers to be unloaded in the hour or two remaining before the train's departure time. Cars packed tightly with prisoners had many dead; some were half filled with corpses. Because survivors were too weak to help in their removal, Totoiescu ordered police to round up Gypsies to do the work. Survivors were desperate for water; Totoiescu recalled seeing someone lower two shirts tied in tandem

TRENURILE MORTUARE (THE DEATH TRAINS)

from a car window in order to reach into a puddle and soak up some of the water. Still, German and Romanian soldiers continued to prevent the systematic distribution of water to the prisoners.

Now the passengers had a rare instance of good fortune. A rail accident on their scheduled route delayed the train's departure and permitted removal of most of the dead. Had there been no accident the train almost certainly would have been sent on its way once Triandaf got there with his gendarmes. Not only was it ready to go, Jews held in the synagogue having been reloaded about 3:00 a.m., but, according to Totoiescu, the general staff's representative at the Iași station, Lieutenant Colonel Mavrichi, called the station chief at Tîrgu Frumos repeatedly between about 6:00 and 7:00 a.m., urging him to get the train moving. Instead, the removal of cadavers went on for some ten hours, from about 6:00 a.m. to 4:00 p.m. Dr. Gheorghiu claimed he "ascertained each death" on Monday night when only a few cars were opened and again on Tuesday. "Among the dead most had their heads broken," he said, "the eyes of some had been poked out, others had deep wounds in their bodies caused by such blows that I had the impression some of them left Iași already dead."[17] The train was in Tîrgu Frumos for about nineteen hours and except for the few cars opened on Monday night and during the time bodies were being removed, car by car, on Tuesday, their doors remained closed. Passengers were desperate for water; some, at great risk and expense, managed to get a few drops. Some survivors recalled seeing prisoners murdered when they tried to get to puddles of water near the tracks or from a nearby stream. Regional Inspector of Police Giosanu, in a report to Director General Leoveanu's office, said, "the number of dead is explained by the absence of medical attention, very many being wounded in Iași by German and Romanian soldiers and even from the absence of enough air."[18] The first cadavers arrived at the Tîrgu Frumos Jewish cemetery about 10:00 a.m., piled in a truck and covered with mats, on top of which sat police commissar Ion Botez armed with a machine gun. Vasile Mandache, conscripted with other men early Monday morning for burial work, recalled that when he was taken to the Jewish cemetery about 8:00 a.m., "the graves had already been prepared overnight by Jews taken there by police and we only threw corpses off the trucks and into the trench which was more than 30 m. long. While we worked other men dug another grave. The corpses . . . were nearly all naked, black, putrefied so that their flesh came off in our hands."[19]

One of several Jews who were thrown alive into the graves cried out for water and was pulled, with difficulty, from among the dead. Workers washed him off and gave him something to drink and a discarded shirt. Mandache, who said he helped extract the man from the corpses, recalled that workers

CHAPTER 8

put the Jew on one of the trucks used to haul bodies and, as far as he knew, returned him to the city. Avram Soloman, another conscripted cemetery worker remembered the incident differently. "[I saw] policemen from Tîrgu Frumos . . . under the command of Commissar Botez . . . take the Jewish citizen, who I myself had pulled alive from the grave, lift him with a mat and leave with him for a nearby place I knew about. A short time later we heard gunshots and then the police returned with the truck and the body of the citizen who, a few moments before, had been pulled from the grave."[20] Soloman and Mandache both recalled that in the evening Mayor Totoiescu, Dr. Gheorghiu, and some others came to the cemetery where the mayor ordered bodies in one of the mass graves be covered with straw, splashed with gasoline, and set on fire. "I don't know who lit the fire," Mandache said, "but I saw it burn. . . . There was a lot of smoke and a terrible stench." Dr. Gheorghiu watched along with the others but, according to Mandache, neither he nor anyone else examined the corpses at the cemetery. Totoiescu was eager to complete the burial by Wednesday morning, having been informed that General Antonescu was soon going to pass through Tîrgu Frumos. So he summoned Gypsies to complete the burials overnight. A few days later members of the Jewish community informed the mayor that because the graves were oozing a putrid liquid they needed an additional covering of earth. Lieutenant Triandaf reported that some 654 Jews were taken from the train and buried in Tîrgu Frumos.[21]

About 4:00 p.m. Tuesday, long before the burying was finished and before all the dead had been removed from the cars or the cars cleaned, the track toward Călăraşi was cleared and the train sent on. After leaving Tîrgu Frumos it was again sent meandering: passing through or stopping at Săbăoani three times and Roman four times. At Mirceşti, about 35 miles (56 kilometers) by rail from Tîrgu Frumos, cars were opened, some for the first time since leaving Iaşi, and 327 cadavers unloaded. These were buried near the village of Lungani-Roman. That same day (Wednesday) the train went on to Roman again and back to Săbăoani where another 170 or 180 dead were removed. Major Simulescu, from Supreme Military Headquarters, and two army doctors, Major Parvulescu and Captain Roiu, supervised the examination of survivors. Among the dead was Ghetzel Buchmann, head of the community's cultural section. He had been arrested with one of his two sons (the other having emigrated to Palestine) and the two were put into the same car. The boy, driven mad by heat and thirst, angry that he had not also been sent to Palestine, reviled and attacked the father. The son survived his father by a day. In Săbăoani, Moşe Herşcovici got his first drink of water since leaving Iaşi.[22]

Removing corpses from the Călărași train at Tîrgu Frumos, July 1, 1941. Romanian Information Service. United States Holocaust Memorial Museum.

Bodies thrown from Călărași train, July 1–6, 1941. Federation of Romanian Jewish Communities and Yad Vashem Photo Archives. United States Holocaust Memorial Museum.

CHAPTER 8

On Thursday morning the train left Săbăoani and arrived again at Roman where it was noticed by Viorica Agarici, president of the local affiliate of the Romanian Red Cross and one of the few Romanian officials who actually helped the tortured passengers. She heard cries for water and determined that the cars had to be opened. The stationmaster and German and Romanian guards opposed her intentions, but at her insistence, the train was moved to a track assigned to a sanitation company and survivors taken out, washed, and disinfected. This operation, as in Săbăoani, was carried out in the presence of an officer from Supreme Military Headquarters.[23] A number of passengers got water for the first time since Sunday. Rabinovici recalled that some were nearly dead from lack of water.

> One was so completely dehydrated, so afflicted, he could only have his lips moistened. I was taken down from the car and put in a bath. They took all our coats but representatives of the Jewish Community of Roman were present in the station and gave us other coats. We did not get food. . . . I was obliged to squat the entire night. In the morning I got coffee for the first time. I was again put into the car; this time there were 40 persons and the expedition again set off. On the way it was possible to buy food and water but at exorbitant prices. In one station we got food from the Jewish Community of that city.[24]

In each place where cadavers were taken off the train, mass graves were dug nearby and the dead trucked to the site. In Roman, Deputy Mayor Pipă refused to give the bodies over to the Jewish community for identification and ritual burial. Instead he had the bodies thrown into two ditches in the Jewish cemetery and forbade, "under severe penalty," anyone going near the graves. After eight days of July heat the possibility of identifying any of the dead was gone. Workers removed fifty-three dead from the train at Roman. Afterward it was sent on, stopping overnight (Friday–Saturday, July 4–5) at Mărăşeşti where workers removed ten dead. At Inoteşti forty dead and dying were taken off during the next night. Dr. Iosef Abraham, who went to the Inoteşti station to give assistance, at the direction of the Roman community, saw ten Jews near death stretched on the ground. "I spoke with the military doctor who told me there was nothing more for us to do and indeed after a short time they all died."[25]

The journey of the first of the two Iaşi trains ended at Călăraşi on Sunday afternoon, July 6. Workers took down twenty-five dead and seventy-four

TRENURILE MORTUARE (THE DEATH TRAINS)

dying from the cars. Triandaf reported that the transport had left Iași with thirty-five cars and 2,530 Jews and that on final evacuation at Călărași there were 1,011 alive, twenty-five dead, five who died the day after their arrival, and sixty-nine others who were near death. Triandaf included in the number of dead two prisoners who were killed allegedly trying to escape. He also pointed out in his final report that "all along the way from Tîrgu Frumos to Călărași drinking water was given to the Jews on the train by the gendarme guards," that bread was provided by the mayor of Tîrgu Frumos, food and clothing by the Roman Jewish community, and that he himself distributed fifty kilograms of sugar to the passengers. This hardly agrees with Triandaf's attitude or conduct as survivors recollect. Some members of Triandaf's own guard unit testified that he ordered them "not to give food or water to those on the train," and that he threatened to court-martial any of them who gave water to the Jews or who opened the cars. According to a number of survivors, several persons were shot attempting to get water by Triandaf or at his orders or in his presence. Guards sometimes fired blindly through the sides of cars or through openings made by prisoners who had managed to pull boards or window shutters loose from inside to get air. In Moșe Herșcovici's car, random shooting had wounded him and killed Dr. Aizicovici, engineer Pulwerman, attorney Simon Garcineanu, and Iosef Lebel.

Triandaf reported that on the first train to leave Iași some 1,519 of the 2,530 Jews perished, including the twenty-five dead and sixty-nine dying taken off at Călărași. The 1,011 survivors, some with little or no clothing, were housed in a hangar belonging to the 23rd Infantry Regiment. About sixty moribund persons were put in a school building to die so as not to burden the public hospital, to which another thirty-five were sent. Despite some medical care, five or six persons perished each day at the school and a few died at the hospital, usually following surgery. Herșcovici, whose memory failed him when some local Jews came to the prison camp to collect names and addresses of survivors in order to inform their families, had the presence of mind to save his wounded and infected foot. Having learned of the doctors' decision to amputate it, he managed to lance the abscess himself. As punishment for this unauthorized self-surgery he was refused food for one day, but the foot began to heal.[26]

At first survivors were kept in deplorable circumstances, lacking sufficient food, clothing, or medical care. After two or three days, however, these conditions began to change for the better as Jews from the area and then the Union of Jewish Communities began helping them. The local community of some three hundred persons could not take care of all the pressing needs of the survivors and knew that helping them might draw trouble on themselves. The previous November (1940) legionary police of Călărași arrested and, for some thirty-six hours, tortured a number of prominent Jewish men. Three of these died as a result; one, Dr. Silviu Cohn, was a twice war-wounded veteran. Despite the danger, when the Iași train arrived, the presidents of the two communities (Ashkenazic and Sephardic) began collecting clothing and food and set up committees to get help to the prisoners. After some initial resistance, local Prefect Colonel Ștefănescu and Captain Pitiș, in charge of the prison camp, began allowing prisoners to receive help, mainly medication, food, clothing, and money. A delegation came from Bucharest on July 9 and arranged to supplement local contributions and to buy the cooperation of various officials.[27]

Two months after their arrival, Herșcovici and the other approximately one thousand survivors were loaded like cattle, forty to a car, into a train at the Călărași station and returned to Iași. They were not allowed to leave the cars during the journey, and soldiers sometimes prevented members of local Jewish communities along the way from delivering provisions, forcing the returnees to pay railway employees and soldiers exorbitantly for food and drink from station buffets just a few steps away. Survivors arrived back in Iași on the night of September 6 and were escorted in groups, some of them pelted with stones, to districts where they lived. At the station, before being sent home, they were told that the military commander of the city, General Dumitru Carlaonț, had ordered all Jews to wear a yellow star. Beniamin Rabinovici, who lost his right eye and hearing in his left ear, learned on his return home that his wife had been murdered. Moșe Herșcovici, who never regained full use of his left foot, learned that a brother had been killed during the chestură massacre and his father had died on one of the trains. Both these men, like other Jewish men and boys, were soon conscripted for hard labor. Rabinovici was able to bribe his way out of the work while Herșcovici was sent to Bessarabia to labor under hellish conditions.[28]

The second train from Iași, carrying eighteen cars, was sent to Podu Iloaiei, about 18 miles (30 kilometers) to the west. Loading of the 1,902 passengers began early Monday morning. Railroad workers, municipal policemen, gendarmes, and German soldiers using guns and clubs packed Jews into the cars. The train left the station about 9:00 a.m. The engineer drove it slowly, forward and back, returning once to Iași to have more prisoners or corpses loaded into the last car. It was more crowded than the Călărași train, and in it conditions were even worse. Many of the passengers who died were probably asphyxiated; several committed suicide. The journey, ordinarily no more

Brothers. Top: Carol and Henrich Grinberg died on the Podu Iloaiei train. Bottom: R. Schvartz "asphyxiated" on the Podu Iloaiei train and M. Schvartz "shot in the Chestură courtyard." June 29–30, 1941. Federation of Romanian Jewish Communities. United States Holocaust Memorial Museum.

CHAPTER 8

Herskowicz family photo, 1929–30 in Podu Iloaiei: grandparents, children, and grandchild. Back row second from left: Minna who married Smuel Azriel in 1937. With one toddler and Minna pregnant she and her husband took into their two-room Podu Iloaiei apartment six survivors of the Podu Iloaiei death train, June 30–July 1, 1941. Courtesy of Minna's daughter Ditsa Goshen. United States Holocaust Memorial Museum.

than thirty minutes long, lasted some eight hours, and those who had been loaded first were enclosed in their cars for as many as twelve hours. When the engineer finally stopped the train and the car doors were opened, the living numbered about 708 and the dead 1,194. Zalman Emil recalled that some of the prisoners "managed with indescribable effort to tear away a plank somehow and tried to squeeze out [but] were killed with bayonets or clubs by soldiers guarding the train." Michel Weisenberg was one of a handful of survivors in his wagon. When the car doors were opened he wanted to pull his father out from under the pile of cadavers on the slight chance that he might still be alive. However, one of the train guards, Iacob Niculae, who had taken 18,000 lei from Michel, with a false promise of water, threatened to shoot him if he did not move away from the car. The fear, heat, lack of air and water, and press of prisoners all contributed to the great number of deaths, as did the extraordinary length of time taken for the journey. Mata-

TRENURILE MORTUARE (THE DEATH TRAINS)

tias Carp pointed out that the Jews could have got to Podu Iloaiei sooner by walking and with many fewer deaths. Officials knew about the great number of deaths on the Podu Iloaiei train even before the Călărași train made its first extended stop in Tîrgu Frumos. Prefect Captaru telephoned the interior ministry at 7:55 p.m., June 30, and described those evacuated from the Podu Iloaiei train as a great pile of corpses, "some killed by asphyxiation," and reported the number of dead to be "about 1,000."[29]

CHAPTER 9

Victims

The burial of Jews murdered in the Iași pogrom began Sunday morning June 29. Vlad Marievici, the city's sanitation chief, on his way to work that morning counted nine cadavers lying in the streets. Because of the continuing violence he decided to keep his workers idle for the time being. The first request for a truck came shortly before noon, that is, before the courtyard mass shooting began. When the driver returned early in the afternoon he said he had taken corpses from the chestură courtyard to the Jewish cemetery. On his way home after work the sanitation chief noticed the streets had been cleared of the dead.

As soon as Marievici got to his office Monday morning he received a call from the police station requesting all available trucks and carts. In his postwar testimony he claimed that before sending out his men and equipment, four dump trucks and twenty-four carts, Garrison Commander Lupu assured him that the dying and wounded would be taken to the Jewish hospital. Still, his drivers and carters told him that "in many cases" the dying were loaded with the dead into their trucks and carts and were smothered either by cadavers on the way to the cemetery or in the graves. Marievici insisted that responsibility for these killings was "in the hands of the military and police," not his workers. He recalled that when he himself entered the chestură courtyard he saw "corpses piled up like lumber. . . . On the ground blood flowed as far as the gate and in it I stepped to the depth of my shoe sole."[1] Vasile Spinosu drove one of the four dump trucks. He recalled the dead stacked like logs in the courtyard and "next to the gate . . . some still alive but mutilated and butchered in a barbarous manner." Each truck

CHAPTER 9

was loaded by scavengers and accompanied to the cemetery by a policeman and two or more German soldiers. Spinosu said he made eight trips with twenty to thirty bodies each time. "Put on the truck were live persons, only wounded, who I heard groaning. At the beginning we unraveled the bodies at the edge of the graves; after this it was decided by the officers and police who were there that this took too long and ordered me to drive the truck up to the edge and empty it like garbage, directly into the grave. First a wave of blood flowed, then all the corpses fell topsy-turvy into the grave." Spinosu claimed he saw one other truck and no carts taking bodies to the cemetery, though he did see carts continuously being loaded at the police station and other trucks carrying the dead. "I assumed they were carting the dead some place other than the Jewish Cemetery. . . . I am convinced there were many more dead than 254 buried at the Jewish Cemetery. Also, I didn't see on this route one other truck carrying corpses—except one. . . . As I said, Sanitation had 4 trucks all of which I saw carrying the dead."[2]

During the roundups and killings on Sunday morning, Oisie Sechter, steward of the Păcurari Jewish cemetery, and three gravediggers went to work, concerned mainly with the unburied victims of the aerial bombardment of Thursday the twenty-sixth. Sechter considered the graves already dug for them insufficient. Another two large ditches had also been prepared but apparently not for the bombing victims. Orders for these mass graves, their size and location, had been made a few days earlier by city engineer Teodorescu and community representatives Herş Gherner and Carol Drimer, both of whom were later murdered, the one from blows received at the chestură gate and Drimer after going mad from heat and thirst on the Călăraşi train. The ditches were dug by a compulsory work crew of young Jews and were finished by June 26. The graves were thirty and twenty-five meters long and each two meters wide and deep.[3]

When Sechter and his workers arrived at the cemetery, a German field kitchen unit was there; it was from one of the unit's soldiers that the gravediggers learned of the mass arrests in the city. Early in the afternoon, the commander of the kitchen, wanting cemetery workers to put the unburied bodies in the ground, sent Sechter and his men to the chestură under guard in order for them to get the "bilet de libera." However, before they were out of the cemetery, Sechter recalled, "a Romanian patrol arrived along with many thugs from the [Păcurari] area to arrest us but the German soldier [in charge of the guard detachment] . . . told us not to go with them . . . because they would shoot us." One of the gravediggers, Ozias Hauzner, remembered seeing "corpses and convoys of tortured people the whole way from the cemetery to the police station and back."

Sechter's crew buried 254 men, women, and children on June 29 and 30. The gravediggers described the dead as "completely distorted as a result of beatings," stripped of valuables and "horribly mutilated," not the victims of aerial bombardment. Around 6:30 Monday morning city sanitation trucks and carts began arriving, accompanied by two policemen, Romilă and Rotaru, to supervise burials. "The cadavers were unloaded by us grave diggers and laid out in the cemetery morgue, as long as there was room, and the rest put outside." Despite the fact that most had been stripped of clothing or had their pockets turned out, scavengers flocked to the cemetery. About 10:00 a.m. seven Jews who lived near the cemetery were brought there by policeman Şchiopu and murdered. Hauzner knew all but one of the seven who, he recalled, "were shot right in the cemetery by a Sgt. Instructor and soldier of the 4th Artillery Reg." The innkeeper Samoil Leibovici was also murdered in the cemetery. After pulling several bodies off a garbage cart, Hauzner uncovered Leibovici who begged him for water. "The same soldier who shot those seven men," said Hauzner, "took out his revolver and shot him."

The gravediggers' accounts agree that they buried 254 cadavers, but there must have been, as Spinosu observed, many more than that buried at the cemetery and elsewhere. Hauzner, like Sechter, recalled engineer Teodorescu's instruction for the preparation of mass graves a few days before the pogrom and noted that besides these two graves was a third, "dug by some 50 pre-military Jews brought by police, even on the 30th of June 1941," that is, the day after the great mass killing. All the gravediggers describe the arrival at the cemetery of a number of garbage carts and trucks. Spinosu, who recalled seeing only one other truck delivering bodies to the cemetery, worked only on Monday. Perhaps Sechter's gravediggers also worked only through Monday and were then replaced by the fifty youth who were conscripted for the larger task.[4]

Itzhac David and other young Jewish men, excluded from the military, served in what he described as a "pre-military organization" regularly obliged to do "socially useful work." On Friday or Saturday, June 27 or 28, he was arrested, held for some hours at the chestură and then, with five other young Jewish men, sent to the Păcurari cemetery. After waiting some hours city garbage carts filled with cadavers began arriving and they got to work putting bodies in graves already dug. Because they could not bury the dead as fast as they came in, more young Jews were brought in to do the burying while Itzhac's group was put to digging three more large graves. Itzhac recalled working four days and nights with his co-workers and burying some six thousand bodies. Afterward he was put in a nearby military prison, along with some 160 other burial conscripts, where he believed he would be executed. Instead he and the others were taken to Stânca Rosnovanu, where the Sculeni Jews had been murdered, and put to work digging trenches, an indication that burials there had been too shallow or incomplete.[5]

The truck driver Spinosu was ill Tuesday, sickened he recalled by the gruesome work of the day before. On Wednesday he and the other drivers went to the chestură where they were sent on to Podu Iloaiei to assist in burying Jews murdered on the second death train. "We got to Podu Iloaiei at 10:00 a.m. The bodies were on a field to the right of the road and were in a state of advanced decay, some inflated five times normal size. The bodies were loaded by persons pressed into service by the gendarmes: Romanians, Gypsies, Jews. Some of the bodies fell apart when touched and were loaded piece by piece. . . . There were some German soldiers who took photos although they didn't take part, being spectators."[6]

The 1947 indictment against those charged with "crimes committed against people in the city of Iași, Stânca Rosnovanu and Tg. Mărculești," states that although the exact number of Iași pogrom victims is not known, "it certainly exceeds by much the number 500."[7] That was the number General Antonescu gave in a communiqué of July 1, 1941, announcing the execution of five hundred Judeo-communists who he claimed had shot at German and Romanian soldiers. We have only a rough idea of the number of Jews murdered in Iași, whereas reports on the number killed on the trains are probably close to being accurate. In general the evidence suggests the following: approximately 1,011 of the 2,530 Jews who were embarked from Iași were alive on arrival at Călărași, and the great majority of these survived there over the next few weeks. Of the 1,902 Jews who were on the train to Podu Iloaiei, about 708 survived. Altogether, out of approximately 4,432 passengers about 2,713 died and 1,719 survived.[8] Official reports concerning the massacre in and around the chestură courtyard on Sunday afternoon generally misrepresent what happened and almost certainly underestimate the number of dead. General Stavrescu telegraphed the interior ministry on Sunday evening that according to Police Chief Chirilovici, German and Romanian soldiers killed about three hundred hostages. Chirilovici himself reported that German troops at the police station, angered by a communist plot to free the Jews, "fired into their ranks (to intimidate them) and some of them were killed." Regional Police Inspector Giosanu, on July 2, reported "some 500 Jews were killed in Iași by German and Romanian soldiers." Only Police Inspector Leahu mentions a massacre; in a "declaration" dated July 2 he states that "the number of Jews in the courtyard was about 3500 when the Germans began to massacre them." Leahu also pointed out that Chief Chirilovici (who estimated there were five thousand Jews in the courtyard at the time the shooting started), Garrison Commander Lupu, Colonel Barozzi, Regional Inspector of Gendarmes Bădescu, and General Stavrescu had come to the police station because of the shooting and saw the dead and wounded. According to Leahu, though the killing stopped while they were there, these officers knew it continued after they left.[9]

German ambassador von Killinger reported four thousand Jews executed in Iași. US envoy Gunther noted "persistent reports" that 4,500 or 5,000 had been killed. Matatias Carp observed that "legal documents have put the figure at 8,000." Gheorghe Zaharia, citing official documents from the interior ministry and elsewhere, concluded that "during the days of the pogrom [June 27–30, 1941] and in the 'trains of death' more than 8,000 persons were murdered." Marius Mircu, in his account of events, also claimed that more than 8,000 Jews were killed in the pogrom (apparently not including those who perished in the trains).[10] A report from the Romanian intelligence service (SSI) in Iași to their commander, Eugen Cristescu, two years after the massacre, claimed that memorial services for those murdered in the pogrom had been held in Iași, families of the victims mourning their losses in their respective synagogues. The authors of the report concluded that "after tabulating all the synagogues . . . the number of those killed was 13,266, of which 40 were women and 180 were children."[11]

The killing in Iași did not end with the Sunday massacre. Early Monday afternoon (June 30) Romanian soldiers, having fired at a building on Stradă I. C. Brătianu from which shots had allegedly come, searched the place and pulled out eighteen Jews. They forced them all, including a child and the child's parents, to lie down on the street and machine-gunned them. According to a "strictly secret" police report, from Chief Chirilovici to Regional Inspector of Police Giosanu, some German soldiers assisted in the killing, executing those who still showed some life. In another report Giosanu said German and Romanian soldiers had shot some fifty or more Jews on Monday but that the night had been calm. A city ordinance, posted that same Monday (June 30), clearly targeted Jews and closely followed the government's misrepresentation of events. It stated that hostile agents had entered Iași on the night of June 28–29 and for that reason all residents were to be off the streets between 7:00 p.m. and 5:00 a.m. Civilians discovered with weapons were to be shot on the spot and ten hostages executed for the wounding or killing of a soldier. The source of this ordinance was an order from General Antonescu, sent out by the army and Ministry of Interior to local police authorities. It claimed that because enemy agents had come into the country and made contact with Judeo-communists and others in order to subvert the war effort, it was necessary to take immediate countermeasures by keeping

CHAPTER 9

Several Jews including parents and child murdered on a Iași street, June 30, 1941. Federation of Romanian Jewish Communities and Romanian Information Service. United States Holocaust Memorial Museum.

Jews off the streets at night, grouping Jews in their own districts, even gathering Jewish men (eighteen to sixty) together in large buildings under guard, and taking hostage leading Jews and communists "who will be immediately shot when an act of rebellion or terrorism occurs."[12]

On Tuesday July 1, a German patrol searched another building from which shots had allegedly been fired and arrested the residents, though they found no evidence of shooting. A large crowd of civilians gathered in front of the building, while the search and arrests were being made, demanding its destruction and execution of the residents.[13] That same day a railway guard shot a Jew he claimed had a revolver, and German soldiers plundered a perfume shop owned by Jews. One of the shop's proprietors, Marcusohn, had been gunned down on Sunday with his wife, child, and another merchant, former Romanian army officer Jean Olivenbaum.[14] Also on or about July 1, a patrol of Romanians and Germans murdered Lupu Melik and his wife and son. A daughter, Estelka, about thirteen, escaped and with great difficulty recounted the murders to sympathetic Reserve Captain Filipescu. Her family had been forced to leave their town of Codăești, south of Iași, at the time of the legionnaire government and had the misfortune to be in Iași at the time of the pogrom. They managed to escape the mass killing, but a day or two afterward the patrol found their cellar hiding place and killed them.[15]

On July 2, Antonescu's charge that five hundred Judeo-communists had been executed in Iași appeared on the front page of *Universul,* and twenty dignitaries of the Iași community, members of the Council and rabbis, were arrested and brought, as hostages, to the compound of the 13th Infantry Regiment on Copou Hill. Those withholding information from, or even failing to report suspicions of subversive activity to, local authorities were threatened with execution "together with their entire families." Fifty Jews were to be executed in retaliation for any shooting at Germans or Romanians.[16] Besides the 7:00 p.m. to 5:00 a.m. curfew, Jews were required to shop in the markets only between 10:00 a.m. and noon, wear a yellow star (ordered on August 6, 1941), attend only one synagogue (located in a wing of the Old Age Home), supply authorities with materials and labor, give up their homes and all furnishings in certain parts of the city, and on pain of death be prohibited from entering these or other off-limit districts. Jews were also forced to make never-to-be-repaid "loans" to the state.[17]

Max Gaer, who suffered the physical and mental torments of the pogrom and Călărași train, was a conscript. He had been badly beaten at the time of his arrest, again when he entered the chestură courtyard, and once more when he clambered into a freight car. He survived the Călărași death train but returned to Iași with his hearing permanently impaired by blows to his head and with images of inexpressible human despair.

> I remember there were in the car with me [the brothers] David Schwartz and Leon Schwartz, and Moritz Avram with his two boys, one of whom died, unable to survive the misery.
>
> It is impossible for me to describe the despair of this father when before his eyes his child flickered out like a candle. I think there is no payment or punishment sufficient for this kind of bestiality.

A month after his return home Gaer was ordered to report to the "Recruiting Center" where men were assigned various kinds of usually heavy and degrading work. He was sent to the Institute of the Deaf and Mute where he cleaned windows, floors, and toilets, all the while subject to beatings and insults. His boss made the work of those employed by him extremely painful and then took payments from them to ease up. For his part Gaer, who earned nothing, not even days off, for his labor, eventually bought his way free by paying his boss a monthly salary. There was no way to beat the system—Jews were forced to work or pay or do both. A commission

CHAPTER 9

existed that could release persons from forced labor, and to this body Jews presented reasons why they should be exempted, but the crucial issue was always how much money could be wrung from them. "Not infrequently . . . people sold the last things from their homes just to get the much coveted *carnet de scutire*, so that . . . being free they would be able in some way to earn a miserable existence. Otherwise there was only the refuge of insulting, exhausting, and brutal work."[18] Conscription caused a double hardship for poor families. Besides providing for themselves they had to provision their menfolk who worked but now earned nothing.

The community assisted where it could but its resources were greatly diminished by the same crises that gave rise to the extraordinary needs. On Monday morning, June 30, women began to gather at the door of the Community Council seeking information about their men. At the time, bookkeeper Froimovici was compiling a list of dead, but police agents warned community secretary Klara Scheinfeld, whose brother Salo had been murdered on Sunday, that any who dared "publish a list . . . would all be shot." To protect itself from or at least mitigate official harassment, the community continued to pay off important officials. A few days after the pogrom President Iacob entrusted Scheinfeld with a packet of two million lei (reckoned by Klara to be about ten times the annual salary of a high official) to be delivered to Police Chief Chirilovici:

> With my heart in my mouth I took myself to the Police Station. . . . Frightened to death I climbed the stairs to the Chestură office, in this place, where, just days before, thousands of persons fell dead under a storm of gunfire.
>
> Col. Chirilovici took the envelope, opened it, glanced inside, pushed it in his pocket, nodded his head and said to me all was in order and that I could relay to Mr. Iosef Iacob that all was perfectly in order.

Chirilovici was replaced as Iaşi police chief by Nicolae Crăciun on September 29, 1941, that is, only a few weeks after pocketing the community's huge bribe.

The work of the community was hampered by continuous roundups designed to catch Jews for labor details and by other threats that restricted the movement of its officials. Klara was again sent to the police station, this time to see Chief Crăciun. Crăciun had been commissar of the city's fifth police district; it was he who sent the five Jews, guarded by the murderer Sergeant Manoliu, to the grounds of the 13th Infantry Regiment, and it was in his district, two days later (Saturday, June 28), that he failed to prevent German and Romanian soldiers, some thirty of the latter under Manoliu's command, from beating and robbing Jews. Klara requested from the new chief permits for eight community officials to circulate freely in order to bring assistance to the neediest. At first Crăciun refused to let "eight Yids" move freely about the city but was finally persuaded that it was in his interest to have the community help preserve order among the Jews.[19] Schools, orphanages, medical clinics, canteens, and other services continued to be supported by the community, which was presented with extraordinary demands, from families whose men had been murdered or conscripted, for example, or from those who had been evicted from their homes. Extraordinary emergencies came one after another, as when the remains of those buried in the Jewish cemetery in Tătărași had to be exhumed and removed to the cemetery in Păcurari, or when General Carlaonț ordered Jews to provide, in forty-eight hours, bedding for a four-hundred-bed hospital and threatened to execute Jewish hostages if they did not comply.

Ten days after the pogrom, on July 9, German and Romanian troops occupied Bălți, northwest of Iași in Bessarabia. Jews who survived the killing there, some eleven hundred men, women, and children, made their way to Iași. Hoping to save some of them from wholesale execution, community leaders persuaded the military commander to allow those whose feet were severely cut and bruised admission to the Jewish hospital. The seventeen patients were to be returned in ten days, but a considerable bribe extended their stay and probably their lives. Organizing aid to the Jews of Iași, including hundreds evacuated to the city, fell largely to Aron Stievel, head of the community's social assistance section. He estimated that as a result of the pogrom 60 percent of the Jewish population of Iași was inscribed for support on the section's lists and the other 40 percent suffered "severe reductions and privations." One of many very demanding tasks was accommodating the whole Jewish community of Podu Iloaiei, some 1,700 persons, evacuated to Iași on such short notice that Stievel only learned of it when the first evacuees began arriving in the city. He immediately sent every kind of truck or cart he could command to Podu Iloaiei and in about twenty-four hours managed to get all the Jews out. Some had relatives or acquaintances in Iași who put them up, but most were without means and had to rely on Stievel's organization to find them places to stay and food, supplied mainly by the Old Age Home kitchen.[20]

Boarding schools were set up for the neediest children, those orphaned by the massacre and death trains and some of those whose fathers were sent away from Iași to do forced labor. The single largest effort to help desperate children occurred in 1943–44. Many thousands of Jews had been deported, by order of the Antonescu government, from Bucovina and Bessarabia to the labor-death camps of Transnistria. Children, especially those orphaned in the bloody process, had less chance than others of surviving for long in the camps. In 1942–43 as prospects of an Axis victory faded, the Antonescu government began to reconsider its program of mass extermination and was persuaded by the Center of Romanian Jews to give it permission to send a rescue mission for the orphans. This work was done through the Iași community, which set up two commissions, one under Fred Șaraga, formerly president of the "Star" girls' school in Iași and the other under Dr. Marcu Bercovici, at the time head of the community's cultural section. Șaraga's group went to Moghilev. Bercovici took his commission of eight persons to Bălți, nearly 125 miles (200 kilometers) east-northeast of Iași. It was at the end of February 1944 when the Bercovici team arrived in Bălți and gathered together 450 children, most of them ill, severely undernourished, and filthy. Eight days passed before freight cars were available for the journey back. During their return Bercovici's commission was able to gather up another fifty orphans in Tiraspol. Some two thousand children were recovered; of these Iași took in about seven hundred. When the transports came through the city children assigned to it were taken off the train. The station was crowded with people ready to hand out candies. The children went through quarantine and then were sheltered in the Old Age Home. "The problems these children had were not ended with gathering them, attending to them, and placing them in schools. The children were undernourished and our doctors had extreme difficulty with their diets. We could not pass over a single detail: the children received good and sufficient food, but all hid pieces of bread under their mattresses."[21]

CHAPTER 10

Perpetrators

In 1990 I asked Dr. Caufman, at the time president of the Jewish community in Iași, to help me set up interviews with survivors of the pogrom. He graciously accepted but warned me that each survivor would give a different account of what happened. True enough. Had I been further along in my research I could have told him that, by contrast, nearly every Romanian police officer and military official who was investigated after the war for crimes related to the pogrom told pretty much the same story, that Germans and their local Nazi toadies were responsible for the killings.[1]

Those directly responsible for the Iași pogrom range from the highest government officials to common citizens. The principal instigators of this and the many other massacres that together constitute the Romanian Holocaust were Ion Antonescu, president of the Council of Ministers and commander of Romania's military forces, and his vice president, Mihai Antonescu. Men in the service of these leaders, assisted by local recruits, ignited the Iași pogrom on the night of June 28, 1941, by simulating an attack on German and Romanian troops in the city. These provocateurs were members of Romania's intelligence services: SSI (Serviciul Special de Informații) and Section II of the Supreme General Staff (military intelligence). Some SSI agents, although assigned only to ignite the pogrom, also joined soldiers, policemen, and civilians in the killing. Top city and district police officials likely had some forewarning of the government's plan; at the very least they failed to protect citizens from being attacked, even murdered, in some cases by men under their command. The same can be said about German and Romanian commanders of military units stationed in the area. They had troops enough to curtail the mayhem; instead, their soldiers were a major force in moving the destruction along. Private citizens who joined in the action were not just social scum but also persons of some wealth and station who saw in the desperate plight of Jewish neighbors an opportunity to do them violence and steal their property.

The Iași pogrom and overall policy of extermination were fueled by a campaign of vilification. As the country moved toward war with the Soviet Union, Romanian Jews, already victimized by draconian laws, were increasingly the target of surveillance by the interior ministry and of propaganda representing them as Bolshevists and enemy partisans. At the same time, in their speeches, Ion and Mihai Antonescu began advocating the violent "ethnic cleansing" of Romanian territory and putting into practice a policy of isolating and concentrating Romanian Jews, making them particularly vulnerable targets for wholesale "cleansing" operations. Mihai Antonescu explained to the Council of Ministers (on June 17, 1941) that purification of Bessarabia and Northern Bucovina, territories about to be taken from the Soviet Union and reincorporated into Romania, required a "total and violent elimination of foreign elements."[2] What the Antonescus contemplated, however, was a comprehensive cleansing, eliminating all Jews under their power, not just those living in conquered territory. This is made clear by the fact that the first concentrations and massacres occurred in the Romanian heartland. As many as 150 "suspicious Jews" of Dorohoi were deported to prisons at Tîrgu Jiu in late May 1941. Some three weeks later, on June 21, Ion Antonescu ordered the wholesale concentration of Moldavian Jews (ages eighteen to sixty). Those living in the countryside were to be removed to nearby cities or deported to prison camps. Moving expenses were to be borne by the deportees and those who tried to destroy or somehow recover their evacuated property were to be "punished with death."[3] The execution of 311 Sculeni Jews at Stânca Rosnovanu took place six days later, on June 27, and the Iași pogrom and death trains immediately followed. What links these murders to the general "cleansing" operation carried out during the invasion of the Soviet Union is the fact that the same government agencies, even the same units, responsible for executing the Sculeni Jews (Romanian 6th Cavalry Regiment) and Iași pogrom (SSI's Echelon 1 and military intelligence) moved on to other mass killings in the conquered territories.

Agencies assigned to take the lead in ethnic cleansing operations were, besides SSI, the army (combat, intelligence, and praetorial or judicial services), and Ministry of Interior (district police, the gendarmerie in particular). The first assignment in this campaign of annihilation, provoking the Iași pogrom, was given to SSI. Its director general was Eugen Cristescu, appointed to that post by Ion Antonescu in November 1940. SSI was established in 1938 to gather information for the chief of state but became also a policing operation of some nine hundred agents, serving both civil and military authorities. On the military side Cristescu's immediate superior was, from February 1941, Colonel Radu Dinulescu, head of military intelligence. The two intelligence agencies worked closely together. An important link between them was Lieutenant Colonel Traian Borcescu, who left the counterintelligence office of military intelligence in April 1941 to become chief of SSI's secretarial service. Both agencies collected information about Jews in Moldavia; military intelligence did this through its statistical bureau with offices in Bucharest, Cluj, and Iași.[4] Dinulescu and Cristescu had close ties with officials in the German legation in Bucharest, and these officials were kept informed about the Iași mission by one of their own, Major Hermann von Stransky, an Abwehr officer who served the legation as its liaison with SSI and was directly involved in preparations to ignite the Iași pogrom.

On June 18, 1941, six days after meeting with Hitler, Ion Antonescu launched SSI's 160-man Operational (or "Special") Echelon toward Iași. There were at least four Echelon teams. The first to reach the city was commanded by Grigore Petrovici; once there he went to the municipal police station presumably to meet with police officials and remained there more than an hour.[5]

On Thursday, June 26, chief of SSI's Romanian-German liaison office, Lieutenant Colonel Micandru, and Major von Stransky arrived in Iași and according to their driver, around noon, immediately after the bombing, went to see General Stavrescu at his headquarters, "where they stayed some time." The presence of Echelon agents in Iași on the twenty-sixth is also affirmed by team member Nicolae Trohani, who said that a number of them found safety from the Soviet bombing that day in Bucium, a resident command post of SSI located just south of and overlooking the city.[6]

On Friday, June 27, a group of legionnaires gathered in the Păcurari district of Iași, singing legion songs and alarming area residents. Police Chief Chirilovici reported the matter to Garrison Commander Colonel Constantin Lupu who went there with some soldiers. He found a group of armed men who scattered at his approach, leaving one or two boxes of carbines, a light machine gun, and two men in civilian clothes who identified themselves to the colonel as officers sent by army high command to arm legionnaires for special duties in rear areas once Romanian forces began their assault on the Soviet Union. Apparently satisfied with their explanation, Lupu returned to his post, where the two men soon reappeared, this time in military uniform. They were SSI agents, Major Emil Tulbure and Captain Gheorghe

CHAPTER 10

Balotescu. Tulbure headed one Echelon team and Balotescu belonged to the one commanded by Petrovici. Chief of SSI's secretarial service, Borcescu, testified that "these two officers with their teams of legionnaires prepared the groundwork in the City of Iaşi . . . for committing the massacre and participated together with military and civil elements in . . . this slaughter."[7] Two other team leaders were Lieutenant Colonel Vasile Palius and Eugen Cristescu's brother, Gheorghe Cristescu-Gica. Overall commander of the teams was Florin Becescu-Georgescu. These men were provided up-to-date information about the Jewish population of Iaşi by Junius Lecca, the chief SSI counterintelligence officer in Iaşi. According to Victor Ionescu, himself a military counterintelligence officer, many Echelon agents wore Romanian military uniforms.[8]

According to Borcescu and his assistant, Vernescu, information about the massacre was sent on June 29 to both Ion and Mihai Antonescu. Borcescu said Echelon 1's mission did not include killing, but Vernescu told him members of at least three Echelon teams, and he himself, had participated directly in the murders. Borcescu also said Cristescu told him later, referring to the pogrom, that he had accomplished a great thing in Moldavia, working with Section II of the Supreme General Staff (military intelligence), especially its chief Colonel Radu Dinulescu and Lieutenant Colonel Gheorghe Petrescu, head of its statistical bureau.[9] The pogrom was the beginning of Echelon 1's "cleansing" actions. From Iaşi it moved to the Bessarabian capital Chişinău (Kishinev), where it joined in a killing operation with one of Einsatzgruppe D's commandos, and from there to Tighina and Odessa.[10] Besides killing Jews in the conquered territories, Echelon 1 had the mission of securing useful movable property, automobiles and trucks, for example. Its agents, however, stretched the meaning of their instructions to include anything movable and valuable, objects of gold and silver of course, but also "pianos, fine lingerie, and rugs."[11]

Both Antonescus, as well as minister of interior General Ion Popescu and director general of police and state security Emanoil Leoveanu, had early and continuing information about the mass killing in Iaşi. On Saturday night, June 28, at 11:00 p.m., approximately two hours after SSI agents had set off the pogrom by simulating an attack on German and Romanian troops in the city, Ion Antonescu telephoned the city's garrison commander, Colonel Constantin Lupu, and ordered the arrest of all persons, except children, found in homes from which shots had been fired at troops and after a summary investigation the immediate execution of the guilty. He also ordered the total evacuation of Jews, "package by package" ("*pe pachete, pachete*"), from the city. The general followed up on this order with two communiqués,

Romanian Civil and Military Command

Chief of State ——————— Ion Antonescu ——————— Commander-in-Chief

V.P. & Minister of Justice Mihai Antonescu
Minister of War Gen. Iacovici (Jan.–Sept. 1941)
Minister of Interior Gen. Dumitru Popescu
Deputy Minister of Interior Gen. Ion Popescu
Dir. Gen. of Police Emanoil Leoveanu
Insp. Gen. of Gendarmes Constantin Vasiliu

Chief of Staff Gen. Ioanițiu (1940–41)
Gen. Iacovici (1941–42)
Praetoral Chief Gen. Ioan Topor

Section II (Military Intelligence)
Chief Radu Dinulescu

Serviciul Special de Informații (SSI) Chief Eugen Cristescu
Secretary Lt. Col. Traian Borcescu

German Legation
Ambassador von Killinger
Col. Erich Roedler
Major von Stransky
Major Wetstein
Gustav Richter
Peterson
Hermann von Ritgen

Section "G"
Col. Ion Lisievici
Lt. Col. Mihail C. I. Micandru
Lt. Col. Alexandru Proca
Radu Galeriu (translator)
Lt. Col. M. C. (Sița) Rădulescu
Eugen Haralamb

Eșalon Operativ I
Florin Bececsu-Georgescu

Counter Intelligence
Constantin Mihalcea
Junius Lecca (Iași)

Eșalon I
SSI Chief Eugen Cristescu
Teams Commander Florin B.-Georgescu
—— Teams (*Echipe*) ——

Major Emil Tulbure
Nemoianu

Grigore Petrovici
Capt. Gheorghe Balotescu
Constantin Petrescu
Victor Marinovici
Traian Rădulescu
Titu Boacă (Teraponte)

Col. Vasile Palius
Nicolae Trohani

Gheorghe Cristescu-Gica
Res. Lt. Ionel Stănescu

Note: CN96, 2: 18–21; 42–61 (postwar depositions of E. Cristescu, T. Borcescu, M. C. Rădulescu, V. Marinovici, C. Petrescu, T. Rădulescu, T. Boca, C. Mihalcea, N. Trohani, R. Galeriu).

issued between June 30 and July 2. The first announced that Soviet agents had infiltrated Romania's border area in order to cause disorders and commit acts of aggression, and that these agents had contacted local incendiaries, some of whom had been caught and punished, including five hundred Judeo-communists in Iași, executed for having fired on German and Romanian soldiers. The second warned that "50 judeo-communists" would be executed for each such attack in the future.[12] At the time the second communiqué was issued Leoveanu was in Iași investigating the killings, assisted by Police Chief Chirilovici. Neither they nor other officials found evidence of Jews having firearms or firing at troops or of German or Romanian soldiers having been shot.[13]

Regarding the "death trains," Popescu authorized and Mihai Antonescu approved evacuating survivors of the pogrom by train, an action that some officials characterized as an effort to save Jews from the Germans. We may never know what government leaders intended for the passenger-prisoners, but even when they learned the trains were death traps and there was time to prevent hundreds more from terrible suffering and death they did nothing. While the Călărași train sat in Tîrgu Frumos station, hundreds of its prisoners already dead and hundreds more dying, the fate of those in the train to Podu Iloaiei became known: nearly two-thirds of its passengers had perished in its superheated boxcars. Only a fortunate accident, not the intervention of sympathetic officials, delayed the departure of the Călărași train from Tîrgu Frumos long enough to permit the removal of most of the dead, giving some relief to those still living. For surviving passengers, however, the consequence of having that train continue on for six more days, its cars like ovens in the July heat, was further great suffering and death.

In their postwar trials, high-ranking police officers and General Stavrescu, whose 14th Infantry Division was headquartered in Iași, were not charged with being directly involved in, or organizing, the massacre, but of "participating effectively in its accomplishment." To summarize the charge against them: although they had no evidence that Jews were engaged in subversive actions and knew that men under their command were, nevertheless, assaulting Jews, they took no effective action to stop the crimes. In the case against General Stavrescu, he "came to the police station where Jews had been driven together and were shot . . . [and] had a conference with the top authorities . . . while his officers and soldiers competed with the gendarmes and Germans in committing atrocities."[14] Stavrescu visited the Iași police station three times on June 29 and may have obtained the release of "women, children, and some non-suspects" around the noon hour during his first visit. He returned in the early afternoon, having been informed that the shooting of prisoners had begun. Two of the area's top police officers, District Prefect Colonel Captaru and municipal Police Chief Chirilovici, joined him. While they were there the gunfire subsided, permitting them "to find in the chestură courtyard along the walls a great number of Jews shot dead" and to witness German soldiers viciously beating survivors and others who continued being herded in through the courtyard gates. Captaru claims he and the other officials complained about the killings. After they left, however, the shooting resumed.[15]

It is likely that General Stavrescu was informed about plans to instigate the Iași pogrom and about the general policy of "ethnic cleansing," a policy largely carried out by the military, including his own troops. As I noted above, he was visited on June 26 by SSI officers who, two days later, were involved in triggering the pogrom. In addition, we know that the first instance of ethnic cleansing was the execution of Sculeni Jews on June 27 by one of his units, the Romanian 6th Cavalry Regiment. As I noted before, Colonel Matieș, the regiment's commander, may have had Stavrescu in mind when he claimed he had "superior orders" to carry out the execution. Eleven days after the murder of Sculeni Jews, during the invasion of the Soviet Union by Romanian, German, and Italian forces, the general personally witnessed Matieș's regiment preparing another such massacre at the Bessarabian village of Mărculești. He did not halt the execution or remain to witness the four hundred or more Jews being stripped of valuables and clothing, lined up ten at a time at the edge of an antitank ditch and machine-gunned, first men and then women and children.[16]

Even before the Călărași death train had made its last stop, Stavrescu and Iași police officials, anticipating criminal charges related to the pogrom and death trains, began preparing a defense, picturing themselves in official reports as helpless witnesses to crimes committed by the Germans and their paid or volunteer local sycophants (legionnaires in particular), helpless because they lacked the authority and/or the manpower to intervene effectively. The harmony of this defense was only shaken by the fact that when pressed about their responsibilities to protect the life and property of residents they had only each other to blame for failing to act. One of the more interesting fabrications is revealed by two reports, both of them by Director General of Police and Security Emanoil Leoveanu. These reports have the same date (July 2, 1941), the same number (53), and the same signature. Each purports to be Leoveanu's summary of his investigation into the Iași pogrom. They are different in some important respects. The "earlier" short version claims Jews fired on troops in the city, killing and wounding some German soldiers according to a German officer, and it was this action that provoked, among other reprisals, the brutal searches ("percheziții foarte severe"). No mention is made of Sergeant Manoliu, who murdered six Jews only hours before the pogrom. As for the deportation of Jews who had survived the mass killing, Romanians carried that out in trains General Stavrescu ordered.[17] According to Leoveanu's "later" revised version, Jews did not start the action, did not fire on troops, and the shooting itself was a pretense, simulated by firecrackers and stage-prop pistols. Search teams found no guns and no shooters, and there was no evidence that German or Romanian soldiers had been shot. The attackers are identified as legionnaires and thieves who created a panic in order to pillage. The only casualties were Jews. Sergeant Manoliu is here singled out as a legionnaire and assassin, who should be court-marshaled. German soldiers are faulted for joining Manoliu on the twenty-eighth in a savage search of Jewish homes, of systematically robbing Jews imprisoned in the chestură courtyard, and of turning General Stavrescu's effort to safely evacuate survivors into a second mass killing.[18] Leoveanu's "first" report corresponds to Ion Antonescu's two communiqués (between June 30 and July 2, 1941) blaming Jews for firing on troops in the city; the "second" and, according to Leoveanu, authentic report harmonizes rather with versions of other top Romanian officials after the war, in blaming the Germans. As a general rule, the earliest official reports about the pogrom and trains, those made between June 28 and 30, before Antonescu made public the official version of events, appear closest to the truth.

In a 1945 court deposition General Stavrescu admitted that on the twenty-ninth, despite being informed about severe disorders and visiting the chestură three times, he was primarily concerned with preparing for the coming invasion and unable to do more about the crimes of German soldiers than appeal to their commanding officer, General von Salmuth, commander of the 30th Army Corps (composed of five German and three Romanian divisions). Stavrescu claimed he could do no more because Salmuth was his military superior.[19] Stavrescu did not lack manpower; he had an abundance of soldiers and military police at his disposal and, given his rank and the fact that his 14th Infantry Division was headquartered in the city, the authority to use local police and garrison troops. He not only failed to prevent disorders with this considerable power but also encouraged the violence, cautioning citizens in the June 27 Iași daily *Prutul* not to panic as a result of the previous day's bombing and promising quick and deadly action against enemy agents. That Jews were the target of his remarks is made clear by the fact that he had Police Chief Chirilovici assemble Jewish leaders in order to accuse their community of helping Soviet bombardiers target the city. Besides regular soldiers and military police Stavrescu could have called on the approximately six hundred regular and reserve municipal police under Chief Chirilovici, some four hundred gendarmes and soldiers under Garrison Commander Constantin Lupu, and other gendarmes commanded by Iași District Prefect Dumitriu Captaru. Regarding Stavrescu's claim about being outranked and thus stymied in his efforts to stop the pogrom: Romania was Germany's ally, not a subject but a sovereign state. During the Romanian-German invasion of the Soviet Union military operations in the south were directed by Hitler and General von Schobert, commander of the German 11th Army,[20] but in Romania Ion Antonescu was the supreme commander, and in Iași his general was chiefly responsible for maintaining order. Perhaps Stavrescu believed he had no authority over German troops in the city, but he failed even to restrain his own soldiers from attacking Jews. He said in a postwar "declaration" that he sent out a company of troops during the pogrom to prevent soldiers from interfering in the operations of police and gendarmes, but he also testified that on one occasion he confronted some of his own soldiers convoying Jews toward the chestură and apparently left them to continue after they told him the Germans had ordered them to do so.[21]

On Saturday, June 28, Grațian Sprinceană, police commissar of Iași district II, received three telephone calls from police headquarters, the first two from deputy chief Gheorghe Leahu. In the first call policemen in his district were ordered to turn in all their weapons, then that order was rescinded, and finally, in the third call "policemen were [instructed] not to interfere in what the army was about to do throughout the city, be it good or bad." Sprinceană claimed that because of this last instruction, he had policemen in his charge remain in the district II station that night.[22]

Saturday evening about 9:30 one or more airplanes launched flares or rockets over Iași. This was followed by scattered or simulated gunfire in different parts of the city. Air-raid sirens and shooting sent people scurrying for shelter. At the time Chief Chirilovici and all other top Iași municipal police officers were at the chestură. Other police and military officials were also there or arrived soon after the shooting commenced; they included Garrison Commander Lupu, chief legal officers (praetors) of the Romanian 3rd Army and 14th Infantry Division, Colonel Gheorghe Barozzi and Major Nicolae Scriban, District Inspector of Gendarmes Colonel Gheorghe Bădescu, and regional police inspector Giosanu and subinspector Matei Cosma.[23] As I noted before, their gathering at that place and time indicates they anticipated what was about to happen. Not long after the shooting commenced calls began coming in to the police station reporting that troops were being fired on. The gathered officials responded by sending out patrols to find and arrest the shooters. Generals Stavrescu and Salmuth were informed of these

CHAPTER 10

decisions and sent out their own search teams. Next morning Prefect Captaru reported to the ministry of interior that the previous night's events appeared to be an attempt "to throw suspicion on the Jews . . . leading towards mass murder." In the same report the prefect also points out that on the afternoon of the twenty-eighth the inspector of gendarmes caught a "young legionnaire . . . who had on him a testament written the day before which indicated he was part of a death squad."²⁴ Captaru was not the only official who suspected that the "shooting" was intended to raise a storm against Jews. Still, the authorities continued to send out search teams that invaded Jewish homes, taking valuables, destroying furnishings, and forcing residents into the streets and driving them toward the chestură, bullying or shooting any who resisted.

General Stavrescu ordered continued and expanded searches and arrests at first light on Sunday the twenty-ninth.²⁵ In his report to the interior ministry that evening the general blamed Judeo-communists for terrorizing the city and told of their arrests and "on the spot" executions by German and Romanian soldiers. He said soldiers from both camps had massacred some three hundred hostages at the police station, but that he himself had stopped the killing, removed "all patrols" from the chestură, and got General Salmuth to order the removal of German soldiers. This despite his claim that he had no authority over the general or his troops. Finally, in an effort to maintain the peace, which he reported had been reestablished by nine o'clock Sunday evening, he ordered the evacuation from Iași of about one thousand hostage Jews, who he said were the targets of angry German soldiers. Stavrescu admitted that besides the Germans, "Romanian soldiers, through excessive zeal to catch the guilty . . . contributed to the public terror." He did not point out that besides a slightly injured policeman, the only victims of the "terror" were Jews. In 1945 the general did not repeat his characterization of Jews as Judeo-communist terrorists and claimed Germans alone were responsible for the pogrom, even ordering Romanian soldiers to participate.²⁶

Reserve Colonel Constantin Lupu became garrison commander in Iași on the nineteenth or twentieth of June 1941 and was, after General Stavrescu, mainly responsible for policing the city with his force of several hundred regulars and reserves. This was, practically speaking, Lupu's only responsibility. When top police officers met at Prefect Captaru's office about 4:00 p.m. on the twenty-ninth, Colonel Lupu was charged with securing and pacifying the city and designated "unitary" commander of local police forces. Whereas Stavrescu blamed the Germans and the need to attend to his military mission for not being able to carry out his garrison obligation, Lupu excused his own failure to act by finding fault with other top officials. He reported taking no action when he saw Romanian gendarmes and Germans pulling Jews from their residences and handing them over to other gendarmes to be convoyed to the police station, "because these gendarmes belonged to the Prefect." Instead he "went immediately to the Chestură" to talk with Police Chief Chirilovici and General Stavrescu about the disturbing events. At the police station he witnessed German soldiers savagely beating prisoners as they entered the courtyard. "I waited to receive orders from General Stavrescu," he said, "on what action was needed." Lupu not only failed to protect victims of the slaughter, he himself led a group of gendarmes in carrying out violent searches and arrests. He claimed his own forces were inadequate for restoring order and said this task properly belonged to General Stavrescu, who did have the manpower. Colonel Lupu also said that Prefect Captaru was primarily responsible "for the situation in Iași at the time of the massacre," and that he failed to "give one order or take any measures to stop what was going on."[27]

Captaru excuses his own inaction on the grounds that his "competence as Prefect was only of an administrative kind." At the police station with General Stavrescu late Sunday morning, the prefect said he "saw stretched out along the courtyard wall a large number of Jews who had been shot to death" and reacted by sending a request to the interior ministry for additional troops and the replacement of Colonel Lupu "with a more competent officer." It was Captaru who arranged, on General Stavrescu's orders, for the death trains. Had he made any real effort to have passengers treated no worse than livestock he would have eased much pain and saved many lives. As I noted before, it was Captaru who reported to the interior ministry on June 29 ("That Sunday") the view that weapons' fire during the previous night was meant "to throw suspicion on the Jews" and thus set the stage for their mass murder and he who had requested "drastic measures" from General Stavrescu, Colonel Lupu, and Chief Chirilovici to "prevent by any means . . . a pogrom against the Jews."[28]

Police Chief Chirilovici came to realize on "That Sunday" that the search for weapons and shooters had turned into a raging vendetta in which his own policemen were engaged and that the police station courtyard was becoming a likely shooting arena as it filled with Jews. In a "report" dated June 30 he points out that about an hour before the mass killing in the courtyard, shots were fired into the crowd of prisoners killing some, an action halted by the efforts of Captain Darie, who commanded a Romanian military police company, and a German officer. But the potential for a great slaughter increased as the courtyard continued swelling to "approximately 5,000" prisoners. It was allegedly this danger, and Ion Antonescu's orders,

CHAPTER 10

that convinced General Stavrescu and Colonel Captaru to have prisoners transported out of the city. Stavrescu and other officials claimed the evacuation was necessary to save survivors from further harm, "for fear the Germans would massacre them anew," as Leahu put it. The evacuation did take place, but it was anything but merciful: German troops and Romanians were both responsible for its brutal conduct, and the trains themselves turned out to be death traps.[29] This was known by Iași officials by Monday evening (June 30) because of the hundreds who had died in the Podu Iloaiei train, yet they did nothing to prevent the same horror in the Călărași train that meandered on for six more days.

Military and police authorities met twice on the morning of Sunday the twenty-ninth. Search teams they sent out included, besides soldiers and gendarmes, policemen who had been forced to withdraw from Bucovina and Bessarabia in June 1940 and were in Iași waiting for the invasion and their return to those territories. Like officers and soldiers who carried out the Sculeni massacre, two days before, they were eager to avenge themselves on Jews for a retreat that had come to be characterized as a national humiliation. The new teams were sent out despite the fact that soldiers had suffered no casualties, searches of Jewish residences had turned up no weapons, and the staged shooting itself had ceased. These patrols added to the violence of others, groups of citizens and troops, and individual soldiers who, Police Chief Chirilovici noted, wandered "about the city robbing and mistreating, torturing and even murdering."[30]

Chirilovici committed suicide on June 27, 1947, six years after the pogrom, at a time when the trial of perpetrators was being prepared. His is a special case; he almost certainly knew something about the impending simulated attack on troops in the city. He was directly involved, together with other top police and military officials, in responding to the violence that ensued, and his policemen, individually or in patrols, contributed to the destruction of Jewish life and property. On the other hand he rescued some Jews from almost certain death. Moise Leib was in a convoy when Chirilovici appeared and ordered the hooligan escorts to free their prisoners. Unfortunately, Leib was again arrested by the same thugs who reappeared at his home accompanied by German soldiers. Filip Dauer recalled being pulled from his residence and driven toward the Bahlui River, where he was forced to join "thousands" of Jews lying face down on its banks, in the presence of machine guns mounted and ready to fire into them. "Suddenly," Dauer recalled, "a miracle happened. There appeared the chief of police Col. Chirilovici, who gave the order for our immediate release." Like other police officials, Chirilovici was regularly paid protection money by the Jewish community of Iaşi. Still, his actions were remarkable, unlike most other bribe takers he actually intervened to save Jews. As I noted before, some private citizens and officials, unprotected by high rank or any rank at all, sheltered Jews at great risk to themselves; a few were murdered trying. Others saw in the mortal plight of Jews a chance to profit. Dr. Menachem Mendelsohn recalled that sometime after the pogrom "a soldier brought me a letter from my brother, from Călăraşi . . . to give him 1000 lei for somehow saving him, getting him a glass of water." As for Dauer, his parents and a brother were arrested. His mother was beaten so savagely she never recovered. His sister, having witnessed the shooting death of a neighbor, "went into nervous shock and ran day and night in the street until with difficulty it was possible to bring her back to the house of her parents. I saw her after a few days," said Dauer, "and did not recognize her."[31]

The participation of German soldiers in the massacre of June 29 is documented in a number of eyewitness accounts.[32] In some instances Germans and Romanians united their efforts. This shared criminality is reflected in Romanian officials' earliest reports on the pogrom, that is, before officials settled on a standard version where Germans where the principal if not the sole villains. Police reports about the beatings and robberies in the slaughterhouse district on Saturday the twenty-eighth blame Romanian soldiers of the 13th Infantry and 24th Artillery regiments, in particular Sergeant Manoliu, and some German troops who answered Manoliu's appeal for assistance. In his account of what happened on the night-morning of June 28–29, Police Inspector Giosanu reported that both Romanian and German troops were involved in criminal actions and urgently called on top officials to calm tempers on both sides. He telephoned Director General of Police Leoveanu at 9:30 a.m. on the twenty-ninth to report that searches and arrests were being carried out according to General Stavrescu's orders and being supervised by Romanian military and civil authorities. As I noted above, Stavrescu himself informed the interior ministry on the twenty-ninth that both German and Romanian troops were engaged in searches and arrests.[33]

Official accounts of the pogrom drawn up by officials at the time it occurred (June 28–29) differ from those made three or four days later. Reports of July 2 continue to accuse both Germans and Romanians of violent actions against Jews but now place greater emphasis on the role and responsibility of the Germans. Giosanu complains, for example, that police work and evacuation of Jews was made difficult because of the "pressure of German troops who have been mixed up in everything." Chirilovici claims the Germans initiated the shootings in the police station courtyard because of their concern some of the Jews might escape. Leoveanu claimed the Germans were so furious toward Jews who were set free with the "Liber" permit that they rearrested and beat them, and when the time came to load Jews into the freight cars they prevented Romanian police from taking part and proceeded to overload and then seal the cars shut. Prefect Captaru changed his story radically. On the twenty-ninth he identified Sergeant Manoliu as a murderer and the disturbances of the night before as an attempt to start a pogrom. By the time he sent his July 2 report to the interior ministry he had been to the chestură, seen the "great many Jews who were shot dead" there, and knew also that several hundred Jews had perished in the death trains. Yet none of this is in his July 2 account where he commends the actions of Manoliu (who had executed six Jews), infers Jews had set off the pogrom by firing on German and Romanian troops, alleges that the great majority of Jews arrested on June 29 had been pulled out of houses from which shots had been fired, and were saved from enraged German or Romanian soldiers "or even Christian citizens" by General Stavrescu, who decided to evacuate them from the city by train. Concerning the trains, Captaru says only that the German commander would not allow anyone off the first train at Tîrgu Frumos, its initial extended stop, and that the second train had reached its destination, Podu Iloaiei, "where it was unloaded." The prefect's July 2 report says nothing of the great catastrophe, of the hundreds of Jews who had been murdered on city streets or in the chestură courtyard or the several hundred who had already perished in the trains. The "unloaded" at Podu Iloaiei included some 1,200 dead and dying, most of that train's passengers.[34]

Police Chief Chirilovici and police secretary Gheorghe Stănculescu, reporting on June 30 about events since the twenty-eighth, say nothing of the mass killings; regional police inspector Giosanu referred only vaguely to "the assassination of the 29th"; Captaru refers to "the mistreatment of those in the Chestură," who, by firing weapons, aroused the anger of "German and Romanian soldiers who were charged with keeping the peace."[35] Officials were waiting, it seems, for General Antonescu to give the official version of what had happened before they made their final reports. As I noted above, he did so in a public announcement on June 30, published next day in the government's official records' journal (*Monitorul Oficial*, no. 153): "In Iași 500 judeo-communists who fired on German and Romanian soldiers from their houses were executed." Prefect Captaru's report of June 29 speculating that actions during the night-morning of June 28–29 were intended to provoke the mass murder of Jews was clearly at odds with Antonescu's communiqué. The prefect's July 2 report harmonized with it perfectly.

Local officials who first accused both Romanians and Germans for the Iași pogrom and then heaped most blame on the Germans in reports they made three or four days later, at last, when they were being questioned after the war, in preparation for criminal trials in 1948, declared that the Germans, almost exclusively, were responsible for the murders.³⁶ SSI chief Eugen Cristescu, shortly after the pogrom, bragged that he and Radu Dinulescu, head of military intelligence, had achieved a great thing in Iași. In his postwar testimony, however, he gave credit for provoking the pogrom to German police agencies and their paid Romanian accomplices and said neither he nor his agents were in Iași on June 29, 1941, nor during the days leading up to the pogrom, nor could he provide records of SSI's investigation of the pogrom because, he said, they had been lost.³⁷ As I stated before, Director General of Police Leoveanu, in the first of his two accounts of July 2, 1941, claimed Jews had started the pogrom by shooting at troops and suggested that Germans were among their victims; in his second report (dated and numbered the same) he spreads the blame among legionnaires, thieves, and Germans and counts Jews as victims. In his 1945 testimony he makes Germans the primary villains and claims the Romanian police, though they participated in the searches, arrests, and forced marches to the police station, had not been involved in robbery or murder. Garrison Commander Lupu, in his court deposition, accuses the Germans mainly for the disorders but also blames General Stavrescu, Chief Chirilovici, and Prefect Captaru for not acting or not ordering him to act: "the Prefect of the Județ made no effort to have me, as commander of the garrison, who had troops ready for the purpose of keeping order, do anything." General Stavrescu, in his postwar deposition, said the chestură courtyard massacre was essentially the work of the Germans, including their commander General von Salmuth, and that Romanian soldiers who participated in the actions were ordered to do so by Germans.³⁸ While questions remain about the extent of German participation in the Iași pogrom, no credible evidence indicates that any Jew fired on Romanian and German soldiers, flagged enemy pilots, or in any other way tried to sabotage the Romanian war effort.

The 1947 war crimes indictment of those responsible for the Iași pogrom and death trains identifies, besides high military and civil officials, the active participation of "policemen and police agents . . . joined by some fascist elements in the urban population of Iași," former legionnaires in particular. The Iași police force at the time of the pogrom numbered 451 persons on active duty and 167 reservists. Most of these were ordinary policemen, *gardieni publici:* 384 active and 128 reserve.³⁹ Policemen invaded homes and shelters, terrorized residents, threatening women and children, robbing, extorting money or valuables, beating the men and pulling them into the streets to be driven off. Policeman Gheorghe Bocancea, in his early thirties, was seen beating Jews in the chestură courtyard and kicking the head of Dr. Avram Rosen, a reserve captain in the Romanian army. Policeman Ioan Mînăstireanu, twenty-eight, together with two gendarmes, broke into a number of residences. He took Lipa Favel to a district police station and beat him savagely until he paid his tormentor several thousand lei. During the war Mînăstireanu continued to extort money from Jews, threatening to arrest them for being communists or for not being in compliance with forced labor requirements. Some he robbed repeatedly. A number of other policemen were seen beating, robbing, and murdering Jews.[40]

Ordinary citizens, like Ioan Raitmayer, thirty-seven, who had a shoe repair and barber shop, and his sons, seventeen-year-old Petru, a legionnaire sympathizer, and fourteen-year-old Constantin also participated in thefts and murders. The Raitmayer brothers and some legionnaire companions broke into Jewish homes on Strada Andrei, where the father had his shops, and took the residents to the chestură. Eliza Marcovici, who knew the Raitmayer family, recalled that many of those who were marched away never returned, "among these were my husband and son, Israel Marcovici and Jack." Ety Cohen had known the Raitmayers since 1934 as being very active in the legionnaire movement. She recalled that Petru was among a band of legionnaires who killed her husband. Another witness to these same events recognized among the attackers two or three policemen and a certain Granatiuc, "who carried in his hand a plank he used to beat Jews and especially the Jewish family Moscovici who did not want to leave their home."[41]

Ion Ștefaniu, about fifty-four at the time of the pogrom, a laboratory assistant in the Iași Medical Faculty, married with two children, murdered several Jews. Some of them he beat to death using a club with a "head of iron." Together with two others, gendarmes or soldiers, he beat Lili Wolf, stole her lingerie and money, then threatened to cut off her finger if she refused him her wedding ring. While Ștefaniu was marching Jews to the chestură, a Jewish woman appeared in the street. He blocked her passage, then "hit her with his club across the back until he left her completely senseless."[42] While the Poltog family was being sent to the police station, Petre Martinescu and his wife Elena robbed their home and only departed when the residents returned. The Martinescus, and a band of thugs they were with, left behind the body of Toivi Ceaușu, a deaf mute, who they had beaten to death.[43]

Those murdered were stripped of money, clothes, jewelry, and shoes. Petty extortion and stealing shoes were, of course, at the low end of the action. Theft on a grand scale was the work of government by means of the Romanianization laws of 1940–41, which, among other restrictions, prohibited Jews from owning rural land and commercial enterprises. As I mentioned earlier, some owners took Christian partners in order to salvage a part of their property. The pogrom was a signal for such associates to take over. On June 29 Rebeca Auerbach and her husband Herman were convoyed to the chestură. She was released before the massacre, but he survived the shooting only to die in the Călărași train. Rebeca, who was beaten into a lifelong invalid, not only received nothing for her husband's share in a mill, which continued operating under his two partners, but was hounded by their Christian associate Fotea for whatever money she still had. Ghetzel Buchmann had taken Iași mayor Bogdan Petrica as an associate, in his attempt to keep some woodland he had inherited. Ghetzel, his son, and his wife Roza were arrested and taken to the chestură on the twenty-ninth. She was released but Ghetzel and his son, like Herman Auerbach, died in the Călărași train. On the day of the pogrom, Roza recalled,

> Bogdan Petrica, my husband's associate in the forest . . . did not come to save my husband but sent someone else . . . that same Sunday—a Romanian man—to ask me for the ownership papers. In my confusion I gave him also a valise in which money was hidden. I begged this man, who was older than me, to go with me to the Chestură, taking me as his daughter to save my husband, my brother, and my husband's son, but he said in horror, "it is not possible to go. What is happening at the Chestură is horrible. . . . It's better to hide yourself! Save yourself!" and he didn't go with me.[44]

Emil Vinovschi, a former actor in the National Theater, had a business office on Stradă Stefan cel Mare and for some time had coveted Elias Leibovici's large grocery store next door, on the corner with Stradă Lozonschi. On the twenty-ninth Vinovschi ordered a Romanian patrol to break into the Leibovici residence and pull out the whole family. On Vinovschi's orders Elias, his wife, their daughter, and two others were shot. Next morning Vinovschi discovered that Emil, though seriously wounded, was still alive and ordered a soldier to put a bullet in his head. The bodies were eventually loaded into a garbage wagon and carted off.[45]

Dumitru Dadarlat and his family lived on Stradă Lăpușneanu in a courtyard of apartments with Jewish residents. The building also housed a tavern that appeared to be Dadarlat's but was held in a partnership with Moise Lazar. Vera Botezatu, who managed the eight or nine tavern employees, recalled that in the early afternoon of the twenty-eighth, Dadarlat returned from being "mobilized" and told her and the others to close the tavern early because something frightful was going to happen that evening. Dadarlat himself was gone the whole night, returning about ten Sunday morning, by which time some Jewish men from the courtyard had already been sent to the chestură (from which they did not return). Later in the morning Moise escaped another roundup, but Dadarlat forced him to give him the tavern. Another resident of the same court was Margaretta Rozinfeld, who lived there with her husband and two grown sons. They had escaped the earlier arrests but about 5:00 p.m. were pulled out and taken to the police station. Before their convoy set off, Margaretta begged Dadarlat to intervene on behalf of her husband and sons, but he was not swayed. Having survived a savage beating at the police station she was released and returned to find her home plundered. Also taken to the chestură was Lupu Zilberman, a man about seventy, who owned the courtyard apartments. He was so badly beaten at the police station that his body was thrown into a garbage wagon to be carted off for burial, but a drayman, finding some life in him, took him to the Jewish hospital. Meanwhile, Dadarlat also took over Zilberman's apartment.[46]

CHAPTER 11

The German Connection

In 1939–40 Romania became a main trading partner of Germany, joined the German-Italian-Japan pact (November 1940), and began inviting German military missions into the country to build up its defenses against the Soviet Union.[1] On their side German leaders, though they did not anticipate much in the way of military support from Romania in the upcoming war against the Soviet Union, did see a need for its oil, and to that end were eager to secure firm political ties and close cooperation between their intelligence services. The economic connection was anchored in a treaty of March 23, 1939, which made Germany Romania's major trading partner. By 1940 about half of Romania's imports and exports were from and to Germany. Oil exports to Germany rose from 255,000 tons in 1934 to 1,196,000 tons in 1940.[2] On their side Romanians hoped the alliance would give them security, and for much the same reason their predecessors had joined Bismarck's Triple Alliance (Germany, Austria-Hungary, and Italy) in 1883, believing Germany could counterbalance Russian power.

Shortly after Germany seized Czechoslovakia in March 1939, Great Britain and France promised to support Romania's independence. But following the German-Soviet nonaggression pact of August 23, 1939, and their invasions of Poland in September, Great Britain backed away from insuring Romania against a Soviet takeover. In mid-June 1940, acting on its secret agreement with Germany (at the time of the August 1939 pact) to divide Eastern Europe between them, the Soviet Union swallowed up Estonia, Latvia, and Lithuania. A few days later France fell to Germany. Now the ax fell on Romania; on June 26 the Soviet Union ordered Romania out of Bessara-

CHAPTER 11

bia and Northern Bucovina and quickly moved in. Carol's government, despite brave words in the past about honor and "to the last man," abandoned the territories without a fight and having already sought ties with Germany drew even closer. Not close enough, however, to dissuade Hitler from having Romania stripped of two more territories: northwestern Transylvania, to Hungary on August 30, 1940, and southern Dobrodgea, to Bulgaria on September 7, 1940.

Public anger in Romania arising from their country being pulled apart was directed against King Carol and Germany. The king was forced to run for his life out of the country, on the day Dobrodgea was amputated. For the Nazi regime, however, the matter was resolved rather well. First of all, a break between Romania and Germany was unlikely, given Romania's isolation, its economic needs, and the Soviet threat. Second, the Carol dictatorship was replaced by the pro-German power-sharing government of Ion Antonescu, a sure-handed fifty-eight-year-old military professional, and the Iron Guard, who saw themselves and the Nazis as ideological kinsmen.[3]

This ideological kinship was part of the glue that, besides political and economic necessities, held the Romanian-German partnership together. On the Romanian side prominent scholars, publishers, churchmen, and ministers, along with Swastika-ornamented fascist Green Shirts and Blue Shirts (Legionnaires and Lancers), were drawn to the Third Reich. A. C. Cuza and his son Gheorghe, a professor, like his father, at the University of Iași, and director of the fascist-racist newspaper *Cetatea Moldovei* (*Fortress Moldavia*), attended a massive Nazi Party rally in Nuremberg in 1934 and came away delighted with what they saw. The following year A. C. Cuza and his political partner, poet Octavian Goga, paid what they considered to be a highly satisfactory visit to Hitler. Both men were early and strong admirers of the Führer and Nazism. Codreanu's legionnaires saw themselves and the Nazis as part of the same fascist brotherhood of militant nationalists, Jew-haters, and anticommunists.[4]

The Nazi revolution appealed especially to a number of prominent Romanian intellectuals. Nichifor Crainic (1889–1972), theologian, philosopher, member of LANC and its successor, the National Christian Party, and minister of propaganda (1940–41), was a great admirer of German culture and the Nazis.[5] He promoted antisemitic ideas in *Gîndirea* (*Contemplation*), an influential literary review he edited. Among Crainic's adherents was the philosopher Nae Ionescu, who edited the daily *Cuvântul* (*The Word*) and himself had a following of young intellectuals, including Iron Guard enthusiast Mircea Eliade (1907–1986) and "exultant" Hitlerist Emil Cioran (1911–1995). A notable exception to the trend was Nicolae Iorga. His ties

THE GERMAN CONNECTION

to Germany included a doctorate from the University of Leipzig, but he opposed Nazism, Hitlerists like Goga, and even the Iron Guard whose leader, Codreanu, considered him an ideological founder of his movement.[6]

Nazi leaders, on their side, began developing ties with prominent Romanian fascists through Alfred Rosenberg's Foreign Office. In June 1934 Rosenberg, Himmler, and other Nazi officials decided to spend 750,000 marks on advancing their aims in Romania, in particular securing oil and other raw materials for Germany. Romanian fascists were quite receptive to this attention, which, from the late 1930s, was largely handled by the SD (SS Security Service: Sicherheitsdienst), part of Heydrich's large police operation. How much money was actually given and to whom is not known. Likely benefactors were leaders of the National Christian Party, Goga and A. C. Cuza, and Iron Guardists. The guardists in particular were seen as allies by SS leaders, including Himmler and Heydrich.[7]

Regarding the "Jewish Problem," Germany's efforts to weaken and dispose of its Jews in the 1930s reinforced the same trend in Romania and not just in modeling some of its anti-Jewish decrees on the 1935 Nuremberg Laws. Even before the monarchy was overthrown in September 1940, the idea of a Romanian final solution involving Germany was being considered by some of the country's leaders. When Carol's minister-president Ion Gigurtu met with Hitler on July 26, 1940, he told the Führer that Romania had begun to solve its own "Jewish question," but that a final solution could not take place without his assistance in carrying out "a total solution for all Europe." Still, he cautioned that any sudden removal of Jews from Romania's economy would harm his country. Hitler replied that Jews in Germany had proven themselves "to be absolutely dispensable." Hours before meeting with the Führer, Gigurtu had raised the same issues with Ribbentrop, who told him Germany would certainly settle her own Jewish question and perhaps find a European-wide solution.[8]

Despite the spiritual and ideological closeness of the SS and Iron Guard, Hitler supported Antonescu in his showdown with the Legion in January 1941. And he got what he wanted: a Romania free of Iron Guard disorders and under the steady hand of a staunch ally who controlled the army. From his first days as head of the National-Legionnaire State, Antonescu had eagerly offered his support to Germany and welcomed visits by top German military commanders. On November 23, 1940, Romania joined the Three-Power Pact (Germany, Italy, Japan) and invited German military missions into Romania to prepare its army to fight. That mission began arriving the following month; its stated purpose was to ready Romanian defenses against a Soviet attack, but its real purpose was to secure the country's supply of oil

CHAPTER 11

and other raw materials for Germany and to get ready for "Operation Barbarossa." German commanders saw the military role of its ally as defensive and secondary because they doubted its combat readiness. In March 1941, German troops in the country began preparing for the invasion, and in May General Eugen Ritter von Schobert, who was to direct operations in the south, took command of all German troops in Romania. His 11th Army was headquartered at Piatra Neamț, a little more than 60 miles (100 kilometers) west of Iași and the Soviet border as the crow flies. Antonescu likely guessed that Germany planned an invasion from the deployment of its military forces along the border (Prut River), but Hitler instructed his officers to explain the buildup as preparation for a Soviet "surprise attack." Not until Antonescu met with Hitler on June 12, 1941, was he officially informed about the invasion, that is, only ten days before the general assault on the USSR and twenty days before Operation München (July 2, 1941), when the German 11th and Romanian 3rd and 4th armies joined the campaign.[9]

At that June 12 meeting Antonescu and Hitler were joined by Armed Forces Chief Field Marshal Wilhelm Keitel, General Alfred Jodl, and Major General Arthur Hauffe, chief of staff of the military mission in Romania. Antonescu expressed his wholehearted desire to have Romania fight alongside Germany from the outset.[10] According to official records of their first two meetings, November 22–23, 1940, and January 14, 1941, Hitler and Antonescu did not discuss the "Jewish question." In fact, the Nazis had not yet devised a comprehensive program for mass extermination. Goering's instructions to Heydrich to draw up such a plan (July 31, 1941), the Wannsee Conference (January 20, 1942), and negotiations between Himmler and the German general staff (beginning in March 1941) on the matter of a military accommodation with the Reichsführer-SS's special mission (annihilating communists and Jews) in conquered Soviet territory, were weeks or months away. However, at their June 12, 1941, meeting, according to Antonescu, the two leaders did discuss the fate of Jews in the conquered territories. Although the official record of their talks is silent on the matter, the general claimed Hitler told him what Germany intended to do. He made this claim during the invasion to verify that the actions of his own forces against Jews in areas that fell under Romanian jurisdiction, namely, mass murder and forced deportation to the east, were in full agreement with the Führer's plans.[11] We do not know if Hitler's revelations at the June meeting persuaded Antonescu that the moment was right for "cleansing" Romanian territory of Jews, but within a week of his return to Romania from the meeting, Antonescu dispatched the 160-man mobile SSI unit (Echelon 1) on its mission, first to set off the pogrom in Iași and then to join the general German-Romanian attack against Jews in conquered Soviet territory.

SSI chief Eugen Cristescu testified after the war that his agents were not in Iași at the time of, nor had anything to do with, the pogrom, and that the perpetrators were Germans, in particular, agents of three German police and intelligence services he said were in the city: Gestapo, SD, and secret field police (Geheime Feldpolizei). Cristescu said the chestură massacre was carried out by Death's Head (Totenkopf) troops deliberately provoked when shots were fired over their heads by Germans and Romanians employed by these intelligence agencies. Cristescu's claims are not credible, but some survivors also accuse the Totenkopf of the chestură massacre. Rebeca Auerbach said Death's Head troops had taken over the police station by the time she was released shortly before the massacre. Evidence that might clear up such matters is gone. SSI records of the Iași pogrom were lost, according to Cristescu, and just hours after Antonescu was deposed, Germans destroyed records of their own intelligence and security services in Romania by bombing (on August 25, 1944) the Bucharest hotel Splendid Parc in which those documents were kept.[12]

Did the Germans, as Cristescu claims, participate in planning and executing the Iași pogrom? We know that the intelligence services of Germany and Romania had established close ties well before June 1941. It is this closeness and the fact that Major Hermann von Stransky, a German military intelligence (Abwehr) officer, was involved in triggering the Iași pogrom, that point to more than an incidental link between agents of the two countries and the massacre. Stransky, a member of the German legation in Bucharest, was assigned to section "G" of Romania's intelligence service (SSI: Serviciul Special de Informații). Section "G" (liaison with the Germans) was commanded by Lieutenant Colonel Constantin Micandru. Stransky came from Vienna but had lived in Romania, spoke the country's language like a native, and carried Romanian papers identifying him as Alexandru Stavrescu. In the German legation he was the assistant of Colonel Erich Rödler, Abwehr chief for Romania. Also in the legation, from April 1941, was Eichmann's representative Captain Gustav Richter. Richter vigorously promoted an anti-Jewish policy in Romania, wanted Romanian Jews tightly concentrated and administered, and to do this pressed for the creation of a Central Jewish Office (Centrală Evreilor) and the appointment of Naziphile Radu Lecca to be its director. Both he and Lecca aimed at having Jews sent to Nazi death camps in Poland. Richter was also a favorite of Mihai Antonescu who saw him as a necessary ally in organizing a Romanian final solution. If members

CHAPTER 11

of the German legation had a hand in initiating and planning the Iași pogrom, their number would most likely have included Rödler, Stransky, and Richter.[13]

The postwar testimony of Traian Borcescu is a principal source of information about the links between intelligence services of the two countries on the eve of the invasion of the Soviet Union and what Romania's intelligence services intended for the country's Jews. Romanian military intelligence (Section II of the Supreme General Staff) employed Borcescu between 1938 and 1941. From there he moved to SSI, first as chief of its secretarial services (May to December 1941) and then as head of its counterintelligence section. Borcescu described Colonel Radu Dinulescu, commander of Section II (1941–43), as a "passionate Germanophile" and the work of Section II early in 1941 as largely occupied with the Jews of Moldavia (number, urban-rural distribution, infiltration of industry, military personnel, communists, spies, and enemy sympathizers), establishing camps or ghettos to imprison dangerous Jews, and preparing to act against Soviet agents parachuted into Romanian territory. When Borcescu came to SSI he was impressed by the importance of Micandru's "G" section as a main link between SSI and the intelligence services in the German legation. He claimed SSI shared all its information on communists and Jews with the legation and shared with Abwehr "all information regarding the status of Romanian military units as well as information about . . . commanders of Romania's major units."

Regarding the Iași massacre, Borcescu said his own secretary, who had participated in the killing, told him that Cristescu was there at the time with the entire SSI Operational Echelon 1 and on the day of the pogrom sent a report (one that Borcescu himself had seen) of the action to General Antonescu. Borcescu also said he saw an album of photographs taken on the day of the pogrom by Cristescu's brother Gheorghe with explanatory notes by Echelon teams' leader Florin Becescu-Georgescu. Most photographs showed streets with bodies of Jews scattered about; some showed walls riddled with bullets, evidence according to the notes that Jews, stirred up by Soviet partisans, had fired on Romanian and German soldiers as they moved through the city on their way toward the front. In two photographs soldiers, "victims" of the Jewish attack, were shown sprawled "murdered" on a street. The executioners of Jews were identified, in the album's notes, as "German SS and Romanian soldiers and police"; those executed at the chestură and elsewhere around the city were estimated to be about twenty thousand. Borcescu believed the pogrom was planned and carried out mainly, but not exclusively, by SSI Echelon 1. As I noted before, Echelon 1

THE GERMAN CONNECTION

got information about the Jewish population (its "hotbeds and centers") in Iași from SSI officers in the city and from Romanian military intelligence. According to Borcescu, it was with this information that SSI chief Cristescu, "together with Section II of the Supreme General Staff and with the German command, worked out plans to bring about the Iași massacre." Assisting SSI Echelon 1 teams assigned the work of setting off the pogrom was Colonel Micandru's German liaison, or "G" unit, officers including Major Stransky. Micandru and Stransky arrived in Iași on June 26 and spent some time with General Stavrescu, likely informing him of the plan to set off the pogrom. The postwar testimony of Constantin Rădulescu, another liaison officer, indicated that Stransky played some role in the action. Rădulescu recalled a December 1941 dinner honoring SSI chief Cristescu where he overheard Micandru say to Stransky "we intend to do away with the Jews, just as we did in Iași . . . not so, Sandu?"[14] As an Abwehr officer Stransky almost certainly kept his boss, Colonel Rödler, informed about the Iași mission, and he would have also shared that information with General von Salmuth whose 30th Army Corps was headquartered in Iași.

German soldiers who took an active part in the pogrom belonged to Salmuth's army corps. As I noted before these soldiers participated in all aspects of the pogrom, including the slaughter inside the chestură courtyard. They worked alongside Romanians in the brutal loading and sealing of the "death trains." At some stations where the Călărași train was halted on its meandering journey German officers and soldiers prevented efforts to aid the captive passengers. Police inspector Leahu reported on July 2 that late on the morning of the twenty-ninth a number of Romanian officials came to the chestură and Stavrescu personally intervened to have "women, children, and other non-suspects" set free. According to Leahu, this so enraged the Germans that after the general left, besides continuing to bludgeon Jews entering the courtyard, they began shooting those inside. This action brought Stavrescu back, accompanied by police officials. While they were there the shooting stopped, but after they left, Leahu reported, "the massacre continued." Rebeca Auerbach, who had been released from the courtyard before the massacre, said it had been completely taken over by Death's Head troops. Community president Iacob claimed German soldiers carried out "the machine-gun massacre." A certain Marcel Braunstein, who recorded in some detail his recollections of the pogrom, wrote that SS Captain Alfred Ringer came into the courtyard and stopped the issuing of "Liber" permits, and after that "German machine guns went to work."[15] Adrian Radu-Cernea (Zwieback), who escaped over the courtyard wall when the shooting began, claims that in the courtyard "with my own eyes I saw Germans wearing the characteristic uniform of the Organisation Todt," and that it was these Germans who began machine-gunning the prisoners when the air-raid siren went off. Other survivor accounts identify Romanians as the shooters. Beniamin Rabinovici was in line for a "Liber" paper when an air-raid warning sounded, followed after a few minutes by gunfire that, he recalled, "suddenly opened up above us from windows in the upper floors and from policemen." Max Gaer was in the courtyard for the second time when, about 2:00 p.m., the gate was closed and a siren went off. Gaer recalled that a few minutes later the shooting began from machine guns mounted on the walls of the station and from "police officers and sergeants stationed in windows of the upper floors firing into the mass with pistols and rifles." Iancu Naftule, like Gaer, in the courtyard for the second time when the mass killing occurred, remembered seeing Germans beat Jews as they entered the courtyard and saw municipal policemen shooting "many" prisoners.[16] Some survivors may have mistakenly identified German soldiers at the chestură as members of the Totenkopf Formation, but I do not recall any survivor account that denies the participation of German soldiers in the general action against Jews outside the police station during the pogrom. Some survivors describe particular instances, for example, the rounding up of Jews in residential courtyards, where German soldiers took part in the action, and most survivors who mention the gauntlet at the chestură gate report German soldiers among those bludgeoning Jews.[17]

In late June or early July, around the time of the pogrom, Sonderkommando 10a (Sk10a) passed through the city of Iași. Sk10a was a subunit of Einsatzgruppe D (EgD), one of the four SS mobile killing teams assigned the task of killing communist officials and Jews during the invasion of the Soviet Union. Sk10a team members who said they remembered Iași, in their postwar depositions, claimed they came into the city after the pogrom, which some understood had been "a Jewish rebellion," but denied having anything to do with it. Erich B____ said he hardly remembered most Romanian towns, but Iași stood out in his memory because there he first experienced "a so-called pogrom" and because it was in Iași that SK10a commander Heinz Seetzen explained to his men "more precisely" their assignment. Erich said when SK10a entered the city he witnessed "an action" by the Romanian military against Jews and saw bodies of murdered civilians lying in the streets. At the train station he said he saw corpses closely packed together in an open freight car.[18] What draws our attention to Sk10a is the fact that one tactic the Einsatzgruppen used to kill Jews was to instigate pogroms by encouraging local antisemites to do the killing for them. An early example of such "self-cleansing actions" occurred on June 25–26, 1941, three days before the Iași pogrom, when Einsatzgruppe A "set in motion" a pogrom in Kovno, Lithuania,[19] in which several hundred Jews were murdered. Abwehr officers like Colonel Rödler and Stransky might have suggested such a method to Romanian intelligence officials as a way to destroy the Jewish community of Iași. Regarding SK10a itself, no evidence has surfaced linking it to the Iași massacre.

Conclusion

Adrian Radu-Cernea (Zwieback) was one of only five Jews admitted to the University of Iași for the 1939 fall term, and he was one of the few Jews who not only escaped from the chestură courtyard when the shooting began but was not recaptured and returned to the ongoing massacre. On "That Sunday" he and his father were among those rounded up and driven to the police station where they managed, keeping close together, to get safely into the courtyard through the gauntlet of club-wielding soldiers at the gate. Inside they were separated, about the time the shooting began. In the first moments of that horror the son scrambled over the courtyard wall and made his way safely home. There, provisioned by his mother, he hid himself in the wreckage of a bathroom damaged during one of the Soviet bombings. On the evening of his second day in hiding, Tuesday, July 1, his mother brought him news about the neighbors. Their grocer Mr. Leibovici and his whole family had been shot to death, their doctor had also been murdered, and Mr. Olivenbaum had been killed and placed in the window of his hat store with a machine gun in his arms—"evidence" that Jews had shot at troops in the city. Newspapers the next two days included official communiqués from Ion Antonescu: first, that "500 Judeo-communists" had been executed in Iași for firing on German and Romanian soldiers, and second, that for each repetition of such acts fifty Judeo-communists would be executed. Writing about these events years later, Adrian describes having been stunned by what was happening: "I said to myself: 'Why must we remain in these cursed places, poisoned by this primitive antisemitism, by so much grief for so long?'"[1]

The poisoning began when early Christians alleged that Adrian's ancient

CONCLUSION

ancestors had murdered Jesus and were the offspring of Satan. Among many later allegations, one especially had horrific consequences—that Jews killed Christian children for their blood to be used in the making of Passover bread. In the late nineteenth century this largely Christian mythology was supplemented or replaced by pseudo-scholars who gave Jew hatred a name (antisemitism) and offered, as scientific fact, that Jews were a race apart. While the new "science" certainly reached Romania, Jew hatred there continued to be driven mainly by the old Christian myths and the particular circumstances of the country's own history.

At the very outset of that history, in the struggle for an independent and unified country, a new crime was added to the ancient and medieval list, namely, the effort of Romanian Jews to become citizens of the emerging state. At first citizenship seemed within reach because a number of Romanian leaders, seeking wide support in 1848 for their national aims, called for the political emancipation of Jews. However, when independence was about to be achieved in the 1860s and a national constitution had to be written, the question of Jewish citizenship presented itself unequivocally. Lawmakers, even some who had earlier called for the Jews' emancipation, said no: no to the appeals of resident Jews, to international Jewry, and to other governments. And though the constitution was revised in 1879 to admit Romanian Jews to citizenship, a demand made by European powers at the Congress of Berlin, the policy remained unchanged, bureaucratic hurdles being raised to effectively deny what the revised law required. Finally, in the aftermath of World War I, the Romanian government bowed to international pressure, sweetened by a gift of territory that doubled the country's size and population, and granted citizenship.

Christian university students led the widespread and clamorous opposition against citizenship. They called for *numerus clausus* or *numerus nullus,* restricting the number of Jewish students in, or eliminating them altogether from, public schools. Out of the student movement grew a broader campaign against Jewish inclusion. Jews were to be removed from, or be given a greatly diminished role in, the political, economic, and cultural life of the country. Some on the right saw removal from the country, a statewide application of *numerus nullus,* as the logical solution to the "Jewish Question." The antisemitic right rode this issue for all it was worth. Fascist militiamen wearing uniforms adorned with swastikas terrorized Jews with impunity. Most successful were members of the Legion of the Archangel Michael, or Iron Guard, founded in 1927 by Corneliu Codreanu. His aim was to cleanse Romania, by murder if necessary, of corruption and Jews. The public disposition toward him and his aims and methods may be gauged by the outcome

CONCLUSION

of two trials, one in 1924 when Codreanu, among others, was tried for conspiring to kill corrupt officials and Jews in Bucharest and another in 1925 for murdering the Iași prefect (district police chief) who was, he claimed, in the pay of Jews. Codreanu was guilty of both crimes, but in court defenders focused the jurors' attention on Codreanu's patriotism, and he was promptly acquitted. Large crowds gathered at each trial and greeted the verdicts and their hero with rousing cheers. Jurors who heard the murder case returned to the courtroom to render their verdict wearing swastika-decorated lapel ribbons. The growing public support for Codreanu showed itself emphatically in the December 1937 national election in which his party, renamed Totul pentru Țară, or All for the Country (to dodge a government ban), got the third largest number of seats in Romania's parliament.

Romania's government moved far in the direction of *numerus clausus* and *numerus nullus* between December 1938 and June 1941, taking from Jews many of their legal and property rights and excluding them from a wide range of occupations. Notable in this process were the Citizenship Revision Law of 1938 and the Nazi-inspired racist laws of August 8–9, 1940. Day by day the Jews' material and political means were diminished, leaving them with no institutions (police, political parties, law courts, legislature, democratic newspapers) outside their own communities, to which they could turn for support or protection. Even the possible benefits of Western influence diminished as Romania drew closer to Nazi Germany.

Before draconian laws had completely stripped Romanian Jews of political and economic means, however, they were staggered, beginning in late June 1940, by a series of murders and a five-month Iron Guard reign of terror. More than a hundred Jews were murdered by Romanian military units during their forced retreat from Bessarabia and Northern Bucovina at the end of June and beginning of July 1940; several Jews were murdered, eleven in Ploiești, and many others around the country were beaten and robbed or had their property stolen or destroyed by legionnaires during the National-Legionnaire government (September 1940–January 1941); and in Bucharest during the legionnaire rebellion of January 21–23, 1941, hundreds of Jews were brutalized and at least 120 murdered while their homes, businesses, and synagogues were vandalized and destroyed. These events were not altogether different from attacks against Romanian Jewish communities in the past or those directed against neighboring Ukrainian and Russian communities around the turn of the century. Still, for Romanian Jews, the magnitude and degree of violence directed against them, all in a period of seven months, was extraordinary and terrifying.

By mid-June 1941 Romanian Jews had become the targets of a national

CONCLUSION

vendetta: individually thrown from moving trains or murdered in mass; stripped of legal rights, property, and employment; in some cases deported to prison camps; watched by the police; reviled in the press. Where could they turn? Not to Antonescu's government, the Orthodox Church, the courts or press, all pillars of antisemitism, or to the generally unsympathetic Christian public, growing more or less accustomed to political violence and crimes against Jews. We know now that at this time, on the eve of war against the Soviet Union, Romanian Jews were in mortal danger. The state had turned them into defenseless aliens and become an ally of Nazi Germany, which was prepared to annihilate Jews in conquered Soviet territories, some of which (Northern Bucovina, Bessarabia, and Transnistria) were to come under Romanian rule. These circumstances presented the country's leaders with an opportunity for finally eliminating their own "Jewish problem."

Direct action began, however, not in the conquered occupied territories but in Moldavia, in the Romanian homeland, the *Regat* or Old Kingdom, on June 27, 1941, at Stânca Rosnovanu, a few miles north of Iași, where officers and soldiers of the Romanian 6th Cavalry Regiment executed 311 men, women, and children taken from the town of Sculeni just across the Prut River in Soviet territory. These Jews were robbed, the men forced to dig ditches, and then all, small children clinging to their mothers' necks, lined up along the trenches and machine-gunned. Regiment Commander Colonel Matieș claimed he had "superior orders" to carry out the execution. The second massacre began the next evening in the nearby city of Iași, a pogrom ignited by Romania's intelligence service (SSI). Jews were murdered in their homes or in the streets; many were beaten with heavy clubs or crowbars; some were raped; homes were plundered; watches and money stolen; jewelry ripped from fingers and ears; several hundred, perhaps thousands, were killed by gunfire in the courtyard of the municipal police station the following afternoon (Sunday the twenty-ninth), and approximately 2,700 survivors of the mayhem died in two trains that some officials claimed were meant to get them out of harm's way. In the case of the earlier massacres of Jews, by Romanian soldiers retreating from Bucovina and Bessarabia in June–July 1940 and by Iron Guardists in Bucharest during the rebellion of January 1941, the Romanian government failed to protect the innocent victims or punish the killers. In the case of the mass murders of Sculeni and Iași Jews, the government itself was responsible.

Romania's turn to a policy of annihilation came following a succession of ruthless antisemitic governments (from December 1937 to June 1941). These governments (Goga-Cuza, King Carol, National-Legionnaire, and Ion Antonescu) enacted laws aimed at destroying the Jews' political rights and

CONCLUSION

their very livelihood and for the most part proved themselves willing observers of the murders, even mass murders, of Jews. In the June–July 1940 massacres that occurred during the reign of Carol II more than a hundred Jews (including children) were murdered, some mutilated before they were killed. One investigator wrote, turning perpetrators into victims and vice versa, that the soldiers killed because they had been "humiliated and mocked" by Jews during the retreat.[2] Ion Antonescu elevated that accusation to a national disgrace, and he used it, during the invasion of the Soviet Union, to justify the punishing attack on Jewish communities in these same territories—a payback for that humiliation. Not only were the killers not punished, some returned during the invasion, through the same towns and villages they had ravaged before, intent on completing their revenge. In the second great prewar massacre, the murder of at least 120 Jews in Bucharest during the Iron Guard uprising of January 21–23, 1941, captured rebels were punished but not for killing Jews. Antonescu, who held the Romanian army back during the massacre, cynically intimated later that he had saved Jews by finally crushing the rebellion but would not save them again should they turn against him.

What likely turned the Romanian government from a passive or acquiescent bystander in the killing of Jews into the chief agency of their destruction was its alliance with Nazi Germany and their united attack on the Soviet Union. The fact that Germany was moving on a parallel course toward solving its own "Jewish problem" attracted the interest of Romanian leaders. That interest was signaled in July 1940 when Prime Minister Ion Gigurtu proposed to Hitler that Romania wanted to eliminate its Jews but could only do so in the context of a Führer-orchestrated "final solution for all Europe."[3] The war itself was propitious; it meant the complete subjugation of Jews in the conquered territories and a screen to hide mass murder and brutal deportations. Thus for Romania, on the eve of war, the way to genocide lay open.

Antonescu likely decided to launch the government's genocidal operation in mid-June 1941 around the time of his June 12 meeting with Hitler or during the week that followed. He claimed Hitler told him at that meeting what Germany planned to do with Jews living in the conquered territories.[4] What did Romania plan to do? Mihai Antonescu answered that question on June 17 when he told the Council of Ministers that "removal of foreign elements" from the occupied territories would be "total and violent."[5] The initial assault came ten days later on June 27 at Stânca Rosnovanu, followed over the next few days by the Iași pogrom and death trains (June 28 to July 6). That the pogrom was a government-staged event is made clear by the testimony of Lieutenant Colonel Traian Borcescu, chief secretary of SSI, and by the fact

CONCLUSION

that around nine o'clock Saturday evening, June 28, 1941, when the shooting began, all top police officials in the area (municipal and district), together with officers representing the two major Romanian military units in and around the city (the 14th Infantry Division and 3rd Army), were gathered at the municipal police station, ready to monitor and direct the action.[6]

Three days after the pogrom, on July 2, before the Călărași death train had reached its last stop, Army Group South (mainly the German 11th and Romanian 3rd and 4th armies) attacked the Soviet Union, advancing into Bucovina and Bessarabia. Actions there against Jews—murder, beatings, rape, theft—were carried out by combat troops and special mobile units, German Einsatzgruppe D and Romanian SSI Echelon 1. Jews who escaped being killed were rounded up and evacuated to camps and ghettoes in Transnistria. Those who survived the brutal detentions and deportations were likely to be killed in the camps: worked to death by their Romanian or German masters or shot, burned alive, or left to perish from exposure, disease, and famine.[7] According to an enumeration by Romanian officials there were 156,121 Jews living in Bessarabia, Bucovina, and the Dorohoi district of northern Moldavia on September 1, 1941. Nine months later that number had been reduced to 19,576 persons.[8]

Romanian military units and other government agencies that carried out mass killings at Stânca Rosnovanu and Iași took part in "cleansing" the conquered territories in a campaign of pogroms, indiscriminate shootings, mass executions, deportations, and internment. In the Transnistrian camps or along the roads leading to them Jews were murdered by "natural death": starvation, sickness, exposure, exhaustion. One constant feature of these actions was theft. The Antonescu government led the way; even before it began killing operations it enriched itself by legalizing the theft of Jewish rural and urban property, prohibiting Jews from owning such property and requiring its transfer to the state. The first victims of the Romanian Holocaust, the Jews of Sculeni, were forced to surrender their valuables before they were executed. One of the unresolved conflicts among perpetrators was the division of spoils. The government claimed proprietorship, but soldiers and police kept what they could of stolen valuables. Greed's constant partner was murder and brutality, including maiming and rape.

Had the war not turned against Romania and her Axis partners the annihilation would almost certainly have been resumed in the Romanian heartland where it began. Some 300,000 Jews remained there during the war; in fear of being killed, sent to Transnistria, having what little remained to them expropriated, or being forced into hard, unpaid, and demeaning labor, and facing a myriad of other discriminations beyond the difficult circumstances brought on by the war. What did Antonescu have in mind for them? Would he give them to the Germans? Because Germany depended heavily on Romanian oil and because he was Hitler's trusted ally, Antonescu's decision in this regard was crucial, not something the SS was likely to override. What he wanted was a Romania rid of Jews, and early in the war, as German and Romanian troops rapidly advanced eastward toward Stalingrad and the Caucasus, prospects for a comprehensive "cleansing" appeared to be within reach. The numbers of Jews killed by Einsatzgruppen (Egs) are astounding: EgC reported on October 2 that units under its command "executed 33,771 Jews in Kiev [at Babi Yar] on September 29 and 30, 1941"; EgD reported that its Kommandos had executed 35,782 Jews and communists in and around the cities of Nikolayev and Kherson between September 16 and 30; at Odessa on October 23–24 as many as 40,000 Jews were murdered by German and Romanian units under Romanian command.[9] So encouraged were Romanian leaders by the early success of the "cleansing" operation that they began to contemplate a near future when not only Jews would be eliminated from their territories. In November 1941 Vice President Mihai Antonescu asked Hitler what was to be done with the many Ukrainians and other Slavic peoples living in conquered territories (between the Prut and Bug rivers) then under Romanian control. "The great difficulty in moving Europe toward a future peace," he said, "is solving the Slavic problem." Despite living in Europe for centuries, claimed Mihai, the Slavs had remained aliens to the spirit and civilization of Europe, and because of their high birth rate were a biological time bomb. "It is necessary," he said, "to find a radical and genuine solution to these problems," a solution in which all Europe should cooperate. Regarding his own country, he said, "the Romanian people are and always have been anti-Slavic just as they have always been inherently anti-Semites."[10]

On August 17, 1942, Martin Luther, a divisional chief in the German Foreign Office, informed his Foreign Ministry that the two Antonescus had consented to have Germany begin deporting Romanian Jews to its Belzec death camp. Radu Lecca, Romania's chief commissar for Jewish affairs, was invited to Berlin to participate, along with Gustav Richter (Eichmann's representative in Romania) in an August 19 conference on the deportations and another meeting in Berlin on September 26–28 to put the plan in its final form. On October 10, 1942, the Romanian government decided to begin deportations. Next day, however, Marshal Antonescu canceled that decision.[11] He may have been offended because Lecca had been snubbed by the Germans back in August when they were planning the deportations. He may have been swayed by pleas of political and religious authorities in and out of Romania: the papacy, the Romanian metropolitan Bălan, Romania's chief rabbi Șafran, and US secretary of state Cordell Hull who, on September 13, 1942, first day of the Jewish New Year, delivered "an emotional message of sympathy . . . from the American people" for the persecuted Jews of Europe.[12]

Apologists for Antonescu liken him to a savior for preventing deportations to Nazi death camps. They also claim he saved tens of thousands of Jews in Transnistria from being slaughtered by retreating German troops. We don't know what the dictator was thinking, but the facts are clear—during the first months of the war he advanced Romania's own solution to its Jewish question, brutal deportations and mass murder. He changed his mind about sending Romanian Jews to the German death camps but not, it seems, because he was stricken with remorse or for the sake of Jews, some of whom were still being killed in Transnistria more than a year after he rejected the Nazi deportation plan. Still, thousands of Jews who were being moved through the killing process lived because the dictator changed course. Perhaps his early confidence in an Axis victory was shaken and he saw some practical advantage for Romania and himself in retreating from genocide, but that he was a savior is nonsense. He was a mass murderer who stopped short of killing all his intended victims.

History never entirely settles on a single starting point. The massacres of 1940–41, which are the harbingers of Romania's wartime policy of annihilation, are themselves legacies of a violent past. Wilhelm Filderman anticipated the coming disaster. In his memoir, under the year 1935, he noted, "little by little the antisemitic excesses transformed themselves into a real collective psychosis. . . . Barbarous myths of 'national purity' of blood, of ritual murder, poisoned the atmosphere."[13] Filderman described the 1890s, decade of the Dreyfus calamity and pogroms in Bucharest and Iași, as a time of ominous rumbling. Two early documented instances of antisemitic violence were the murder of five Jews of Tîrgu-Neamț in 1710 and two more in Roman four years later.[14] Religious feelings, stirred by charges of ritual murder, helped promote the killings, but other motives must explain the sadistic beatings and thievery. A sad irony of such actions, then and later, was reporting that often inverted victim and perpetrator, making victims out to be agents of their own deserved suffering. History never entirely settles on a stopping place. The Iași massacre is linked to Romania's antisemitic past and is not altogether different from earlier pogroms, but it also belongs to what came after, the state-administered genocidal crimes of the twentieth century and beyond.

Notes

PREFACE

1. K. Treptow and M. Popa, eds., *Historical Dictionary of Romania* (London: Scarecrow Press, 1996), 25–27.

2. See Victor Eskenasy, "The Holocaust and Romanian Historiography: Communist and Neo-Communist Revisionism," in *The Tragedy of Romanian Jewry*, ed. R. L. Braham (Boulder, CO: East European Monograph CDIV, 1994), 173–236; for the politics behind postwar denial of the Romanian Holocaust, see R. L. Braham, *Romanian Nationalists and the Holocaust: The Political Exploitation of Unfounded Rescue Accounts* (Boulder, CO: East European Monograph CDLXXXIII, 1998).

3. "Wiesel Commission," *Final Report of the International Commission on the Holocaust in Romania* (Yad Vashem, 2004) (Wiesel Commission—Wikipedia).

4. *Cartea Neagră: Suferințele evreilor din România, 1940–1944*, 2nd ed., 3 vols. (București: Diogene, 1996), CN96, sponsored by B'nai B'rith Foundation and the Goldstein-Goren Center for the History of the Jews in Romania, Tel Aviv.

5. See, for example, J. Alexandru et al., eds., *Martiriul evreilor din România, 1940–1944: Documente și mărturii* (București: Hasefer, 1991); and Lya Benjamin, comp., *Evreii din România între anii 1940–1944*, vol. 1, *Legislația-Antievreiască* (București: Hasefer, 1993).

INTRODUCTION

1. C. Troncotă, *Eugen Cristescu, asul Serviciilor Secrete Românețtii: Memorii, mărturii, documente* (București: R. A. I. and Roza Vânturilor, 1994), 118–19; see also M. Carp, *Cartea Neagră*, 2nd ed., 3 vols. (București: Diogene, 1996) (hereafter CN96), 2: 13; Yad Vashem record group (YVA rg) 0–11/73, War Crimes indictment: Republică Populară Româna, Parchetul Curții din București, Cabinetul Criminalilor de război, dos. Nr. 5260/1947, "Rechizitor . . . pentru cercetarea crimelor săvârșite asupra populației din orașul Iași, Stânca Rosnovanu și Tg. Mărculești în lune Iunie 1941" ("Rechizitor"), 11.

2. CN96, 2: 25–26, 74–83; "Rechizitor," 44–46.

3. S. Manuila and W. Filderman, "Regional Development of the Jewish Population in Romania," *Genus* 13 (1957), 153–65; E. Illyes, *National Minorities in Romania: Change in Transylvania* (Boulder, CO: East European Monographs CXII, 1982), 48–54.

4. A. Karețki and M. Covaci, *Zile Însîngerate la Iași (28–30 iunie 1941)* (București: Politică, 1978) (hereafter *Zile*), 89.

5. Y. Arad et al., eds., *The Einsatzgruppen Reports: Selections from the Dispatches of the Nazi Death Squads' Campaign against the Jews, July 1941–January 1943* (New York: Holocaust Library, 1989), 34.

6. CN96, 2: 48–51 (Borcescu deposition 1945), 75–76 (Matieș reports July 1941).

CHAPTER 1

1. A. Ciorănescu, *Vasile Alecsandri* (New York: Twayne, 1973), 44, 121, 128–29; Leon Volovici, *Nationalist Ideology and Antisemitism: The Case of Romanian Intellectuals in the 1930s* (Oxford: Pergamon Press, 1991), 3, 15, 173.

2. C. Iancu, *Les Juifs en Roumanie (1866–1919): De l'exclusion à l'émancipation* (Aix-en-Provence: Université de Provence, 1978), 34–36.

3. Ibid., 59–62; R. W. Seton-Watson, *A History of the Roumanians from Roman Times to the Completion of Unity* (Cambridge: Cambridge University Press, 1934; reprint, Archon Books, 1963), 262–68, 301–13.

4. Iancu, *Les Juifs en Roumanie (1866–1919)*, 50–54; Seton-Watson, *Roumanians*, 221–23.

5. Iancu, *Les Juifs en Roumanie (1886–1919)*, 95–98; A. Levy, *L'Occident et la persécution israélite en Roumaine* (Paris: Noblet, 1870), 4–16.

6. Iancu, *Les Juifs en Roumanie (1866–1919)*, 214–17.

7. Nicolae Iorga, *Drumuri și orașe din România*, 2nd ed. (București: Pavel Suiu, 1916), 160.

8. Seton-Watson, *Roumanians*, 207–11.

9. A. D. Xenopol, *Istoria partidelor politice în România*, vol. 1 (*al Istoriei Românilor*, vol. 9), Partea II, *dela 1848 până la 1866* (București: Baer, 1911), 448–49.

10. *Règlement organique de Moldavie*, chap. 3, art. 94, cited in Iancu, *Les Juifs en Roumanie (1866–1919)*, 47.

11. *Timpul*, 13 Oct. 1881, in M. Eminescu, *Opere*, XII, *Publicistică 1 ianuarie–31 decembrie 1881* (București: Academiei Republicii Socialiste România, 1985), 367.

12. C. Codreanu, *For My Legionaries: The Iron Guard* (Madrid: "Libertatea," 1976, trans. of 1936 Sibiu edition, *Pentru Legionari*), 6–7, 91–101.

13. Iorga, *Drumuri*, 159, 172–73.

14. United States Holocaust Memorial Museum (hereafter USHMM), RG 25.004M, reel 32, dos. 40010, vol. 9 (Consiliu de Miniștri, June 17, 1941).

15. CN96, 3: 95.

16. Codreanu, *My Legionaries*, 82.

17. J. Ancel, "The 'Christian' Regimes of Romania and the Jews, 1940–1942," *Holocaust and Genocide Studies* 7 (Spring 1993): 19–21.

CHAPTER 2

1. L. A. Cohen, "The Jewish Question in Moldavia and Wallachia, 1848–1866," in *Romania between East and West: Historical Essays in Memory of Constantin C. Giurescu*, ed. S. Fischer-Galati et al. (Boulder, CO: East European Monograph CIII, 1982), 197–200.

2. Telegram of 13/25 Dec. 1864, in *Arhivă Cuza-Voda*, 16, no. 136, cited in Cohen, "The Jewish Question," 211.

3. A. D. Xenopol, *Istoria partidelor politice în România*, vol. 1 (*al Istoriei Românilor*, vol. 9), Partea II, *de la 1848 până la 1866* (București: Baer, 1911), 448–49. A. Ciorănescu, *Vasile Alecsandri* (New York: Twayne, 1973), 121, 128–29; Volovici, *Nationalist Ideology*, 3, 15, 173.

4. E. Schwarzfeld, "The Jews of Roumania from the Earliest Times to the Present Day," *American Jewish Yearbook 5662* (September 14, 1901–October 1, 1902): 63; J. Starr, "Jewish Citizenship in Rumania, 1878–1940," *Jewish Social Studies* 3, no. 1 (1941): 58.

5. David Mitrany, *The Land and the Peasant in Romania* (Oxford: Oxford University Press, 1930), 50–62.

6. Iancu, *Les Juifs en Roumanie (1866–1919)*, 66–74, 91–92.

7. F. Israel, ed., *Major Peace Treaties of Modern History, 1648–1967*, vol. 2 (New York: Chelsea House, 1967), 992.

8. C. Iancu, *Jews in Romania, 1866–1919: From Exclusion to Emancipation*, trans. C. de Bussy (Boulder, CO: East European Monograph CDXLIX, 1996), 101–5.

9. Five hundred twenty-nine according to Schwarzfeld, "The Jews," 68–69, a number that Iancu claims is not exact, *Les Juifs en Roumanie (1866–1919)*, 187–89; J. Starr, "Jewish Citizenship," 59–62, gives a figure of 361, all members of the upper class, naturalized between 1879 and 1912.

10. I. C. Butnaru, *The Silent Holocaust: Romania and Its Jews* (New York: Greenwood, 1992), 195–205.

11. Iancu, *Les Juifs en Roumanie (1866–1919)*, 192–96.

12. Wilhelm Filderman, "My Life: The Memoirs of Doctor W. Filderman, L.L.D.," typescript (Jerusalem: Yad Vashem Archives), 78.

13. Schwarzfeld, "The Jews," 69–79.

14. Iancu, *Les Juifs en Roumanie (1866–1919)*, 220–21 and note.

15. *L'indépendance Roumaine*, November 25–December 7, 1897, cited in Iancu, *Les Juifs en Roumanie (1866–1919)*, 225; Filderman, "My Life," 12–14.

16. Letter of French Vice-Consul Lucien Piat to Minister Delcasse, May 29, 1899, in Iancu, *Les Juifs en Roumanie (1866–1919)*, 316–17.

17. Edward Judge, "The Russian Government and the Kishinev Pogrom: A Review of the Evidence," mimeo, 1–10, and see his *Easter in Kishinev: Anatomy of a Pogrom* (New York: New York University Press, 1992).

18. Filderman, "My Life," 49–51; *Jewish Encyclopaedia*, 14, "Romania," 390–92.

19. Iancu, *Les Juifs en Roumanie (1866–1919)*, 226–29, 230–33, 322–25; Filderman, "My Life," 84.

20. N. Iorga, "Istoria evreilor în țările noastre," in *Analele Academiei Române*, Ser. II,

Tom. XXXVI (1913–14), *Memoriile Secţiei Istorice* (Bucureşti, 1914), 168–69, 185–87, 193–94.

21. N. Iorga, *România cum era pînă la 1918*, 2, *Moldova şi Dobrogea* (Bucureşti, n.d.), 73.

22. Iorga, *Drumuri*, 161.

23. Bela Vago, *The Shadow of the Swastika: The Rise of Fascism and Anti-Semitism in the Danube Basin, 1936–1939* (London: Saxon House, 1975), 21–22.

24. E. Natanson, "Romanian Governments and the Legal Status of Jews between the Two World Wars," *Romanian Jewish Studies* 1, no. 1 (1987): 55.

25. Filderman, "My Life," 84; J. Starr, "Jewish Citizenship," 65–68.

26. Vago, *Shadow*, 22.

27. Filderman, "My Life," 103–25.

28. Volovici, *Nationalist Ideology*, 10–44.

29. Irina Livezeanu, *Cultural Politics in Greater Romania: Regionalism, Nation Building, and Ethnic Struggles, 1918–1930* (Ithaca, NY: Cornell University Press, 1995), 8.

30. Iancu, *Les Juifs en Roumanie (1866–1919)*, 47.

31. Livezeanu, *Cultural Politics*, 195, 238.

32. Codreanu, *My Legionaries*, 84.

33. Filderman, "My Life," 84–88.

34. Codreanu, *My Legionaries*, 3–4, 8–14, 80, 84.

35. Ibid., 82.

36. Volovici, *Nationalist Ideology*, 28–30.

37. Codreanu, *My Legionaries*, 87–88.

38. J. Starr, "Jewish Citizenship," 67–68.

39. Codreanu, *My Legionaries*, 118, 132–36, 149–50, 190.

40. Ibid., 159, 178, 139–81.

41. Ibid., 211.

42. Ibid., 288–302, 319.

43. Vago, *Shadow*, 29; N. M. Nagy-Talavera, *The Green Shirts and the Others: A History of Fascism in Hungary and Rumania* (Stanford, CA: Hoover Institution, 1970), 284–85; Henri Prost, *Destin de la Roumanie (1918–1954)* (Paris: Berger-Levrault, 1954), 66–70.

44. K. Hitchins, *Rumania, 1866–1947* (Oxford: Oxford University Press, 1994), 419–20.

CHAPTER 3

1. Victor Eskenasy, ed., *Izvoare şi mărturii referitoare la evreii din România* [hereafter *Izvoare*], vol. 1 (Bucureşti: Federaţia Comunităţilor Evreieşti din Republică Socialistă România, 1986), 65–67, Appendix 2, "*Prezente judaice în Dacia Română*," 141–44, and the preceding three pages of photographs of monuments, and vol. 2, part 1, Mihai Spielmann, ed. (1988), 183–235; Schwarzfeld, "The Jews," 25–37; Iancu, *Les Juifs en Roumanie (1866–1919)*, 37–40. *Encyclopaedia Judaica* (Jerusalem: Keter, 1971–72), 14: 1479–81.

NOTES TO CHAPTER 3

2. W. F. Reddaway et al., eds., *The Cambridge History of Poland (to 1696)* (Cambridge: Cambridge University Press, 1950), 513–16; G. Vernadsky, *A History of Russia*, vol. 5, *The Tsardom of Moscow, 1547–1682*, part 1 (New Haven, CT: Yale University Press, 1969), 444–57; Schwarzfeld, "The Jews," 35.

3. M. A. Halevy, "Comunitățile evreiești din Iași și București, până la Zaveră (1821)," in *Sinai: Anuar de studii Judaice*, ed. M. A. Halevy (București: Institutul de Istorie Evreo-Română, 1931), 37; *Abyss of Despair*, English trans. of *Yeven Metzulah* by A. J. Mesch (New Brunswick, NJ: Transaction Books, 1983).

4. Iancu, *Les Juifs en Roumanie (1866–1919)*, 40–41.

5. *Izvoare*, 2, part 1, 23–25 and 2, part 2, 518.

6. Ibid., 2, part 1, 108–9.

7. *Izvoare*, 2, part 1, xxix–xxxiii, xliii–xliv, 163; part 2, 19–20, 64–65, 140–43, 177–79, 341, 351–52, 358; Schwarzfeld, "The Jews," 55–58; Halevy, "Comunitățile," 57–66.

8. *Izvoare*, 2, part 2, 15–17, 104, 123–28; Halevy, "Comunitățile," 78–79.

9. Halevy, "Comunitățile," 75–78.

10. *Izvoare*, 2, part 2, 441–45.

11. Schwarzfeld, "The Jews," 35–52; *Izvoare*, 2, part 2, 522–24.

12. *Izvoare*, 2, part 1, 52–54.

13. Iorga, "Istoria evreilor," 197.

14. Iancu, *Les Juifs en Roumanie (1866–1919)*, 46–47, 145; Schwarzfeld, "The Jews," 51–53, 57–58.

15. Halevy, "Comunitățile," 86–87. In the late eighteenth century antisemitic writings began showing up in Iași. *Înfruntarea Jidovilor* (The Insolence of the Jews) appeared there in 1803. In it Halevy found "all the outrageous lies . . . uttered about Jews in the course of history with exception of ritual murder." Metropolitan Iacob Stamate promoted the pamphlet, encouraging a storm of Christian anger, which might have turned deadly had his successor, Veniamin Costache, not given Jews protection and pacified the attackers; Schwarzfeld, "The Jews," 42.

16. *Recensământul general al populațiunii României din decembrie 1899* (București: Serviciul statisticii generale, 1905), 82, 98.

17. Verax (Radu Rossetti), *La Roumanie et les Juifs* (București: Socecu, 1903), 43, 102–3, 107, 372–77.

18. Iancu, *Les Juifs en Roumanie (1866–1919)*, 148; Schwarzfeld, "The Jews," 59; "Jassy," *Encyclopaedia Judaica*, 14: 1293–96.

19. Schwarzfeld, "The Jews," 59–62; *Encyclopaedia Judaica*, 14: 1029–30 ("Schwarzfeld"), 398 ("Rumania").

20. Israel Marcus, *Șapte momente din istoria evreilor în România* (București: Glob, 1977), 83.

21. Schwarzfeld, "The Jews," 59; M. Halevy, "Jacob Psanter, the First Chronicler of Rumanian Jewry," *YIVO Annual of Jewish Social Science* 7 (1952): 204–11.

22. Yad Vashem, The Holocaust Martyrs' and Heroes' Remembrance Authority, Archives (Jerusalem), record group (hereafter, YVA rg) 3-0/2463 (Bercovici), 1–2.

23. YVA rg 0-3/1739 (Moscovici), 1–12 and 0-3/1748 (Barzilay), 1–3; "Jassy," *Encyclopaedia Judaica*, 9: 1293–96; see also C. Barzilay and B. Causanscky, eds., *Almanachul ziarului Tribuna Evreiască pe Anul 5698 (1937)* (Iași: "Progresul," 1937).

24. *Almanachul* . . . *1937,* 45–46, 48–50, 51; N. Bogdan and C. Eremia, *Cel Mai Nou GHID al Iașului* (Iași: "Damaschin," 1932), 133–34; YVA rg 3–0/1748 (Barzilay), 3-7 and 3-0/1742 (Kelpner), 4.

25. *Almanachul* . . . *1937,* 212–16.

26. YVA rg 0-3/1739 (Moscovici), 10–13; Filderman, "My Life," 13.

27. YVA rg 0-3/1748 (Barzilay), 7; P-6/48 (Wm. Filderman papers: Braunstein, "Rebeliunea din 29 iunie 1941 dela Iași"), 63; no. 57.300 (Iţic Rubin, "Aşa a Fost . . . Masacrul dela Iași. *Duminică 29 Iunie 1941*"), 21–22.

28. YVA rg 0-3/1223 (Iosef), 4–5, 9.

29. YVA rg 0-3/1739 (Moscovici), 9.

30. YVA rg 0-3/1731 (Wahrmann), 3.

31. YVA rg 0-3/1747 (Stievel), 4–11; *Almanachul* . . . *1937,* 220–21.

32. YVA rg 3-0/2463 (Dr. Bercovici), 1–6.

33. "Iași," in *Pinkas Ha-Kehilot* (Register of Jewish Communities), vol. 1, *Romanyah* (Jerusalem: Yad Vashem, 1969), 141–76, trans. from Hebrew by Silviu Sanie (pp. 16–17 of his translation).

34. YVA rg 3-0/1742 (Kelpner), 2–4.

35. *Roumania, Ten Years After* (Boston: Beacon Press, 1929), 20–21.

36. Filderman, "My Life," 352–53.

37. YVA rg 3-0/1449 (Dauer), 3–5; 0–3/1495 (Leib), 2.

38. Filderman, "My Life," 46–51, 303–4.

39. Ibid., 304–10; B. Vago, "The Jewish Vote in Romania between the Two World Wars," *Jewish Journal of Sociology* 14, no. 2 (1972): 232–34.

40. Raphael Vago, "Romanian Jewry during the Interwar Period," in *The Tragedy of Romanian Jews,* ed. R. Braham (Boulder, CO: East European Monograph CDIV, 1994), 47–55; B. Vago, *Shadow,* 57; *Politics and Political Parties in Roumania* (London: International Reference Library Publishing, 1936), 283–91; Filderman, "My Life," 310.

41. YVA rg 3-0/1739 (Moscovici), 10–11; *Politics and Political Parties,* 241–42.

42. *Politics and Political Parties,* 242–66; B. Vago, "Jewish Vote," 229–44.

CHAPTER 4

1. Vago, *Shadow,* 23, 32; Radu Ioanid, *The Sword of the Archangel: Fascist Ideology in Romania,* trans. P. Heinegg (Boulder, CO: East European Monograph CCXCII, 1990), 43; A. Vaida-Voevod, *Cuvântare către naţiunea română* (Cluj: Ofensiva română, [1937]), 117–28.

2. Adrian Radu-Cernea, *Pogromul de la Iași: Depoziţie de martor* (București: Hasefer, 2002), 130.

3. Vaida-Voevod, *Cuvântare,* 20–30, 32; Ioanid, *Sword,* 53.

4. Hoare to A. Eden, September 26, 1936, in Vago, *Shadow,* 191–92.

5. Nagy-Talavera, *Green Shirts,* 289.

6. Wilhelm Filderman, *Adevărul asupra problemei evreieşti din România, în lumina textelor religioase şi a statisticei* (București: Triumful, 1925), lxvi; Ioanid, *Sword,* 127–28; Mircea Eliade, *Autobiography,* vol. 1, *1907–1937, Journey East, Journey*

West, trans. M. Ricketts (San Francisco: Harper, 1981), 280–81; Volovici, *Nationalist Ideology*, 70–75; Butnaru, *Silent Holocaust*, 48–49.

7. Jean Ancel, ed., *Documents Concerning the Fate of Romanian Jewry during the Holocaust* (New York: Beate Klarsfeld Foundation, 1986), 1: 148–82; Vago, *Shadow*, 24, 28; Codreanu, *My Legionaries*, 31, 56; *Politics and Political Parties*, 262–64; Filderman, "My Life," 665.

8. Butnaru, *Silent Holocaust*, 50–51; Vago, *Shadow*, 29; Nagy-Talavera, *Green Shirts*, 285.

9. Hoare to Eden in 1936: January 29, April 4 and 27, September 10, in Vago, *Shadow*, 26, 167–68, 173, 178, 188.

10. Vago, *Shadow*, 25–26, 30, 50, 60; Michel Sturdza, *The Suicide of Europe* (Belmont, MA: Western Islands, 1968), 100–101; Joseph Rothschild, *East Central Europe between the Two World Wars*, vol. 9 of P. Sugar and D. Treadgold, eds., *A History of East Central Europe* (Seattle: University of Washington Press, 1974), 312.

11. Ancel, *Documents*, 1: 203–4, 208–9, 217–18, 219–23.

12. Starr, "Jewish Citizenship," 66–68, 72–80.

13. Emil Dorian, *The Quality of Witness: A Romanian Diary, 1937–1944* (Philadelphia: Jewish Publication Society of America, 1982), 22.

14. Vago, *Shadow*, 49–51; Henri Prost, *Destin de la Roumanie (1918–1954)* (Paris: Berger-Levrault, 1954), 110–11, 116–17, 123; Rothschild, *East Central Europe*, 311–12, 316

15. Vago, *Shadow*, 62, 67–69, 71; Prost, *Destin*, 114–15; Nagy-Talavera, *Green Shirts*, 296; Ancel, *Documents*, 1: 241–52.

16. S. Stanciu, chief ed., Centrul pentru studiul istoriei evreilor din România, *Martiriul evreilor din România 1940–1944. Documente și mărturii* (București: Hasefer, 1991), 18–19.

17. Ibid., 3–13, 18–21.

18. Ibid., 15.

19. Seton-Watson, *Roumanians*, 347–49, 352, Appendix 2, 566.

20. *American Jewish Yearbook* 40 (1938–39), 285.

21. Filderman, "My Life," 638–43; Vago, *Shadow*, 38, 58.

22. *American Jewish Yearbook* 39 (1937–38), 434, 438–39 and 40 (1938–39), 285.

23. YVA rg 3-0/1449 (Dauer), 3–5, and 3-0/1495 (Leib), 2–4.

24. YVA rg 0-3/1414 (Scheinfeld), 2–4.

25. *Politics and Political Parties*, 186–89.

26. *American Jewish Yearbook* 39 (1937–38), 447–48; and 40 (1938–39), 189.

27. *American Jewish Yearbook* 41 (1939–40), 315–20 and 42 (1940–41), 399–400; Starr, "Jewish Citizenship," 74–76; Vago, *Shadow*, 68–70.

CHAPTER 5

1. Filderman, "My Life," 5–8, 13–14.
2. *Pinkas Ha-Kehilot*, 1: 51–56.
3. YVA rg 0-3/1739 (Moscovici), 6.

4. Filderman, "My Life," 584–88.

5. A. Adams, *Bolsheviks in the Ukraine: The Second Campaign, 1918–1919* (New Haven, CT: Yale University Press, 1936), 235–36.

6. Filderman, "My Life," 115–28.

7. Ibid., 146–51; Codreanu, *My Legionaries*, 44–45.

8. YVA rg 3-0/1748 (Barzilay), 4–5.

9. Codreanu, *My Legionaries*, 89; Starr, "Jewish Citizenship," 66–67; Filderman, "My Life," 166–67.

10. Filderman, "My Life," 319–29; Butnaru, *Silent Holocaust*, 41–42; *Romania, Ten Years After*, 128, 131; Livezeanu, *Cultural Politics*, 68–87.

11. *Romania, Ten Years After*, 119–32.

12. Ibid., 23–24.

13. Filderman, "My Life," 359, 369, 388.

14. Ibid., 326, 345, 377, 390–91, 523–27.

15. Ibid., 329; *Egalitatea* (December 14, 1923), quoted in C. Iancu, *Les Juifs en Roumanie (1919–1938)*, 219.

16. Vago, *Shadow*, 240 (Hoare to Eden, February 12, 1937, "Annual Report" of 1936).

17. Rothschild, *East Central Europe*, 313–14; Vago, *Shadow*, 51; Titu Georgescu, "La cinquieme colonne in Roumanie," *Revue d'Histoire de la Deuxieme Guerre mondiale* 18, no. 70 (1986): 33–34.

18. CN96, 3: 28–30.

19. M. Mircu, *Pogromurile din Bucovina și Dorohoi* (București: "Glob," 1945), 133–35 (report to the "Procurer General" "in connection with the events of July 1, 1940"), cited in J. Alexandru et al., eds., *Martiriul evreilor din România, 1940–1944: Documente și mărturii* (București: Hasefer, 1991), 25–32.

20. Alexandru, *Martiriul*, 29–39; CN96, 3: 46–48; Butnaru, *Silent Holocaust*, 66–67; I. Șerbănescu et al., eds., *Evreii din România între anii 1940–1944*, vol. 3, *1940–1942: Perioda unei mari restriști* (București: Hasefer, 1997), part 1, 37–48.

21. Radu Ionid, *The Holocaust in Romania: The Destruction of Jews and Gypsies under the Antonescu Regime, 1940–1944* (Chicago: Ivan R. Dee, 2000), 38–43; Wiesel Commission, *Final Report*, in section "The June/July 1940 Romanian Withdrawal from Bessarabia and Bucovina."

22. CN96, 1: 78.

23. YVA rg 0-3/1722 (R. Auerbach), 1–3.

24. S. C. Cristian, *Patru ani de urgie: Notele unui evreu din România* (București: "Timpul," 1946), 7–32.

25. Ancel, *Documents*, 1: 542–43; YVA rg 0-11 (80) (Hahamu), 8–9; *Pinkas Ha-Kehilot*, 1: 77–78.

26. Alexandru, *Martiriul*, 44, 49–50.

27. Filderman, "My Life," 710.

28. Alexandru, *Martiriul*, xxi, 3–21.

29. Rothschild, *East Central Europe*, 315–16; Filderman, "My Life," 153.

30. I. Calafetanu, *Români la Hitler* (București: Univers Enciclopedic, 1999),

74–81; A. Hillgruber, *Hitler, König Carol, und Marschall Antonescu: Die deutsch-rumanischen Beziehungen, 1938–1944* (Wiesbaden: Steiner, 1965), 117–18.

31. Hillgruber, *Hitler, König Carol, und Marschall Antonescu*, 119–21; Nagy-Talavera, *Green Shirts*, 310–28; M. Broszat, "Das Dritte Reich und die rumänische Judenpolitik" in *Gutachten des Instituts für Zeitgeschichte* (München, 1958), 121–26; and "Die Eiserne Garde und das Dritte Reich," *Politische Studien* 9 (1958): 628–36; H. Hohne, *The Order of the Death's Head*, trans. R. Barry (New York: Ballantine, 1971), 289; W. Hoetle, *The Secret Front* (London: Weidenfeld-Nicolson, 1953), 175–76.

32. Radu Ioanid, "The Pogrom of Bucharest," *Holocaust and Genocide Studies* 6, no. 3 (1991): 377–80.

33. Dorian, *Quality of Witness*, 138–39.

34. CN96, 1: 181–202, 259–62; Alexandru, *Martiriul*, 68–83.

35. Ancel, *Documents*, 2: 358–61; Ancel, "The 'Christian' Regimes," 18.

36. Lya Benjamin, ed., *Evreii din România între anii 1940–1944*, vol. 1, *Legislația Antievreiască* (București: Hasefer, 1993), 122–38.

37. YVA rg 0-3/1721 (Buchmann), 3–4.

38. YVA "The Dr. W. Filderman Archives," doc. no. 51, 94–101 (Filderman to Ion Antonescu, January 2, 1941).

CHAPTER 6

1. YVA rg 0-3/898 (Herșcovici), 1.
2. YVA rg 0-3/1233 (Gaer), 1–2.
3. Max Volovici, interviewed by his brother Leon Volovici (Israel 1986).
4. L. Benjamin, ed., *Evreii din România, între anii 1940–1944*, vol. 2, *Problema evreiască în stenogramele consiliului de ministri* (București: Hasefer, 1996), 214.
5. United States Holocaust Memorial Museum Archives, Record Group (hereafter USHMM, RG 25.004M), reel 35, dos. 40010 ("Activitatea Serviciului Secret al Misionarilor," June 7, 1941).
6. Alexandru, *Martiriul*, 37–38.
7. USHMM, RG 25.004M, reel 32, dos. 40010, vol. 9 (Consiliu de Ministri, June 17, 1941).
8. Flavius Josephus, *The Jewish War*, trans. G. A. Williamson (Baltimore: Penguin, 1959), 337–39.
9. CN96, 2: 40.
10. USHMM, RG 25.004M, reel 35, dos. 40010, vol. 89 (Ministerul Afacerilor Interne, Nr. 4147, June 21, 1941).
11. Ibid., Nr. 4362 and 4467, June 28, 1941.
12. Radu-Cernea, *Pogromul*, 7–12.
13. Mrs. Volovici interviewed by her son Leon Volovici (Israel 1986).
14. USHMM, RG 25.004M, reel 32, dos. 40010, vol. 9 (Stenographic report, June 23, 1941).
15. Radu-Cernea, *Pogromul*, 13–14.
16. YVA rg 0-3/1731 (Wahrmann), 5, and 0-3/1413 (Aaron), 2.

17. YVA rg P-6/48 (Filderman papers, Braunstein, "Rebeliunea"), 60; CN96, 2: 24.

18. USHMM, RG 25.004M, reel 35, dos. 40010, vol. 89 ("Nota," no. 234, June 20, 1941: Regional Insp. of Police to Chief Insp. of Iasi Police and Dir. Gen. of Police to Regional Insp. of Police [Iaşi], both dated June 24, 1941).

19. M. Mircu, *Pogromul de la Iaşi din 29 Iunie* (Bucureşti, 1945), 6; YVA rg 0-3/1721 (Buchmann), 4, and P-6/48 (Filderman papers, Braunstein, "Rebeliunea"), 61; and 0-3/1223 (Iacob), 5; USHMM, RG 25.004M, reel 43, dos. 108233, vol. 38 (depositions: Iacob 19 July 1945 and Gen. Ionescu 6 Aug 1945).

20. CN96, 2: 24, 74, 139; YVA rg P-6/48 (Filderman papers, Braunstein, "Rebeliunea"), 61.

21. CN96, 2: 115 (Police Inspector Leahu July 2, 1941 report); YVA rg P/6 18a (Filderman papers, Schleier account), 25.

22. CN96, 2: 24–25, 70–71; YVA rg 0–11/73, "Rechizitor," 5.

23. YVA rg 0-3/1722 (Auerbach), 3–4.

24. YVA rg 0-3/1721 (Buchmann), 3, and P/6 18a (Filderman papers, Schleier account), 25–26; USHMM, RG 25.004M, reel 43, dos. 108233, vol. 37 (Leon Haimovici declaration, n.d.).

25. CN96, 2: 68, 92–93 (depositions: Hahamu 1945 and Schleier postwar, n.d.); YVA rg 0-3/1722 (Auerbach), 3 and 0-3/1223 (Iacob), and 0-3/1721 (Buchmann), 4–5; Radu-Cernea, *Pogromul,* 20.

26. USHMM, RG 25.004M, reel 43, dos. 108233, vol. 37 (Ionescu August 6, 1945 deposition); CN96, 2: 67; YVA rg 0–11/73, "Rechizitor," 4.

27. CN96, 2: 27, 71; YVA rg 0-3/73, "Rechizitor," 6.

28. RG 2500M, 108233, reel 46, vol. 120 (Petraru 15 June 48 declaration).

29. RG 2500M, dos. 18209, reel 78, vol. 2 (Prepoliţă 4 Aug 45 declaration); CN96, 2: 76 (Matieş 30 July 41 report).

30. CN96, 2: 25–26, 74–83; YVA rg 0-3/73, "Rechizitor," 44–46.

31. CN96, 2: 75–76 (Matieş 20 July 41 report); see also L. Benjamin, S. Stanciu, et al., eds., *Evreii din România între anii 1940–1944,* vol. 3, *1940–1942: Perioada unei mari restrişti* (Bucureşti: Hasefer, 1997), 342–43 (Matieş and Stihi 28 July 41 report).

32. RG 2500M, dos. 108233, reel 44, vol. 46 (Matieş, "Memoriu").

33. RG 25.004M, dos. 108233, reel 46, vol. 131 (Captaru 30 June 41? Report).

34. Popricani, Romania, mass grave: for example, http://www.ejpress.org/article/50151.

CHAPTER 7

1. CN96, 2: 92–93 (Schleier postwar deposition, n.d.); YVA rg 0-3/1745 (Stievel), 13; Radu-Cernea, *Pogromul,* 22.

2. CN96, 2: 70–71, 89–90, 112, 119; YVA rg 0–11/73, "Rechizitor," 6–7; USHMM, RG 25.004M, reel 43, dos. 108233, vol. 36 (Captaru, "Darea de Seamă," n.d.).

3. I take up this matter in chapter 10.

4. USHMM, RG 25.004M, reel 48, dos. 108233, vol. 29 (Lupu, "Ordin tele-

NOTES TO CHAPTER 7

fonic"); reel 48, dos. 108233, vol. 30 ("Parchetul Curtii Marțiale al Comandamentului II Teritorial" no. 8820).

5. CN96, 2: 84, 87–89 (Chirilovici 30 June 1941 reports), 69 (G. Sprinceană 19 July 1945 deposition).

6. Ibid., 102–4 (Stavrescu 29 June 1941 report).

7. USHMM, RG 25.004M, reel 35, dos. 40010, vol. 89 (Giosanu and Captaru reports: 23621 and 10420).

8. CN96, 2: 84, 87–89, 111–14 (Chirilovici 30 June 1941 report), 121–22 (Leoveanu 2 July 1941 statement; see chapter 10 on Leoveanu's two reports for this date).

9. YVA rg 0-3/1426 (Marcovici), 5; 0-3/1722 (Auerbach), 4–5; 0-3/897 (Rabinovici), 1.

10. Max interviewed by Leon Volovici (Israel 1986).

11. YVA rg 0-3/1233 (Gaer); Mircu, *Pogromul,* 36.

12. YVA rg 0-3/1721 (Buchmann), 5–6; CN96, 2: 93 (Schleier account).

13. CN96, 2: 69–70 (Sprinceană 19 July 1945 deposition), 73, 109–11 (Giosanu 29 June and 2 July 1941 reports); YVA rg P-6 18a, 38 (Filderman papers, Giosanu's report).

14. YVA rg 0-3/898 (Herșcovici).

15. Interview February 6, 1991 (Tibia spoke English during parts of the interview).

16. Radu-Cernea, *Pogromul,* 26–32, 120.

17. YVA rg 0-3/897 (Rabinovici), 1–2.

18. CN96, 2: 88, 113 (Chirilovici 30 June 1941 reports).

19. YVA rg 0-3/1721 (R. Buchmann), 6, and P-6/48 (Filderman papers, Braunstein, "Rebeliunea"), 62.

20. Mircu, *Pogromul,* 35–36.

21. Max Volovici interview (1986).

22. YVA rg 0-3/1495 (Leib), 3-4; 0-3/898 (Herșcovici), 1–2; 0-3/1233 (Gaer), 4.

23. CN96, 2: 89 (Captaru 29 June 1941 report); YVA rg 0-3/1463 (Natansohn), 3.

24. YVA rg 0-3/1722 (Auerbach), 4–5.

25. CN96, 2: 108–9 (Captaru 1947 deposition).

26. Ibid., 105, 114, 117 (2 July 1941 reports: Captaru, Chirilovici, Leah).

27. YVA rg 0-3/1495 (Leib), 3-4; 0-3/1233 (Rabinovici), 4–5; 0-3/898 (Herșcovici), 2–3.

28. YVA rg P-6/48 (Filderman papers, Braunstein, "Rebeliunea"), 63; A. Karețki and M. Covaci, *Zile Însîngerate la Iași (28–30 iunie 1941)* (București: Politică, 1978), 81.

29. USHMM, RG 25.004M, reel 43, dos. 108233, vol. 36 (Captaru 29 June 1941 report to Ministry of Interior).

30. CN96, 2: 139–40 (Goldstein 28 March 1945 deposition).

31. USHMM, RG 25.004, reel 17, dos. 100399, vol. 1 Tribunalul Capitalei Colegiul II Penal, Deciziune penală nr. 2289 (1955), two reports: Procuratura Generală a R.P.R., witness Clara Szepessy, 1955 and dosar nr. 136/1953).

32. CN96, 2: 93–95 (Schleier, "Duminica Ceea," n.d.).
33. YVA rg 0-3/1722 (Auerbach), 5–6.
34. CN96, 2: 68–69, 96, 98–102; I. C. Butnaru, *The Silent Holocaust: Romania and Its Jews* (Westport, CT: Greenwood Press, 1992), 152–53; Radu-Cernea, *Pogromul,* 60–68.

CHAPTER 8

1. USHMM, RG 25.004M, reel 48, dos. 108233, vol. 29 (Ion Antonescu to Lupu 28 June 1941, 11 pm).
2. CN96, 2: 123–25 (Captaru 20 May 1947 deposition) and 125–26 (Interior Ministry 13 Sept. 1941 report and Chirilovici 15 Sept. 1941 report to Int. Min.); USHMM, RG 25.004M, reel 48, dos. 108233, vol. 29 (Parchetul Curții Marțiale al Comandamentului II Teritorial 13 Sept. 1941); reel 43, dos. 108233, vol. 36 (Captaru 29 & 30 June 1941 to Int. Min. & Int. Min. to Captaru, Captaru 1 July 1941 to Insp. of Transp., C.F.R., Iași); reel 35, dos. 40010, vol. 89 (Int. Min. 30 June 1941 to Captaru).
3. YVA rg 0-3/898 (Herșcovici), 3–4.
4. CN96, 2: 95–96 (Schleier).
5. YVA rg 0-3/1233 (Gaer), 5.
6. YVA rg 0-3/898 (Herșcovici), 3–4, and 0-3/1413 (Leib), 6.
7. USHMM, RG 25.004M, reel 43, dos. 108233, vol. 38 (Săvinescu 6 Sept. 1945 deposition).
8. CN96, 2: 120 (Leoveanu 2 July 1941 report), and 114 (Chirilovici 30 June 1941 report).
9. USHMM, RG 25.004M, reel 43, dos. 108233, vol. 38 (Săvinescu, 6 & 8 Sept. 1945 depositions); reel 35, dos. 40010, vol. 89 (Giosanu 30 June 1941 to Leoveanu); CN96, 2: 116–17 (Leahu 30 June 1941 report).
10. USHMM, RG 25.004M, reel 43, dos. 108233, vol. 37 (Haimovici declaration, n.d.).
11. YVA rg 0-3/1413 (Leib), 6–7.
12. YVA rg 0-3/1722 (Mittelman), 6–7; 0-3/898 (Herșcovici), 4–5.
13. *Zile Însingerate la Iași (28–30 iunie 1941)* (București: Politică, 1978), 97–100.
14. Ottmar Trașcă and Dennis Deletant, eds., *Al III-lea Reich și Holocaustul din România, 1940–1944,* Documente din archivele germane (București: Editura Institutului Național pentru Studierea Holocaustului din România "Elie Wiesel," 2007), 160–61.
15. USHMM, RG 25.004M, reel 41, dos. 108233, vol. 31 (1945 depositions: Totoiescu, Ionescu); CN96, 2: 126–36 (1945 depositions: Totoiescu, Petrea, Gheorghiu, Teodorescu).
16. USHMM, RG 25.0004M, reel 17, dos. 39912, vol. 1 (court findings 1948 on Vătăjanu); reel 41, dos. 108233, vol. 31 (1945 depositions: Atudorei, David, Freitag).
17. USHMM, RG 25.004M, reel 41, dos. 108233, vol. 31, and CN96, 2: 126–35 (Totoiescu and Gheorghiu 1945 depositions).

18. CN96, 2: 139–41 (Goldstein 1945 deposition), USHMM, RG 25.004M, reel 35, dos. 40010 (Giosanu 1 July 1941 report no. 23777).
19. CN96, 2: 136–38 (Solomon and Mandache 1945 depositions).
20. USHMM, RG 25.004M, reel 17, dos. 39912, vol. 1 (Soloman 17 June 1948 deposition).
21. CN96, 2: 126–32 (Totoiescu 16 Aug. 1945 deposition), 141–44 (Triandaf 9 July 1941 report).
22. YVA rg 0-3/898 (Herşcovici), 5; 0-3/1721 (Buchmann), 7; P-6/48 (Filderman papers, Braunstein, "Rebeliunea"), 64; CN96, 2: 142, 144 (reports on dead removed at Săbăoani: Triandaf about 300, Ştefănescu 172); USHMM, RG 25.004M, reel 43, dos. 108233, vol. 38 (Fentz Perca 26 July 1945 testified he saw buried 180 bodies taken from the train at Săbăoani).
23. Mircu, *Pogromul*, 11–14; CN96, 2: 142 (Triandaf 9 July 1941 report).
24. YVA rg 0–3/897 (Rabinovici), 4–5.
25. USHMM, RG 25.004M, reel 43, dos. 108233, vol. 38 (Perca, Rediu, Beram, Abraham 26 July 1945 depositions); CN96, 2: 142 (Triandaf 9 July 1941 deposition).
26. CN96, 2: 139–41, 142–43 (Goldstein 1945 deposition & Triandaf 9 July 1941 report); YVA rg 0-11/73 "Rechizitor," 40–42, and 0-3/898 (Herşcovici), 4–6.
27. Ancel, *Documents*, 2: 26, 472–74; YVA rg 0-3/1490 (Elias), 1–3; P-6/46 (Filderman papers), 74; 0-3/897 (Rabinovici), 5–6; Mircu, *Pogromul*, 86–97.
28. YVA rg 0–3/897 (Rabinovici), 6–7; 0-3/898 (Herşcovici), 6–7.
29. USHMM, RG 25.004M, reel 41, dos. 108233, vol. 33 (Maer 1946 deposition); reel 41, dos. 108233, vol. 34 (Emil 1945 declaration); reel 46, dos. 108233, vol. 109 (Weisenberg and Bercovici 1950 depositions); YVA rg 0-11/73, "Rechizitor," 43–44: CN96, 2: 35–36, 117 (Leahu 2 July 1941 declaration), 120 (Leoveanu 2 July 1941 report), 148 (Captaru 30 June 1941 report).

CHAPTER 9

1. CN96, 2: 149–50 (Marievici 1945 deposition).
2. CN96, 2: 151–52 (Spinosu 1945 deposition).
3. Mircu, *Pogromul*, 5–6.
4. USHMM, RG 25.004M, reel 43, dos. 108233, vol. 37 (depositions: Sechter 1945, Hauzner and Herşcovici n.d.).
5. YVA rg 0-3/1472 (Itzhac David).
6. CN96, 2: 151–52 (Spinosu 1945 deposition).
7. YVA rg 0-11/73, "Rechizitor," 11.
8. CN96, 2: 32–38, 141–43 (Triandaf 9 July 1941 report).
9. CN96, 2: 102–22, 149–52; *Zile*, 103–5.
10. Ancel, *Documents*, 3: 42–43, 102; CN96, 2: 13; "Quelques données concernant la terreur fasciste en Roumanie (1940–1944)," in I. Popescu-Puţuri et al., *La Roumanie pendant la Deuxième guerre Mondiale: Études* (Bucharest: Éditions de l'Académie de la RPR, 1964), 51; Mircu, *Pogromul*, 32, 47.
11. Arhivă Serviciului Român de Informaţii, dosar nr. 11.3143, f. 28, quoted

NOTES TO CHAPTER 10

in Cristian Troncotă, *Eugen Cristescu, asul Serviciilor Secrete Românești: Memorii, mărturii, documente* (București: R.A.I. and Roza Vânturilor, 1994), 118–19.

12. USHMM, RG 25.004M, reel 35, dos. 40010, vol. 89 (Armata IV-a, Gen. Ioanițiu to Regional Insp. of Police, Iași, no. 206.82; Min. of Int. 30 June 1941 telegram no. 4599 to all Prefects of Moldavia and others; Giosanu 1 July 1941 report no. 23729 to Director Gen. of Police); CN96, 2: 109–11, 152–54.

13. USHMM, RG 25.004M, reel 35, dos. 40010, vol. 89 (Chirilovici 2 July 1941 to Giosanu).

14. YVA rg P-6/48 (Filderman papers, Braunstein, "Rebeliunea"), 66–67 and no. 57.300 (Iţic Rubin, "Așa a Fost"), 14; CN96, 2: 155–56 (Captaru 2 July 1941 report to Min. of Int).

15. CN96, 2: 101–2 (Filipescu account of the pogrom, n.d.).

16. USHMM, RG 25.004M, reel 35, dos. 40010, vol. 89 (Consiliul de Colaborare 3 July 1941 Proces-verbal); Mircu, *Pogromul*, 83; YVA rg 0-3/1742 (Kelpner), 43–44; CN96, 2: 41 (I. Antonescu 2 July 1941 communiqué).

17. YVA rg P-6/48 (Filderman papers, Braunstein "Rebeliunea"), 74–75; CN96, 2: 156–57 (Gen. Carlaonţ, 6 Aug. 1941 "Order no. 7"; Ancel, *Documents*, II, 505.

18. YVA rg 0-3/1233 (Gaer), 3–10.

19. YVA rg 0-3/1414 (Klara Scheinfeld), 4–10.

20. YVA rg 0-3/1463 (Natansohn); 0-3/1747 (Stievel), 5–6.

21. YVA rg 0-3/2463 (Bercovici), 7–10; 0-3/1747 (Stievel), 5–11; CN96, 3: 473–78.

CHAPTER 10

1. See J. Ancel, *Preludiu la asasinat: Pogromul de la Iași, 29 iunie 1941* (Iași: Polirom, 2005), 411–74 (discussion of the falsification of official reports on the pogrom).

2. Consiliu de Ministri 17 Iunie 1941 in USHMM, RG 25.004M, reel 32, dos. 40010, vol. 9.

3. CN96, 2: 40; USHMM, RG 25.004M, reel 35, dos. 40010, vol. 89, Ministerul Afacerilor Interne (MAI), Nr. 4147 (21 June 41), Nrs. 4362 and 4467 (28 June 41).

4. CN96, 2: 19, 48–54 (Borcescu 12 Nov. 1945 deposition).

5. CN96, 2: 48–57 (Marinovici, Petrescu, Rădulescu, Borcescu 1945–47 depositions).

6. YVA rg 0-11/73, "Rechizitor," 13–14; CN96, 2: 19, 60 (Nicolae Trohani 22 Feb. 1946 deposition).

7. CN96, 2: 52–53, 54–56 (Borcescu 1945–1946 depositions); YVA rg 0-11/73, "Rechizitor," 6, 13; USHMM, RG 25.004M, reel 45, dos. 108233, vol. 73 (Marele Stat Major, Serviciul Secret S.S.I., 18 May 1947), and vol. 29 (Lupu 8 Aug. 1945 deposition).

8. USHMM, RG 25.004M, reel 32, dos 40010, vol. 10 (Ionescu 31 Aug. 1945 deposition).

9. CN96, 2: 51–53 (Borcescu 12 Nov. 1945 deposition); YVA rg 0-11/73, "Rechizitor," 15.

10. J. Ancel, "The Solution of the 'Jewish Problem' in Bessarabia and Bucovina, June–July 1941," *Yad Vashem Studies* 19 (1988): 227–30; CN96, 2: 53–54 (Borcescu deposition).

11. USHMM, RG 25.004M, reel 32, dos. 40010, vol. 10 (Ionescu 1945 deposition).

12. J. Ancel, *Contribuţii la istoria României: Problema evreiască* (Bucureşti: Hasefer and Yad Vashem, 2001–3), vol. 2, pt. 2, 84; CN96, 2: 41 (Ion Antonescu 1 & 2 July 1941 "communiqués").

13. CN96, 2: 118–22.

14. YVA rg 0-11/73, "Rechizitor," 12–20.

15. CN96, 2: depositions: 64–66 (Stavrescu 1945), 108–9 (Captaru 1947), 116 (Leahu 2 July 1941).

16. Ibid, 75–76; YVA rg 0-11/73, "Rechizitor," 48–55.

17. CN96, 2: 118–22.

18. Troncotă, *Eugen Cristescu*, 247–48; Ancel, *Pogromul*, 415–16, 433.

19. CN96, 2: 64–66; Dennis Deletant, *Hitler's Forgotten Ally: Ion Antonescu and His Regime, Romania 1940–44* (New York: Palgrave Macmillan, 2006), 80, 131.

20. Deletant, *Hitler's Forgotten Ally*, 131

21. *Zile*, 45–48; CN96, 2: 64–66 (Stavrescu 1945 "declaration"), see also 68, 91–92, 115–18; YVA rg 0-3/1721 (Buchmann), 3 and p/6-18a (Filderman papers, Schleier account), 25–26; "Rechizitor," 18–19.

22. CN96, 2: 69 (Sprinceană 1945 deposition).

23. Ibid., 2: 28, 71–73, 84, 87–89, 112–13.

24. Ibid., 2: 28–32, 84, 86–91, 109, 112, 119; "Rechizitor," 7.

25. Ibid., 2: 71–73 (Giosanu 29 June 1941 to Director Gen. of Police).

26. Ibid., 102–4 (Stavrescu to Int. Ministry, 29 June 1941), 64–67 (1945 deposition).

27. USHMM, RG 25.004M, reel 43, dos. 108233, vol. 36 (Iaşi Prefect to Interior Ministry 29 June 1941 and Subprefect Isacovici 1945 deposition), reel 48, dos. 108233, vol. 29 (Lupu 1945 deposition); CN96, 2: 65 (Stavrescu 1945 deposition).

28. CN96, 2: 89–91 (Captaru 29 June 1941 to Int. Min.), 123–25 (Captaru, extract from a 1947 deposition about the "death trains"), 62–64 (Lupu 1945 declaration).

29. Ibid., 114 (Chirilovici 30 June 1941 report to Director General of Police Leoveanu).

30. Ibid., 69–70 (Sprinceană 1945 deposition), 87–89, 111–14 (Chirilovici 30 June 1941 reports), 115–18 (Leahu 2 July 1941 report), 119–22 (Leoveanu 2 July 1941 report to Gen. Antonescu).

31. YVA rg 0-3/1413 (Leib), 3; 0-3/1449 (Dauer), 6–7; 0-3/1429 (Mendelsohn), 4.

32. *Documents on German Foreign Policy, 1918–45* (London: H. M. Stationery Office, 1957), Series D (1937–45), 12: 864–66; *Zile*, 47.

33. CN96, 2: 29 June 1941 reports: 71–73, 86–87 (Giosanu), 102–4 (Stavrescu).
34. Ibid., 104–6 (Captaru 2 July 1941 report).
35. Ibid., 73 (Chirilovici and Stănculescu 30 June 1941 report), and 2 July 1941 reports: 109–11 (Giosanu), 118–22 (Leoveanu), 104–7 (Captaru).
36. Ibid., 64–66 (Stavrescu and Lupu 1945 declarations), 108–9 (Captaru 1947 deposition).
37. Ibid., 42–47; and USHMM, RG 25,004M, reel 32, dos. 40010, vol. 10 (Cristescu, postwar declarations).
38. Ibid., 121–22 (Leoveanu 2 July 1941 account), 61–67 (Leoveanu, Lupu, Stavrescu 1945 accounts).
39. YVA rg 0-11/73, "Rechizitor," 20–35; CN96, 2: 117.
40. YVA rg 0-11/73, "Rechizitor," 26–27, 31, 32; USHMM, RG 25.400M, reel 43, dos. 108233, vol. 45 (depositions of several witnesses, 21 July 1945).
41. USHMM, RG 25.004M, reel 46, dos. 108233, vol. 112 (reports concerning Constantin Raitmayer, 8 Sept. 1950).
42. Ibid., reel 44, dos. 108233, vol. 45, part II (witnesses regarding Ion Ştefaniu).
43. Ibid., reel 41, dos. 108233, vol. 32 (reports on Elena and Petru Martinescu).
44. YVA rg 0-3/1721 (Buchmann), 3–7.
45. YVA rg 0-11/73, "Rechizitor," 21 and P-6/48 (Filderman papers, Braunstein, "Rebeliunea"), 237; Radu-Cernea, *Pogromul*, 33.
46. USHMM, RG 25.004M, reel 41, dos. 108233, vol. 33 (Margaretta Rozinfeld, Moise Lazar, and Vera Botezatu 1946 depositions).

CHAPTER 11

1. Vago, *Shadow*, 50; Rothschild, *East Central Europe*, 312; Hillgruber, *Hitler, König Carol und Marschall Antonescu*, 247–54.
2. Vago, *Shadow*, 50; Rothschild, *East Central Europe*, 312; Hillgruber, *Hitler, König Carol und Marschall Antonescu*, 247–54.
3. Hitchins, *Rumania 1866–1947*, 426–60.
4. M. Broszat, "Die Eiserne Garde," *Politische Studien* 9 (1958): 631; Volovici, *Nationalist Ideology*, 155.
5. Volovici, *Nationalist Ideology*, 130.
6. Ibid., 70–75, 130–31, 154–62; Iancu, *Les Juifs en Roumanie (1919–1938)*, 201–4; N. Manea, *On Clowns: The Dictator and the Artist* (New York: Grove Weidenfeld, 1992), 91–93.
7. Iancu, *Les Juifs en Roumanie (1919–1938)*, 201–4; Manea, *On Clowns*, 91–93; Armin Heinen, "Die Legion 'Erzengel Michael,'" in *Rumanien: Soziale Bewegung und politische Organisation* (Munich: Oldenbourg, 1986), 337–42 ("Geld und Politik"); T. Georgescu, "La cinquienne colonne in Roumanie," 26; Ancel, "German-Romanian Relations," in *The Tragedy of Romanian Jewry*, ed. R. L. Braham (Boulder, CO: East European Monograph CDIV, 1994), 58; Hillgruber, *Hitler, König Carol, und Marschall Antonescu*, 247–49; Ancel, *Documents*, 1: 218; Broszat, *Das Dritte Reich*, 106–8.

NOTES TO CONCLUSION

8. *Documents on German Foreign Policy, 1918–1945,* Ser. D (1937–45), vol. 10, 301–16.

9. Jürgen Föster, "Germany's Acquisition of Allies in South-East Europe," 387–406, and "The Decisions of the Tripartite Pact States," 1021–28, in *Germany and the Second World War,* vol. 4, ed. Militärgeschichtliches Forschungsamt (Oxford: Clarendon Press, 1996).

10. Ion Calafeteanu, *Români la Hitler* (București: Univers Enciclopedic, 1999), 81–93.

11. Von Killinger to the Foreign Ministry in Berlin 16 Aug. 1941 (Bucharest), *Akten zur deutschen auswärtigen Politik, 1918–1945,* serie D, 1937–1941, Band XIII (1970), do. 207, p. 264, cited in Ancel, "Antonescu and the Jews," *Yad Vashem Studies* 23 (1993): 231–32.

12. CN96, 2: 18, 42–43 (Cristescu 1945? Deposition); YVA rg 0-3/1722 (Auerbach), 5.

13. Deletant, *Hitler's Forgotten Ally,* 121, 205, 212, 334–35 (notes 1 and 18); J. Ancel, "The German-Romanian Relationship and the Final Solution," *Holocaust and Genocide Studies* 2, no. 2 (2005): 260–63.

14. CN96, 2: 48–54 (depositions: Borcescu 1945, Rădulescu 1947); USHMM, RG 25.004M, reel 32, dos. 40010, vol. 10 (Haralamb and Ionescu 1945 depositions).

15. CN96, 2: 31 (M. Carp), 116 (Leahu 2 July 1941 report); YVA rg 0-3/1722 (Auerbach), 5; 0-3/1223 (Iosef), 2–3; P-6/48 (Filderman papers, Braunstein "Rebeliunea"), 62, 70.

16. YVA rg 0-3/897 (Rabinovici), 3, and 0-3/1233 (Gaer), 4–5; CN96, 2: 138–39 (Naftule 1945 deposition); Radu-Cernea, *Pogromul,* 28, 100.

17. Radu-Cernea, *Pogromul,* 28, 100; Ioanid, *Holocaust,* 67, 76; Ancel, *Pogromul,* 117–18.

18. YVA, Einsatzgruppe D testimonies, file TR 10/11492, folders: III, 774–91; IV, 821–25, 837, 850, 870–71; V, 1161–62; VI, 1301, 1904, 1911–13; VIII, 1756; and X, 2078.

19. *Trial of the Major War Criminals before the International Military Tribunal (Nuremberg; 14 Nov. 1945–1 Oct. 1946),* IV, Proceedings, 17 Dec. 1945–8 Jan. 1946, 313–19, 463–65; Ronald Headland, "The Einsatzgruppen: The Question of Their Initial Operations," *Holocaust and Genocide Studies* 4, no. 4 (1989): 401–12.

CONCLUSION

1. Radu-Cernea, *Pogromul,* 27–32, 43–44; CN96, 2: 41.
2. Alexandru, *Martiriul,* 25.
3. *Documents on German Foreign Policy, 1918–1945,* Series D, X, 305, 308–9, 316.
4. Von Killinger to the Foreign Ministry in Berlin 16 Aug. 1941 (Bucharest), *Akten zur deutschen auswärtigen Politik, 1918–1945,* serie D, 1937–1941, Band XIII (1970), do. 207, p. 264, cited in Ancel, "Antonescu and the Jews," *Yad Vashem Studies* 23 (1993): 231–32.

5. L. Benjamin, ed., *Evreii din România între anii, 1940–1944,* vol. 2, *Problema Evreiasca în stenogramele consiliului de Miniştri* (Bucureşti: Hasefer, 1996), 234–58.

6. CN96, 2: 48–54, 87–89, 112–13.

7. CN96, 3: 235–70 (deportations to Transnistria in 1942), 271–414 (Transnistria).

8. CN96, 1: 23–26; 3: 45–46.

9. *Einsatzgruppen Reports,* 168; Ioanid, *Holocaust,* 182.

10. Calafeteanu, *Români la Hitler,* 97–99.

11. CN96, 3: 241–42, 253–70; Hilberg, *Destruction,* 501–3; Ancel, "Antonescu and the Jews," 273–76; Ancel, *Documents,* 4, no. 60, 111 and no. 65, 120.

12. Ioanid, *Holocaust,* 246; CN96, 3: 245–46; Ancel, "Plans for Deportation of the Romanian Jews and Their Discontinuation in Light of Documentary Evidence, July–October 1942," *Yad Vashem Studies* 16 (1984): 381–420; Ancel, *Documents,* 10, no. 91, 210, 215, and 4, no. 119, 252, and no. 138, 276, and no. 203, 299.

13. Filderman, "My Life," 633.

14. Schwarzfeld, "The Jews," 37–38; *Izvoare,* 2: 2, 522–24.

Bibliography

Alexandru, J., et al., eds. *Martiriul evreilor din România, 1940–1944. Documente și mărturii.* București: Hasefer, 1991.

Ancel, J. *Contribuții la istoria României: Problema evreiască.* 2 vols. Bucharest: Hasefer / Yad Vashem, 2001–3.

———. *The Economic Destruction of Romanian Jewry.* Translated by L. Schramm. Jerusalem: Yad Vashem, 2007.

———. "German-Romanian Relations." In *The Tragedy of Romanian Jewry,* edited by R. L. Braham. Boulder, CO: East European Monographs CDIV, 1994.

———. *Preludiu la asasinat: Pogromul de la Iași, 29 iunie 1941.* Translated by C. Bines. Iași: Polirom, 2005.

———. *Transnistria.* 3 vols. Bucharest: Atlas, 1998.

Ancel, J., ed. *Documents Concerning the Fate of Romanian Jewry during the Holocaust.* 12 vols. New York: Beate Klarsfeld Foundation, 1986.

Arad, Y., et al., eds. *The Einsatzgruppen Reports: Selections from the Dispatches of the Nazi Death Squads' Campaign against the Jews.* New York: Holocaust Library, 1989.

Benjamin, Lya, et al., eds. *Cum a fost posibil?: Evreii din România în perioada Holocaustului.* București: Institutul Național pentru Studierea Holocaustului din România, 2007.

———. Federația Comunităților Evreiești din România, Centrul pentru studiul istoriei evreilor din România. *Evreii din România între anii 1940–1944, Izvoare și mărturii referitoare la evreii din România.* București: Hasefer, 1993, 1996, 1997. Vol. 1, *Legislația-Antievreiască;* vol. 2, *Problema evreiască în Stenogramele consiliului de miniștri;* vol. 3, *1940–1942: Perioada unei mari restriști.*

Braham, Randolph. *Romanian Nationalists and the Holocaust: The Political Exploitation of Unfounded Rescue Accounts.* Boulder, CO: East European Monographs CDLXXXIII, 1998.

Braham, Randolph, ed. *Destruction of Romanian and Ukrainian Jews during the Antonescu Era.* Social Science Monographs. New York: Columbia University Press, 1997.

———. *The Tragedy of Romanian Jewry.* Boulder, CO: East European Monographs CDIV, 1994.

Broszat, M. "Das Dritte Reich und die rumänische Judenpolitik," in *Gutachten des Instituts für Zeitgeschichte.* (München 1958).

BIBLIOGRAPHY

———. "Die Eiserne Garde und das Dritte Reich." *Politische Studien* 9 (1958).

Butnaru, Ion. *The Silent Holocaust: Romania and Its Jews.* Westport, CT: Greenwood Press, 1992.

———. *Waiting for Jerusalem: Surviving the Holocaust in Romania.* Westport, CT: Greenwood Press, 1993.

Carp, Matatias. *Cartea Neagră: Suferinţele evreilor din România, 1940–1944.* 2nd ed. Bucureşti: Diogene, 1996; 3 vols.: 1, *Legionarii şi Rebeliunea;* 2, *Pogromul de la Iaşi;* 3, *Transnistria.*

Codreanu, Corneliu. *For My Legionaries (the Iron Guard).* Translation of 1936 Sibiu edition, *Pentru Legionari.* Madrid: "Libertatea," 1976.

Cristian, S. C. *Patru ani de urgie: Notele unui evreu din România.* Bucureşti: Timpul, 1946.

Deletant, Dennis. *Hitler's Forgotten Ally: Ion Antonescu and His Regime, Romania 1940–44.* New York: Palgrave Macmillan, 2006.

Dorian, Emil. *The Quality of Witness: A Romanian Diary, 1937–1944.* Philadelphia: Jewish Publication Society of America, 1982.

Filderman, Wilhelm. "My Life: The Memoirs of Doctor W. Filderman, L.L.D." Typescript. Jerusalem: Yad Vashem Archives.

Friling, T., et al., eds. *Final Report of the International Commission on the Holocaust in Romania.* Yad Vashem, 2004; and Iaşi: Polirom, 2005); and Wikipedia, "Wiesel Commission."

Halevy, M. A. "Comunităţile evreieşti din Iaşi şi Bucureşti, până la Zaveră (1821)." In *Sinai: Anuar de studii Iudaice,* edited by M. A. Halevy, 11–112. Bucureşti: Institutul de Istorie Evreo-Română, 1931.

Heinen, A. Die legion "Erzengel Michael." In *Rumänien: soziale Bewegung und politische Organisation.* München: Oldenbourg, 1986.

———. *Rumänien, der Holocaust und die Logik der Gewalt.* München: Oldenbourg, 2007.

Hillgruber, A. *Hitler, König Carol, und Marschall Antonescu: Die deutsch-rumänischen Beziehungen, 1938–1944.* Wiesbaden: Steiner, 1965.

Hitchins, K. *Rumania, 1866–1947.* Oxford: Oxford University Press, 1994.

Hohne, H. *The Order of the Death's Head.* Translated by R. Barry. New York: Ballantine, 1971.

Iancu, Carol. *Les Juifs en Roumanie (1866–1919): De l'exclusion à l'émancipation.* Aix-en-Provence: Université de Provence, 1978.

———. *Les Juifs en Roumanie (1919–1938): De l'émancipation à la marginalization.* Paris-Louvain: Peeters, 1996.

Ioanid, Radu. *The Holocaust in Romania: The Destruction of Jews and Gypsies under the Antonescu Regime, 1940–1944.* Chicago: Ivan R. Dee, 2000.

———. *The Sword of the Archangel: Fascist Ideology in Romania.* Translated by P. Heinegg. Boulder, CO: East European Monographs CCXCII, 1990.

Kareţki, A., and M. Covaci. *Zile Însîngerate la Iaşi (28–30 iunie 1941).* Bucureşti: Ed. Politică, 1978.

Livezeanu, Irina. *Cultural Politics in Greater Romania: Regionalism, Nation Building, and Ethnic Struggles, 1918–1930.* Ithaca, NY: Cornell University Press, 1995.

BIBLIOGRAPHY

Marcus, Israel (Marius Mircu). *Pogromul de la Iași din 29 Iunie.* București, 1945.

———. *Șapte Momente din Istoria Evreilor în România.* București: Glob, 1977.

Mitrany, D. *The Land and the Peasant in Rumania.* Oxford: Oxford University Press, 1930.

Nagy-Talavera, N. M. *The Green Shirts and the Others: A History of Fascism in Hungary and Rumania.* Stanford, CA: Hoover Institution, 1970.

Pinkas ha-kehilot (Register of Jewish Communities). Vol. 1, *Romanyah.* Jerusalem: Yad Vashem, 1969.

Politics and Political Parties in Roumania. London: International Reference Library Publications, 1936.

Radu-Cernea, Adrian. *Pogromul de la Iași: Depoziție de martor.* București: Hasefer, 2002.

Republica Populară Română. Parchetul Curții din București, Cabinetul Criminalilor de război, dos. Nr. 5260/1947, "Rechizitor . . . pentru cercetarea crimelor săvârșite asupra populației din orașul Iași, Stânca Rosnovanu și Tg. Mărculești în luna iunie 1941." Yad Vashem record group 0–11/73, War Crimes Indictment.

Roumania, Ten Years After. Boston: Beacon Press, 1929.

Schwarzfeld, E. "The Jews of Roumania from the Earliest Times to the Present Day." In *The American Jewish Yearboook,* 5662 (September 14, 1901–October 1, 1902).

Seton-Watson, R. W. *A History of the Roumanians from Roman Times to the Completion of Unity.* Cambridge: Cambridge University Press, 1934; Archon Books, 1963 reprint).

Sebastian, Mihail. *Journal, 1935–1944.* Translated by P. Camiller. London: Pimlico, 2003.

Stanciu, S., chief ed. Centrul pentru studiul istoriei Evreilor din România. *Martiriul evreilor din România 1940–1944.* Documente și mărturii. București: Hasefer, 1991.

Starr, J. "Jewish Citizenship in Rumania, 1878–1940." *Jewish Social Studies* 3, no. 1 (1941).

Troncotă, Cristian. *Eugen Cristescu, asul Serviciilor Secrete Românéștii: Memorii, mărturii, documente.* București: Roza Vânturilor, 1994.

Trașcă, O., and D. Deletant, eds. *Al III-lea Reich și Holocaustul din România, 1940–1944.* Documente din archivele germane. București: Editura Institutului Național pentru Studierea Holocaustului din România, 2007.

USHMM RG. United States Holocaust Memorial Museum Record Group, Library and Archives.

Vago, Bela. *The Shadow of the Swastika: The Rise of Fascism and Anti-Semitism in the Danube Basin, 1936–1939.* London: Saxon House, 1975.

Volovici, Leon. *Nationalist Ideology and Antisemitism: The Case of Romanian Intellectuals in the 1930s.* Translated from Romanian by C. Kormos. Oxford: Pergamon Press, 1991.

YVA rg. Jerusalem, Yad Vashem (Holocaust Martyrs' and Heroes' Remembrance Authority). Archives record group.

Index

all numbers in italics refer to illustrations

Abraham, Iosef, 104
Adevărul (The Truth), 45, 56, 57
Agarici, Viorica, 103
agrarian reform of 1864, 18
Aizicovici, Max, 98, 105
Alecsandri, Vasile: *The Village Bloodsuckers (Lipitorile Satelor)*, 9, 18
Alexandrescu, Major, 91
Alexandru I. Cuza University, 10
"All for the Fatherland" (Totul Pentru Țară), 28, 151
Alliance Israélite Universelle, 17
American Committee on the Rights of Religious Minorities, 38–39, 59
Anti-Jewish Universal Alliance, 20
The Antisemite (Antisemitul), 22
Antisemitic League, 61
antisemitic parties and organizations, 43–44, 61
Antisemitic Romano-European Congress, Bucharest, 20
Antonescu, Ion, 15, 140; accusation of Jews mocking Romanian troops, 153; call for "ethnic cleansing," 4–5, 66, 72–73, 122; communiqués misrepresenting Iași pogrom, 114, 117, 128, 134, 149; in Cristea government, 48; dismantling of Iron Guard, 67; dispatch of Echelon I to Iași after meeting with Hitler, 142–43, 153; legal destruction of Jewish community, 68, 152–53, 154; and mass murders of Jews of Odessa, 4; and National-Legionnaire State, 63, 67; order that all Jews be deported from Iași, 73, 95, 124; and plan for deportation of Romanian Jews to Belzec death camp, 155–56; prewar anti-Jewish actions, 65–66, 122; principal instigator of Romanian Holocaust, 121; received early and continuing information about Iași pogrom, 124; relations with Nazi Germany, 67, 141
Antonescu, Mihai, 68, 74; approval of death trains, 126; call for "ethnic cleansing" or "purification," 4–5, 13–14, 72–73, 122, 153; and evacuation of Jews from Iași, 95; principal instigator of Romanian Holocaust, 121; and Richter, 143; and "Slavic problem," 155
Apărarea Națională (The National Defense), 44–45
Army Group South, invasion of Soviet territory, 2, 4, 13, 153, 154
Association of Christian Students, 57
Atudorei, Dumitru, 100
Auerbach, Herman, 64, 98, 137
Auerbach, Isaac, 34
Auerbach, Rebeca, 64, 84, 90, 98, 137, 145
Avram, Moritz, 117
"Awake Romania!", 20
Azriel, Smuel, 108

Bădescu, Colonel, 91, 115
Bahlui River Valley, 3, 132

INDEX

Bălan, Lazar, 68
Bălan (policeman), 74
Balkan Wars, 21–22
Balotescu, Gheorge, 123–24
Bălți, murder and evacuation of Jews by German and Romanian troops, 119
Bărnuțiu, Simion, 15
Barosi, Colonel, 91
Barozzi, Gheorghe, 115, 129
Basel Congress of 1897, 35
Becescu-Georgescu, Florin, 124, 144
Beilis, Mendel, 32
Bercovici, Emil, 62
Bercovici, Marcu, 35, 120
Bessarabia, 21; annexed by Soviet Union, 3, 50; Jewish exiles from Russian Civil War, 56–57; mass murder Jews during Romanian withdrawal from, 62–63; mass murder of Jews during Romanian/German invasion of Soviet Union, 4, 13; under Romanian rule, 3, 152
Bismarck, Otto von, 139
Bloody Days in Iași (28–30 June 1941) (Karețki and Covaci), 99
Blue Shirts (Lancers), 44, 46, 140
B'nai B'rith, 21
Bocancea, Gheorghe, 135–36
Bolschwing, Otto von, 67
Borcescu, Traian: postwar testimony about links between intelligence services of Germany and Romania, 123–24, 144–45, 153–54
Botez, Ion, 100, 101, 102
Botezatu, Vera, 137
Botoșani, 3
Brăilescu-Gotlieb, Dr., 72
Brătianu, Gheorghe, 46
Brătianu, Ion, 11, 18, 20, 23
Braunstein, Marcel, 75, 145
Breasla jidovilor, 30
Bucharest, 13; massacre of Jews during 1941 rebellion of Iron Guard, 6–7, 72, 151, 152, 153; rampage of Christian university students in Jewish quarter of, 20
Bucharest Bar Association, 51

Buchmann, Ghetzel, 35, 69, 76, 85, 98, 102
Buchmann, Roza, 69, 75, 76, 88, 98
Bucium, SSI command post, 123
Bucovina, 4; annexed by Soviet Union, 3, 50; mass murder of Jews during Romanian withdrawal from, 62; mass murders of Jews during Romanian/German invasion of Soviet Union, 154; mass murders of Jews in 1940, 6; under Romanian rule, 3, 152
Bulgaria, annexation of southern Dobrogea, 63, 140
Buna Vestire (Good News), 45

Căinari, Gura, 78
Călărași death train, 2, 4, 95, 96–106, *103*, 109, 117, 126, 127, 132; survivors, 105–6
Călinescu, Armand, 48
Câmpulung, 59
Canaris, Wilhelm, 64
Cantacuzino (Iron Guard leader), 44
Cantemir, Prince, 31
Captaru, Dumitriu (prefect of Iași district), 129; conflicting reports of Iași pogrom, 79, 88, 90, 134; excuses for actions in Iași, 131; meetings with police officials during Iași pogrom, 91, 127; orders for death trains, 95, 96, 99, 100, 131; suspicion of ruse to attack Iași Jews, 130
Carlaonț, General, 91, 119
Carol II, King, 28, 43; abdication, 63, 71, 140; accord with Germany, 53; anti-Jewish legislation patterned after Nuremberg laws of 1935, 5, 48–49, 62, 65, 152; efforts to destroy Iron Guard, 6, 44; and Goga-Cuza government, 46, 48, 53; murder of Codreanu, 6; shift to fascist right, 46, 61–62; visit to Hitler, 46
Carp, Matatias, 108–9, 115
Carp, Valeriu, 62, 63
Casă Verde (Legion headquarters in Iași), 64
Ceaușu, Toivi, 136

INDEX

Central Council of Jews in Romania (Consiliul Central al Evreilor din România), 40, 41, 120
Cernăuți (Cernowitz), 4, 58–59
chestură, 1. *See also* Iași pogrom of 1941
Chirilovici, Constantin (chief police inspector), 36, 82–84, 129; and accusations that Jews were collaborating with Soviet bombers, 76, 126; conflicting reports of *chestură* massacre and Iași pogrom, 83–84, 114–15, 131–32, 133–34, 135; and evacuation of Jews of Iași, 96; failure to find evidence of Jews having firearms or firing at troops in Iași, 126; meetings at *chestură* on That Sunday, 85, 90, 127; payoffs to by Jewish community, 118, 132–33; rescue of some Jews of Iași, 132; suicide, 132; 1945 testimony about Iași pogrom, 135
Chișinău (Kishinev), 4, 124
Choir Temple, Bucharest, 18
Christian guilds, 33
Christian lawyers and doctors, efforts to exclude Jews from professions, 44, 48, 51
Christian National Defense League (Liga Apărării Național-Creștine [LANC]), 25, 43, 44, 59
Christian Nationalists, 23
Christian university students: antisemitic demonstrations, 5–6, 15; 1927 attack on Jewish students, 39; 1899 attack on Jews, 55–56; competition from Jewish students, 6; demand for *numerus clausus* (restricted admission) and *numerus nullus* (no admission), 6, 25, 44, 57; 1922 mass demonstration, 25, 57, 61; opposed citizenship for Jews, 10, 43, 58; rampage in Jewish quarter of Bucharest, 20; and rise of Romanian fascism, 24; "the generation of 1922," 24, 57–58
Cîmpoeș, Gheorghe, 77
Cioran, Emil, 140

Cîrlig, killings at, 79
Citizenship Law of 1924, 23–24, 47–48
Citizenship Revision Law of 1938, 6, 47–48, 52, 53
Ciudei, murders at, 62, 63
Ciurchi cemetery, Iași, 66
"cleansing the ground," 13
Codreanu, Corneliu, 36; arrests and acquittals for murders of PM and police, 6, 25–27, 45, 48, 58, 150–51; assassination of, 6, 27, 48, 60; and Association of Christian Students, 57; creation of Iron Guard, 10, 25–26, 27, 43; defense of Totu, 58; exhumation of, 66; and extreme nationalist movements of 1920s and 1930s, 24–25; and mass demonstration to oppose constitutional change of 1923, 25; and mass meeting in Iași to protest constitutional change, 14–15; and political murder, 56; praise of state heroes who fought against citizenship for Jews, 12–13; promise to expel Jews from Romania, 60, 150; urged students to expand antisemitic program, 25
Cohen, Ety, 136
Cohn, Silviu, 106
Cojocaru, Iosub, 75, 76
Constantinescu (health minister), 52, 53
Copou Park, Iași, 11, 12
Cosma, Matai, 91, 129
Cossacks, 29
Crăciun, Nicolae, 118–19
Crainic, Nichifor, 140
Cries, Solomon, 64
Crimean Tatars, 29
Cristea, Miron, 46, 48, 53
Cristescu, Eugen (head of SSI), 115, 122–23, 124, 135, 143, 145
Cristescu-Gica, Gheorge, 124, 144
Cultural Association of Jewish Women, 35
Curierul Israelit (Israelite Courier), 21, 59
Cuvântul (The Word), 140

181

INDEX

Cuza, Alexandru C., 20, 24, 61, 140; 1907 call for exclusions or expulsions of Jews, 22; and Goga-Cuza government, 6; defense of Totu, 58; and extreme nationalist movements of 1920s and 1930s, 24–25; and mass meeting in Iași to protest constitutional change, 14–15; and 1897 meeting in Bucharest, 55; opposed citizenship for Jews, 10, 47; *Poporația*, 56; and solution to "Jewish problem," 13; split with Goga over policy, 47
Cuza, Alexandru I. (prince of Romania), 6, 10, 17
Cuza, Gheorghe, 47, 140
Czechoslovakia, German takeover of, 61

Dadarlat, Dumitru, 137–38
Daniel brothers (Chaim, Leon, and Albert), 34
Darie, Captain, 131
Dauer, Filip, 132, 133
David, Mendel, 100
Death's Head units. *See* Totenkopf (Death's Head) Formation
death trains. *See Trenurile mortuare* (The Death Trains)
Delaporte, Henri Pacifique, 18
Der Veker (The Alarm Clock), 37, 40
Deșteptarea (Awakening), 20
Dimineața (Morning), 45, 57
Dinulescu, Radu, 123, 124, 135, 144
Dniester River, 4
Dobrogea, southern, annexation by Bulgaria, 63, 140
Dolhasca, murder of Jews at, 63
Dorian, Emil, 68
Dorohoi, 3; May 1941 deportation of Jews to Tîrga Jiu prisons, 72, 122; pogrom of July 1, 1940, 4, 62–63
Dreyfus trial, 55, 156
Drimer, Carol, 112
Duca, Ion, 28, 45
Duminica ceea (That Sunday), 2, 3, 81–94. *See also* Iași pogrom of 1941

education: exclusion of Romanian Jews from public schools, 6, 65; Iași Jewish community, 34, 37–38; Jewish Romanian schools, 33, 37
Einsatzgruppe A, 147
Einsatzgruppe D, 4, 124, 146–47, 154
Einsatzgruppen, number of Jews killed by, 155
Eliade, Mircea, 140
Emek Israel, 35
Emil, Zalman, 108
Eminescu, Mihai, 12
Engels, Friedrich, 40
epitropi (administrators), 33
ethnic "purification" or "cleansing," 3, 4–5, 13–14, 66, 72–73, 122, 153

Fallick, David, 58
Fălticeni, 3
fascist antisemitic political parties and groups, 5–6; campaign against democratic papers, 45; campaign against so-called Judeo-Bolshevik journalists, 45; and Christian university student movement, 43; favored statewide *numerus nullus*, 44; publications of, 44–45
fascist states, murder of political opponents, 60
Favel, Lipa, 136
Federation of Jewish Communities, 68
Ferdinand, King, 23
Fermă de Hachshara (preparation farm), 35
Filderman, Wilhelm, 20, 22, 39, 41, 55, 58, 61, 65, 68, 69, 156
Filipescu, Richard, 93–94, 116
Focșani, pogrom of 1925, 58
France: fall to Germany, 139; promise to support Romanian independence, 139
Franco, Francisco, 46, 58
Fraternitatea, 34
Freitag, Solomon, 99, 100
Frontul Renașterii Naționale (Renaissance National Front), 61
Frontul Românesc (The Romanian Front), 43
fussgayer, 21

INDEX

Gaer, Max, 71, 85, 88, 96, 117–18, 146
Galați, murder of Jews in, 63
Garcineanu, Simon, 105
Gaster, Moses, 34, 35
Gavrilovici, Constantin, 92
Geheime Feldpolizei, 143
Geller, Leon, 40
General Association of Romanian-Born Jews, 20, 21
"the generation of 1922," 57–58
Georgescu, Commissar, 52
German military forces: Einsatzgruppe A, 147; Einsatzgruppe D, 4, 124, 146–47, 154; instigation and participation in Iași massacre, 121, 133–35; number of Jews killed by Einsatzgruppun, 155; Sonderkommando 10a (Sk 10a), 146
German military intelligence *(Abwehr)*, 64, 123, 143, 144, 145, 147
German-Soviet nonaggression pact of 1939, 139
Germany, attack on Soviet Union, 73, 74, 152
Gestapo, 143
Ghelerter, Dr., 22, 36, 40
Gheorghiu, Constantin, 100, 101, 102
Gheorghiu, Ioan, 93
Gherner, Herș, 85, 88, 112
Ghica, Alexandru, 65
Gigurtu, Ion: decrees of August 8–9, 1940 (patterned after Nuremberg laws of 1935), 5, 48–49, 62, 65; meeting with Hitler, 141, 153
Gîndirea (Contemplation), 140
Giosanu (regional police inspector), 83, 85, 86, 91, 101, 114, 129, 133
Goering, Hermann, 142
Goga, Octavian, 6, 46; defense of Totu, 58; National Agrarian Party, 44, 45; visit to Hitler, 140
Goga-Cuza government, 10, 37, 152; Citizenship Revision Law, 47–48; promise to confiscate Jewish property, 46–47; promise to expel Jews from country, 47

Goilav, Major, 62
Goldfaden, Avram, 9
Goldstein, Nathan, 92
Golimus, Aurel, 65
Great Britain, promise to support Romanian independence, 139
"Great Synagogue" (Sinagoga Mare), 30
Greeks and Ottoman janissaries, conflict of, 31
Green Shirts (Legionnaires), 44, 140
Green Tree cabaret, Iași, 9
Grigore Ghica, Prince, 30
Grinberg, Carol and Henrich, *107*
Grițic, Dumitru, 100
Gruenberg-Moldvan, David, 37
Gypsies, 65, 85, 98, 100

hahambasha (chief rabbi), 30, 33
Hahamu, Abraham, 65, 76
Haimovici, Leon, 97
Hannover, Nathan, 29–30; *Yeven Metzulah (Abyss of Despair)*, 30
Hansen (Wehrmacht General), 67
Hasidim: opposition to *haskalah*, 34; vs. modernists, 33
haskalah (enlightenment), 33, 34
Hasmonaea, 35, 91
Hauffe, Arthur, 142
Hauzner, Ozias, 112, 113
Herșcovici, Moșe, 71, 86, 91, 95–96, 102, 105, 106
Herskowicz family, *108*
Herța, 63
Herzl, Theodor, 35
Heydrich, Reinhard, 141, 142
Himmler, Heinrich, 1, 4, 141, 142
Hitler, Adolph, 69; Antonescu's meeting with, 142–43, 153; Carol II's visit with, 46; Gigurtu's meeting with, 141, 153; Goga's visit with, 140; and partitioning of Romania, 61; support for Antonescu, 66–67, 141; viewed by Romanians as hero, 15
Hoare, Reginald, 44, 45–46, 51, 61
Holy Land (Țara Sfântă), 31
Horthy, Miklós, 69
Hull, Cordell, 156

INDEX

Hungary, 1; and alleged ritual murder of Christian child by Jews of Tiszaeszlar, 20; annexation of northwestern Transylvania, 63; expulsion of Jews from in 1367, 29

Iacob, Iosef, 36, 76, 118, 145
Iancu, Carol, 12, 22
Iași, Jewish community, 30–31; attacks by Cossacks in 1650, 31; attacks by Russians and Turks in 1870s and 1880s, 31; Breasla jidovilor, 30; commercial enterprise, 31; Communal Council, 30, 35–36, 37; craftsmen and artisans, 31; cultural flowering in nineteenth century, 33–35; economic community, 38–39; education, 34, 37–38; Great Synagogue, 31; guilds, 31, 33; *hahambasha* (chief rabbi), 30, 31; internal divisions, 33; Jewish hospital, 33; Jewish merchants and artisans in 1831 and 1839, 33; lack of wealth, 38–39; leaders attracted to socialist movement, 40; number of registered Jewish heads of household, 30–31; offices of Great Elder and Regional Chief, 30; organized intellectual life, 33–35; population growth in nineteenth century, 33; protection money to police and other government officials, 36; in seventeenth century, 29; social assistance section, 36–37; "Society for helping the sick," 31; Yiddish theater, 9. *See also* Iași pogrom of 1941
Iași Bar Association, expulsion of Jewish lawyers, 39, 51
Iași pogrom of 1941, aftermath: burial of murdered Jews, 111–14; community assistance to survivors, 118–20; conscription of Jews for forced labor, 117–18; estimates of number of Jews murdered, 114–15; government misrepresentation of events, 115–16; payments of Jewish community to city officials, 118; refugees from Podu Iloaiei, 119; requirement that Jews make "loans" to state, 117; requirement that Jews wear yellow star, 106, 117; rescue of orphans from Transnistria death camps, 120

Iași pogrom of 1941, 1–2, 7, 36, 38, 153–54, 156; beginning of widespread assault against Jews, 82; Călărași death train, 2, 4, 95, 96–106, *103*, 109, 117, 126, 127, 132; *chestură massacre, 2, 84–94, 89,* 95, 106, 127; Duminica ceea *(That Sunday),* 2, 3, 81–94; fueled by campaign of vilification, 72, 123; harassment of Jews in days following declaration of war on Soviet Union, 74–75; Jews cleaning cobblestones in *chestură after massacre, 93;* "Liber" permits, 86–87, 90, 92, 134, 145; official reports about *chestură massacre, 114–15, 132, 145; orders that all Jews be evacuated from city, 82; parents and child murdered in street, 116;* planes launching of flares or rockets over city, 75, 129; plundering of Jewish properties by Christians, 5; Podu Iloaiei death train, 2, 95, 106–8, 114, 126, 132; Romanian soldiers seeking revenge upon Jews, 75, 132; rumors of Jewish collaboration with Soviets, 72, 75–76, 81, 83; suspicions of Jewish leaders that action against Jews was imminent, 76, 81; Trenurile mortuare *(The Death Trains),* 2, 3, 4, 7, 38, 95–109, 153; victims of, 111–20; warnings to Jews by non-Jews, 93–94, 133. *See also* Iași, Jewish community

Iași pogrom of 1941, perpetrators, 121–38; conflicting official accounts, 133–35; Echelon units, 122, 123, 124, 142–43, 144–45, 153; Iași police force, 135–36; 1947 indictment against those charged with crimes, 114, 135–36; local officials' blame of Germans, 134–35; participation of

INDEX

ordinary citizens, 136–38; principal instigators of, 121; simulated attack on German and Romanian troops in city, 5, 82–84, 121, 129, 130
Iliescu, Ion, 9
Inotești, 104
Ionescu, Constantin, 75, 99, 100
Ionescu, Nae, 140
Ionescu, Victor, 124
Iorga, Nicolae, 11, 12; anti-Jewish articles, 22; and antisemitic Cultural League, 20; assassination of, 66, 68; 1907 call for exclusions of Jews from political expression, 22; "The History of Jews in Our Country," 23; and 1897 meeting in Bucharest, 55; "national union," 39–40; opposition to Jewish citizenship, 10; proposal that Jews leave Iași or starve, 13; severing of political association with Cuza, 56; ties to Germany, 140–41; and treaty obligation to grant rights to Jews, 25
Iorga-Cuza party, antisemitic in origins, ideology, and platform, 22–23
Iron Guard (Legion of the Archangel Michael), 61, 140, 150; attacks on synagogues, 64–65; *Casă Verde,* 64; extortion from Jews for halting terror, 64–65; and 1937 general election, 46; government executions of, 48; green shirts, 44, 140; killing of prime minister Duca, 28; massacre of Bucharest Jews during 1941 rebellion, 4, 6–7, 72, 151, 152, 153; mass murder of government officials, 6, 60, 66; murder of Jews in Ploiești, 4, 65; and National-Legionnaire State, 63, 65–66, 67, 151, 152; perceived brotherhood with Nazis, 140; seen as allies by SS, 141; threat to Romanian Jews, 27–28; unrestricted police power under Antonescu, 63
Isacovici (subprefect of Iași), 91
Israelite Hospital (Spitalul Israelit), 35, 36
Italy, 1

Itzhac (Jewish man digging graves), 113–44
Ivancu, Herșcu, 93

Janissaries, 32
Jewish commercial guilds, 31, 33
Jewish Khazar state, 29
Jewish medical students, 60
Jewish money changers, 33
Jewish Parliamentary Club, 40
Jewish political parties, in Transylvania and Bessarabia, 39
Jewish Romanian schools, 33, 37
Jewish schools, harassment by state officials, 20
Jewish tailors, 38
Jezequel, Jules, 59–60
Jilava massacre, 68
Jilava Prison, 66
Jodl, Alfred, 142
Joint Distribution Committee, 36
Josephus, 73
Judeo-Bolshevik journalists, 45

kabbalist (mystic), 30
kamelaukions, 31
Kaufman, Mose, 76
Keitel, Wilhelm, 142
Khmelnitsky, Bogdan, 29, 30
Kishinev pogrom of 1903, 21, 32, 55
Kogălniceanu, Mihail, 10–11, 12, 15, 18, 20
Kopstuck, Osias, 68
Korot Haitim (Current Events), 34
Kosak, Walter, 100
kosher meat, taxes on, 33
Kovno, Lithuania pogrom, 147

LANC. *See* Christian National Defense League (Liga Apărării Național-Creștine [LANC])
Lance Bearer (L‡ncier), 44, 46, 140
Lazar, Moise, 137, 138
League of Nations, 62
Leahu, Gheorghe, 36, 64, 74, 76, 83, 86, 129; official reports about *chestură massacre, 114,̇ 132,* 145

INDEX

Lebel, Iosef, 105
Lecca, Junius, 124
Lecca, Radu, 143, 155
Legion of the Archangel Michael (Iron Guard). *See* Iron Guard (Legion of the Archangel Michael)
Leib, Iancu, 88, 90–91
Leib, Moise, 96, 97–98, 132
Leibovici, Elias, 137, 149
Leibovici, Samoil, 113
Leoveanu, Emanoil, 82–84, 86, 101, 124, 126, 127–28, 133–34, 135
Lespezi, 97
Liberal government, 27
Liberal Peasants, 39
Lippe, Karpel, 35
Livezeanu, Irina, 24, 43
Lumea, 57
Lungani-Roman, 102
Lupta, 57
Lupu, Constantin, 85–86, 91, 111, 115, 123, 124, 129; accusations of blame for Iași pogrom, 135; excuse for actions in 1945 depositions, 130–31; leading of police in violent searches and arrests, 131; as military commander of Iași, 82, 130
Luther, Martin (German foreign office), 155

Maccabis, 57
Madgearu, Virgil, 66
Manciu, C. G., 26–27
Mandache, Vasile, 101–2
Maniu, Iuliu, 28
Mannerheim, Carl Gustaf Emil, 15
Manole, Silvia, 86
Manoliu, Mircea, 75, 76, 81–82, 93, 118, 128, 134
Mântuirea, 57
Marcovici, Eliza, 136
Marcovici, Israel, 136
Marcovici, Jack, 136
Marcovici, Oscar, 84
Mărculești, massacre at, 78, 79, 127
Marcusohn (perfume shop owner), 116

Marievici, Vlad, 111
Marin, Vasile, 46
Marinescu, Danubiu, 99, 100
Martinescu, Elena, 136
Martinescu, Petre, 136
Marx, Karl, 40
Mârzescu, Gheorghe, and son, 15
Matieș, Colonel, 2, 77, 78–79, 127, 152
Mayer, Leon, 87
Melik, Estella, 116–17
Melik, Lupu, 116
Mendelsohn, Ilie, 36
Mendelsohn, Menachem, 133
Micandru, Constantin (chief of SSI German liasion office), 123, 143, 144, 145
Micescu, Istrate, 51
Mihailescu, Lieutenant, 78, 79
Mihailov, Vasile, 78
Mihai Racoviță, Prince, 31–32
Mihoreni, murders of Jews, 62
militant nationalism, 24–25, 43, 44
Mînăstireanu, Ioan, 136
Ministry of Interior, Romanian, major force in deporting and killing Jews, 13–14
Minorities Treaty of 1919, 23, 24
Mircești, 102
Mircu, Marius, 75, 115
Mittleman, David, 98
Moldavia, principality of, 3; growing number and prominence of Jews in, 5; Jewish population growth in nineteenth century, 33; shift of capital from Suceava to Iași, 29; uniting with Wallachia, 9–10
Moldavia, Republic of, 3
Moldavia Règlements, 24; racsist propaganda against Jews, 11–12; used to provide legal authority to drive Jews from Romania, 12
Monitorul Oficial, 134
Moscovici, Isac, 62
Moscovici, Moshe, 36–37, 55
Moța, Ion, 26, 46
Mussolini, Benito, 69

INDEX

Naftali Cohen, 30
Naftule, Iancu, 146
Natansohn, Nehema, 88
National Agrarian Party, 44, 45
National Center for Romanianization, 68
National Christian Party, 44, 45, 46, 47, 51, 141
National Committee of Students of Iași, and attack on Jewish community in 1899, 21
National Defense (Apărarea Națională), 25
National-Democratic Party, 22, 25
nationalism, militant, 24–25, 43, 44
Nationalist-antisemites, 22
National Jewish Party (Partidul Național Evreiesc), 40
National-Legionnaire State, 36, 53, 63; abolishment and replacement by military dictatorship, 67; antisemitic laws, 65–66, 151, 152
National Liberal Party, 28, 41
National-Peasant government, 27
National Peasant Party, 28, 39, 45, 52
National Romanian Christian Student Union, 59
National Theater, Iași: fiftieth anniversary of pogrom and death trains, 9; trial of Codreanu, 26–27
Nazis. *See* Romania, and Nazi Germany
Neamul Românesc (Romanian People), 25
Neubacher, Hermann, 66
Neuschatz, Iacob, 34
Nicodim, Patriarch, 15
Nicolae Mavrocordat, Prince, 30
Nicolau, Stefan, 75, 76, 82
Niculae, Iacob, 108
Northern Bucovina. *See* Bucovina
numerus clausus: and education, 60; law of July 16, 1934, 47; and law profession, 51; nationwide, 48, 150
numerus nullus, 6; call for by Christian lawyers, 44; nationwide, 48, 150
numerus Valahicus, 44

Odessa, mass murders of Jews of, 4
Ohalei Șem society, 35

okhrana (Okhrannoe Otdelenie), 21
Olivenbaum, Jean, 116, 149
Onițcani, 31
Operational ("Special") Echelon, SSI, 122, 123, 124, 144–45, 154
Operation Barbarossa, 142
Operation München, 2, 4, 13, 75, 142, 153, 154
Opinia, 57
Organizație sionistă, 35
Organization Todt, 87, 146
Orthodox Jews, opposition to *haskalah,* 34
Ottoman Empire, defeat of, 11, 17

Păcurari Jewish Cemetery, Iași, 75, 112
Pale of Settlement, 53
Panciu, 52
Paris Peace Conference, 23
Parti de la Nație, 61
Parvulescu, Major, 102
Pascal, Iancu, 98
Pașcani, 63, 97
Passover, 31
Patriotul Strămoșesc (The Ancestral Patriot), 60
Paulescu, Nicolae, 25, 26
"Peasant Guard," 45
peasants: Jews as targets for, 18; Liberal Peasants, 39; National Peasant Party, 28, 39, 45, 52; pressure on Jewish farmers to leave rural holdings, 47; Radical Peasants Party, 52; revolt of 1907, 22
Perju, Colonel, 99
Petraru, Ioan, 77–78
Petrescu, Gheorghe, 124
Petrica, Bogdan, 69, 137
Petrica, Ghetzel, 137
Petrica, Roza, 137
Petrovicescu, Constantin, 67
Petrovici, Grigore, 123–24
Piață Unirii, Iași, 85
Piatra Neamț, 142; pogrom of 1925, 58
Pipă (deputy mayor of Roman), 103
Pitiș, Captain, 106
Ploiești, murder of Jews in, 4, 65, 151

INDEX

Podu Iloaiei death train, 2, 95, 106–8, 114, 126, 132
Poland: German-Soviet conquest of, 61, 139; Jews displaced in 1648–49 wars, 29
Poliacu (mayor of Iași), 64–65
Polihroniade, Ioan, 20
Poltag family, 136
Popescu, Ion, 95, 124, 126
Popescu, Stelian, 45, 46, 71, 91, 95
Popricani, mass murders in, 79
Porunca Vremii, 68
Pripoliță, Andronic, 78
Profir, Grigore, 94
The Proletarian (Proletarul), 36
Prut River, 2, 3, 142, 152
Prutul, 76, 128
Psanter, Jacob, 35
pseudoscientific racism, 43
Pulwerman (engineer), 105

Rabinovici, Benjamin, 84, 87–88, 91–92, 103, 106, 146
Rabinovici, Etty, 88
Radical Peasants Party, 52
Radulescu, Ilie, 68
Raitmayer, Constantin, 136
Raitmayer, Ioan, 136
Raitmayer, Petru, 136
Răzmerița (Orthodox priest), 93
Regat (Old Kingdom), 3, 50, 152
Règlement organique, 11, 33
Reichsführer-SS, 142
Revistă Izaelița, 34
Ribbentrop, Joachim von, 141
Richter, Gustav, 143, 144, 155
Ringer, Alfred, 145
Rödler, Erich, 143, 144, 145, 147
Roiu, Captain, 102
Roman, 97, 102, 103, 156
Romania: agrarian reform of 1864, 18; formation of independent state, 9–10; intellectual elite as national heroes, 10; loss of southern Dobrogea to Bulgaria, 63, 140; loss of Transylvania to Hungary, 50; loss to Soviet Union of Bessarabia and Northern Bucovina, 3, 50, 62, 139–40
Romania, and Nazi Germany, 1, 5, 43, 139–47; German destruction of records of actions in Romania, 143; German "final solution" for Jews as model for Romanians, 5, 141; German need for Romanian oil, 53, 139, 141–42, 155; and invasion of Soviet Union (Operation München), 2, 4, 13, 75, 142, 153, 154; links between intelligence services of, 144–45; Romanian entry into German-Italian-Japan pact, 139, 141; SSI (Serviciul Special de Informații) Section "G," 143, 144; treaty making Germany Romania's major trading partner, 139
Romania, antisemitic history, 1–2, 5; accusations of ritual murder against Jews, 31–32; anti-Jewish intellectual elite, 12, 140; anti-Jewish legislation of 1938, 3; Christian myth of Jewish satanism, 15, 150; Christian myths of Jewish deicide and blood libel, 9, 15, 20, 31–32, 44, 45, 149–50; contrast of Jews with virtuous Romanian peasant, 44; image of Jews as Bolsheviks, 15, 44; image of Jews as foreign parasites, 33, 44; image of Jews as undesirable aliens, 5–6, 11–12, 18, 24, 44, 150; images of Jews as greedy merchants and cowards, 9; images of Jews practicing usury and tax evasion, 44; increase in antisemitism in interwar period, 24, 43–53, 56; Jews as targets for angry peasants, 18; legal barriers to public education and health care for Jews, 6, 19–20, 65; overstatement of number of Jews in country, 49; post-WWII antisemitism, 3; wide acceptance of extreme solutions to "Jewish question" in 1920s and 1930s, 3–4
Romanian Bar Association, 51
Romanian Christians: antisemitism,

INDEX

5; boycotts of Jewish businesses in Iași, 20; Christian Nationalists, 23; encouraged crimes against Jews, 60; historical violence against Jews, 3; perception of flood of Jews invading country, 15. *See also* Christian university students

Romanian civil and military command, *125*

Romanian Cultural League, 20, 52

Romanian fascism, 24

Romanian Front, 44

Romanian Holocaust: agencies involved in, 122–23; Călărași death train, 2, 4, 95, 96–106, *103,* 109, 117, 126, 127, 132; Cîrlig killings, 79; Dorohoi pogrom of July 1, 1940, 62–63; ethnic cleansing of occupied Soviet territories, 3; government campaign to vilify Jews as aliens, communists, and allies of Soviet Union, 6, 71; Iron Guard massacre of Jews in Bucharest, 6–7, 67–68, 72, 151, 152, 153; Jilava massacre, 68; Mărculești massacre, 78, 79; mass murder as state policy, 7; mass murders of Jews during Romanian retreat from territories, 4, 62–63, 151, 152; Podu Iloaiei death train, 2, 95, 106–8, 126, 132; Popricani massacre, 79; pre-war violence, 55–69; principal instigators of, 121; requirement that Jews wear yellow star, 106, 117; Romanian denial of, 9; and Romanianization Laws of 1940-41, 136–37; Stânca Rosnovanu massacre of Sculeni Jews, 4, 7, 77–79, 122; terror and mass murders, 1–2, 4, 6–7, 151–52; Trenurile mortuare *(The Death Trains),* 2, 3, 4, 7, 38, 95–109, 153. *See also* Iași pogrom of 1941

Romanian intellectuals, appeal of Nazis to, 140

Romanianization Laws of 1940-41, 136

Romanian Jews: considered themselves as Romanian and worked for citizenship, 34; cultural flowering in eighteenth century, 33–35; dismissed from military in August 1940, 51; domination of small businesses in Moldavia between 1830 and 1860, 33; driven into Moldavia in 1648-49, 29; emigration in 1890s and early 1900s, 20, 56; identified in law at country's inception as undesirable aliens, 11–12, 18; in late nineteenth and early twentieth centuries, 3; little political influence, 39–41; lived in region of Romania for centuries, 29; military service in WWI, 23; population in 1930, 50; in Romania during WWII, 3, 154–55; tripling of population after WWI, 24. *See also* Iași, Jewish community; Romania, antisemitic history

Romanian Jews, laws against, 6; anti-Jewish legislation patterned after Nuremberg laws of 1935, 5, 48–49, 62, 65, 151; Citizenship Revision Law of 1938, 6, 47–48, 52, 53; expropriation of rural property, 66; under National-Legionnaire State, 65–66, 151, 152; prohibition against intermarriage, 49, 65; prohibition against ritual slaughter, 65; prohibition against taking Romanian names, 65; requirement that Jewish stores be open on Saturday and Jewish holidays, 65; transfer of urban property of Jews to state, 68

Romanian Jews, question of citizenship, 5; Citizenship Law of 1924, 23–24; Citizenship Revision Law of 1938, 6, 47–48, 52, 53; 1879 constitution, 15, 18, 19, 23, 39, 150; granting of citizenship after WWI under pressure from allies, 14, 56, 150; and increase in hatred toward Jews, 14, 56; and Moldavia Règlement, 11–13; promises of citizenship to Jewish WWI soldiers, 14; 1848 proposal of and withdrawal of citizenship, 10, 150

INDEX

Romanian military: instigation of and participation in Iași pogrom, 121–22, 133–35; 16th Infantry Regiment, murder of Jews during retreat through Northern Bucovina, 62, 63; 6th Cavalry Regiment massacre of Sculeni Jews, 127, 152. *See also* Section II (military intelligence) of the Supreme General Staff; SSI (Serviciul Special de Informații)
Romanian Orthodox Church, 15, 30, 46, 152
The Romanian People (Neamul Românesc), 22
Romanian press, antisemitic slander, 19
Romanian Red Cross, 103
Romanian unification, 5, 10, 11, 13, 17
Romanian Union of Native Jews, 56–57
Romanization, of Jewish businesses, 47–48
Romilă (policeman), 113
Rosen, Avram, 136
Rosenberg, Alfred, 141
Rosenthal, Henry, 68
Rosenthal, Leon, 67–68
Rosenthal, Rebecca, 68
Rotaru (policeman), 113
Rozinfeld, Margaretta, 138
Russia: defeat of Ottoman Empire, 11, 17; dominant foreign power in Romanian principalities, 11; Kishnev pogrom of 1903, 55; occupation of Iași, 1826-34, 32–33; pogroms following assassination of Tsar Alexander, 55
Russian Civil War, 56

Săbăoani, 97, 102, 103
Sabar River, 68
Șafran, Chief Rabbi, 156
Saineanu, Lozar, 35
Salmuth, von (German 30th Army Corps commander), 82, 95, 128, 129, 135, 145
Santorio, Augusto, 64
Șaraga, Fred, 120
Săvinescu (train station manager), 96, 97

Schachter, Leon, 75, 76
Scheinfeld, Klara, 52, 118, 119
Șchiopu (policeman), 113
Schleier, Israel, 75, 81, 85, 92–93, 96
Schobert, Eugen Ritter von, 142
Schvartz, M., *107*
Schvartz, R., *107*
Schwartz, David, 117
Schwartz, Leon, 117
Schwarzfeld, Benjamin, 34
Schwarzfeld, Elias, 34, 35
Schwarzfeld, Moses, 34, 35
Schwarzfeld, Wilhelm, 34
școală jidovilor, 30
Scriban, Nicolae, 82, 85, 129
Sculeni Jews, massacre of, 2, 4, 7, 77–79, 127, 152, 154
Sechter, Oisie, 112
Section II (military intelligence) of the Supreme General Staff, 2, 144; charged with extermination of Jews, 4; instigation of Iași pogrom, 121
Seetzen, Heinz, 146
"self-cleansing actions," 146–47
Șerbăuți, murder of Jews in, 63
Șerban, Petru, 94
Seton-Watson, R. W.: *History of the Roumanians,* 50–51
Sima, Horia, 48, 61, 63, 65, 67
Simulescu, Major, 102
Slavs, 155
Social Democratic Party (SDP), 40, 41
Social Democrats (SD), 40
Socialist Workers' Party, 36
Socor, E.: *Shame of the University: The Plagiarism of A. C. Cuza,* 56
Solomon, Avram, 102
Solomon, Iancu, 62
Solomovici, Herman, 36
Sonderkommando 10a (Sk 10a), 146
Southern Bug River, 4
Soviet Union: invasion of by German and Romanian troops, 2, 4, 13, 75, 153, 154; invasion of Estonia, Latvia, and Lithuania, 139; ordered Romanian withdrawal from Bessarabia and Northern Bucovina, 62, 139–40

INDEX

Spain, expulsion of Jews from, 29
Spanish Civil War, 46, 58
Spinosu, Vasile, 111–12, 113, 114
Splendid Parc, Bucharest, 143
Sprinceană, Grațian, 129
SSI (Serviciul Special de Informații), 21, 63, 123; charged with extermination of Jews, 4; instigation of Iași pogrom, 121, 124; lost records of Iași pogrom, 143; Operational ("Special") Echelon, 122, 123, 124, 144–45, 154; ordered to provoke Iași pogrom, 5, 122; report of number killed in Iași pogrom, 115; Section "G," 143, 144
SS Security Service (SD), Romania, 67
St. Spiridon Hospital, Iași, 20, 75–76
Staerman, Henry, 75
Stălucitorul (The Shining One), 61
Stânca Rosnovanu, 2; burial of murdered Jews, 114; massacre of Sculeni Jews, 4, 7, 77–79, 122, 152, 153; one of first mass executions to include women and children, 78
Stănculescu, Gheorghe, 134
"Stars" girls school, Iași, 37, 120
Statut Law Code of 1864–65, 17
Stavrescu, Alexandru, 143
Stavrescu, Gheorghe, 76, 95, 123, 145; charges against in postwar trial, 126–27; commander of 14th Infantry Division, 78; 1945 court deposition, 128–29, 130; defense of actions at Iași, 127; meetings at *chestură* on That Sunday, 85, 88–89, 91, 115; official reports about *chestură* massacre, 114; order for evacuation of hostage Jews from Iași,130; orders for death trains, 128; orders for patrols to seek out alleged shooters, 82, 83, 129–30, 133; saving of some Jews, 145
Ștefănescu, Colonel (Călărași prefect), 106
Ștefaniu, Ion, 136
Stievel, Aron, 37, 81, 119
Stihi, Captain, 78, 79
Stînciulescu (police secretary), 36
Stradă Vasile Alecsandri, Iași, 85

Straja Țării (Guards of the Fatherland), 43
Stransky, Hermann von, 143, 144, 145, 147
Sturdza, Ilie, 64
Sturdza, Prince Mihail, 11, 33, 46
Sukkot, festival of, 31
Svastica de Foc (Swastika of Fire), 43
Swastika, 58

Talmudic learning, 33
Talmud-Torah school, 30
Tătărași cemetery, Iași, 119
Tătărescu, Emanuel, 43, 44, 46, 62
Tatars, invasion of Moldavia in 1650, 29
Teodoreanu, Ionel, 51
Teodorescu, (city engineer), 112, 113
Teodorescu (praetor in Tîrgu Frumos), 99
textile production, Jewish industrialists, 38
That Sunday. *See Duminica ceea* (That Sunday)
Three Hierarchs Monastery, 30
Tîrgu Frumos, 95, 97, 99, 105; Jewish Cemetery, 101–2
Tîrgu Jui prison camp, 72, 73, 82
Tîrgu-Neamț pogrom, 31, 156
Titulescu, Foreign Minister, 45–46
Torah study, 31
Totenkopf (Death's Head) Formation, 90, 92, 143, 145, 146
Totoiescu, Aurel, 99–100, 100–101, 102
Totu, Nicolae, 58–59
Totul Pentru Țară ("All for the Fatherland"), 28, 151
Toynbee House, Iași, 35
Transnistria, under Romanian rule, 3, 152
Transnistria labor-death camps, 4, 37, 120, 154
Transylvania, northwestern, annexation by Hungary, 50, 63, 71, 140
Treaty of Berlin, 1878, 17, 19, 23
Trenurile mortuare *(The Death Trains)*, 2, 3, 4, 7, 38, 95–109, 153; Călărași death train, 2, 4, 95, 96–106, *103*, 109, 117, 126, 127, 132; Podu Iloaiei death train, 2, 95, 106–8, 114, 126, 132

Triandaf, Aurel, 100, 105
Trifeşti, 97
Triple Alliance (Germany, Austria-Hungary, and Italy), 139
Trohani, Nicolae, 123
Tulbure, Emil, 123–24

Ukraine, 29
Union of Jewish Communities, 105
Union of Native Jews (Uniunea Evreilor Pământeni [UEP]), 21, 39, 41
Union of Romanian Jews (Uniunea Evreilor Români, or UER), 21, 24, 39–40, 41, 45
Union of Romanian Lawyers, 51
Union Plaza (Piaţă Unirii), Iaşi, 10
Unitary Socialist Party of Romania, 36
University of Bucharest Medical Faculty, attacks against Jewish students, 60
University of Iaşi: 1927 attack of Christian students on Jewish students, 39; Jews admitted in 1939-40, 44; role in post–WWI antisemitic war, 24
Universul (The Universe), 45, 117
Utopian socialism, 40

Văcăreşti prison, 25, 27
Vaida-Voevod, Alexandru, 28, 43, 44
Valahi (Wallachians), 44
Vasile Lupu, Prince, 30
Vătăjanu, Ioan, 100
Ventonic, Alexandru, 36
Vernescu (assistant to Borcescu), 124
Vinovschi, Emil, 137
Volovici, Max, 71, 84–85, 88

Von Killinger, Manfred, 67, 115
Von Schobert, Ritter, 95, 129

Wahrmann, Rabbi, 37, 74
Wallachia, united with Moldavia, 9–10
Wallachians (Valahi), 44
Wallachia Règlements, 11, 24
Wannsee Conference, 142
Wechsler, Max, 40
Weisenberg, Michel, 108
Wiesal, Elie, 9, 13–14
Wolf, Herşu, 75, 76
Wolf, Lili, 136
The Worker (Muncitorul), 40

Xenopol, A. D., 11

yeshiva, 30
Yeven Metzulah (Abyss of Despair) (Hannover), 30
Yiddish, restriction on use of, 53
Yiddish theater, 9
Ypsilanti, Alexander, 31

Zahareşti, murder of Jews in, 63
Zaharia, Gheorge, 115
Zarifopol, Iaşi, 92
Zilberman, Lupu, 138
Zionism, 35, 36, 40, 41
Zionist Hebrew newspaper, first in Romania, 35
Zionist organizations, 39, 40
Zwieback, Adrian, 87, 145–46, 149
Zwieback, Tobias, 74, 87

www.ingramcontent.com/pod-product-compliance
Lightning Source LLC
Chambersburg PA
CBHW071820230426
43670CB00013B/2509